THE HEALTH
INFORMATION
HANDBOOK

For Thomas and Jack

The Health Information Handbook

Resources for self care

Robert Gann

Gower

Published by
Gower Publishing Company Limited
Gower House
Croft Road
Aldershot
Hants GU11 3HR
England

Gower Publishing Company
Old Post Road
Brookfield
Vermont 05036
USA

ISBN 0 566 03549 9

British Library Cataloguing in Publication Data

Gann, Robert
 The health information handbook: resources
 for self care.
 1. Self-care, Health —— Information services
 2. Self-care, Health —— Bibliography
 I. Title
 613'.07   RA776.95

Library of Congress Cataloging-in-Publication Data

Gann, Robert.
 The health information handbook.

 Bibliography: p.
 Includes index.
 1. Health—Information Services—Great Britain.
2. Self-care, Health—Information services—Great
Britain. 3. Health—Information services. 4. Self-
care, Health—Information services. I. Title.
RA773.6.G36   1986   613'.0941   86-14872

Printed and bound in Great Britain by
Biddles Ltd, Guildford and King's Lynn

Contents

Acknowledgements

This book is based on the experiences of the Help for Health Information Service over the past seven years. I should like to take this opportunity to record my thanks to those who have assisted in the preparation of the book and have contributed to the years of development of Help for Health.

I am grateful to my employers, the Wessex Regional Health Authority, for funding Help for Health and for giving me the opportunity and freedom to develop the contacts which have been essential to the compilation of this book. Help for Health has also been funded by the British Library (Research and Development) and by the Hampshire Area Health Authority, and my thanks are due to them too.

Many people have provided me with useful pieces of information. In particular I am grateful to Donna Flake and David Evans for details of American activities, and to Elaine Kempson for information on the Scandinavian scene. It is a particular pleasure to record my appreciation to fellow librarians in the Wessex Regional Library and Information Service and Wessex Medical Library for obtaining so many, sometimes obscure, items for me. The expert assistance of Jacquie Welch with literature searching is especially appreciated. The figures on pages 6 and 100–1 have been redrawn by the Department of Teaching Media, Southampton General Hospital. I have drawn on a large number of published sources. *Participation in Health* by James McEwen, Carlos J.M. Martini and Nicky Wilkins, and *Developing*

Consumer Health Information Services by Alan M. Rees have been especially valuable.

My special thanks are reserved for three people. I owe an enormous debt of gratitude to Roy Tabor, Regional Librarian of Wessex. The early discussions on patient information in Wessex and the establishment of Help for Health were due to his vision. He introduced me to many of the concepts explored in this book and his imaginative direction guided Help for Health through the first years of its life. The manuscript has been ably typed by Marilyn Jamieson, but her contribution to the book has been far greater than this. She has worked with me on the development of information, contacts and ideas in Wessex since 1979. Much of the day-to-day work of the service has been hers while I have received much of the kudos. I am pleased to put the record straight by acknowledging an unsung heroine. Finally, I am indebted to my wife, Jane, for all her support and encouragement, not only while I have been writing this book but over the whole period of Help for Health. She has been patient and understanding through seven fixed-term contracts in as many years. She has selflessly extended her social life to give me quiet evenings to complete the book. Without her it would never have been written.

Author's Note

I have on occasions referred to the recipient of health information as 'the patient'. This is not intended to convey the image of helpless subservience implicit in *Roget's Thesaurus* ('weakling, invalid, case, hypochondriac; meek, acquiescent, submissive'). For reasons of familiarity I have used the term 'patient' when the individual is in hospital or receiving professional health care (see Chapter 2). On other occasions I have used 'individual' or 'member of the public'. Of course most health care is carried out by people themselves. For this reason I have on the whole avoided the term 'health care consumer' which is common in the United States. Individuals are active producers, as well as passive consumers, of health care.

For reasons of economy I have usually referred to the patient as 'he'. This of course means he or she. In view of the pejorative connotations of 'patient' I hope that it is acceptable to use the masculine pronoun.

Preface

The last ten years have seen an unprecedented explosion of interest in the participation of people in their own health care. Governments and health authorities have experienced increasing concern over escalating health costs and have emphasised preventive medicine, health promotion and community-based care as a response. On the part of people themselves there has been a growing health consumerism and a demand for recognition of the competence of lay people in dealing with many health and social problems for themselves.

These developments have been supported by the World Health Organization whose 1978 Declaration of Alma Ata recognised the right and duty of people to participate individually and collectively in their own health care. There has been a realisation that medical science and technology have come to a point where further improvements in health can only come about by people becoming active and informed partners in health protection and promotion. In the United States the 1973 Patients' Bill of Rights was a milestone on the road to active patient participation and informed consent in that country. In the United Kingdom the 1976 Department of Health and Social Security report *Prevention and Health: Everybody's Business* stressed individual responsibility for health, while in 1981 the handbook of policies and priorities for the health services *Care in Action* emphasised the involvement of patient organisations and self-help groups, and an educated public. International Year of Disabled People 1981 had as a major aim the dignity and integration into society of disabled people, and their involvement in decisions affecting their own lives.

The key to increased involvement is access to information and since the mid-1970s a number of organisations have addressed themselves to the public demand for information on health and illness. The 1974 reorganisation of the National Health Service in the UK saw community health councils established as 'patients' watchdogs' and channels of information. In 1976 the first hospital-based citizens' advice bureau was set up and the following year the first DIAL (Disablement Information and Advice Line) opened its doors in Derbyshire. 1977 also saw the National Consumer Council's report on information *The Fourth Right of Citizenship* and the beginnings of community information services in public libraries with the Library Association's Community Information Project. In 1979 the British Library-funded Help for Health project in Southampton joined the Health Information Service at the Lister Hospital, Stevenage, as the pioneers of hospital-based patient information services. Throughout the 1970s and 1980s community health projects were springing up. The first patient participation group was established in 1972 and numbers soon rose to more than sixty. The 1980s saw even more emphasis on self help and health care consumerism with the birth of the National Self Help Support Centre and the College of Health. These British developments have been mirrored in a number of other countries round the world.

This wealth of activity has been recorded in a growing body of literature relating to information provision in health care. But although valuable guides exist to the American scene there has been no comprehensive British publication which reviews the published literature and current projects in the field of health information for the public. This book aims to fill that gap. It is directed at librarians and other information providers, health care practitioners, and those involved in health promotion and community development approaches to health. Its purpose is to communicate the work and experiences of researchers and practitioners from many disparate fields, to promote contacts between them and to provide a catalyst for further activity.

1

Responsibility for health

Information is the first step to every healthy choice. Improvements in our health depend on us taking control over, and responsibility for, health as an important component of our everyday lives. This active participation requires full and continuing access to information: information about our bodies, their workings in health and illness, and the services available to us in treatment and care, support and cooperation.

In 1980 the American Surgeon General produced an influential report *Healthy People*. The report states 'You, the individual, can do more for your own health and wellbeing than any doctor, any hospital, any drug, any exotic medical device.' This is not such a radical statement as it might at first seem. As we approach the year 2000 there is a growing recognition that, following eras of advances in public health and medical science, the key to further real improvements in health is the involvement of the informed individual in his own wellbeing. The British Department of Health and Social Security had produced a similar statement four years earlier, *Prevention and Health: Everybody's Business* (DHSS, 1976) which placed responsibility for health firmly on the individual. The central message was clear – only you can make the decision to choose a healthy lifestyle.

Our health in Western developed countries has been improving for two hundred years. Vickery (1982) has examined death rates in relation to medical advances in the United States over the last century.

Over 75 per cent of the decline in death rate between 1875 and 1975 occurred before medicine's most significant discoveries became available. The discovery of antibiotics in the 1930s ushered in a period during which the decline in the death rate accelerated. This acceleration is usually credited to the number of significant medical advances at the time. However, the trend of several centuries came to an end in the early 1930s and for the next fifteen years, there was no reduction in death rate and no increase in life expectancy. This fifteen-year period in fact coincided with the advent of high technology medicine. Death rates only began to decline again in the 1970s. In the United States this was due to a drop in deaths attributable to heart disease and stroke and coincided with a reduction in the use of tobacco, decreased consumption of fat, and increased exercise among Americans. In other words continuing improvements in health were beyond the reach of medicine, and only came about through a better educated and informed public taking a greater responsibility for its own health.

A similar pattern can be followed in the United Kingdom. The Public Health Movement which developed from the pioneering work of Chadwick (1842) and other reformers was very effective in combating communicable disease. The reforms were based on engineering methods and there were tremendous advances in safe water supply, sewerage, better housing and more efficient agriculture leading to cheaper food. In turn these advances paved the way for the 'medical era' of the first half of the twentieth century, a period characterised by mass vaccination, the use of antibiotics and direct therapeutic intervention giving the possibility of rapid and usually complete recovery from acute illness (McKeown 1965).

The World Health Organization has been at pains to emphasise the importance of society and the environment to health, rather than medical intervention. In a celebrated article in *The Lancet* the Director General Halfdan Mahler writes:

If one looks back to the last century in England, the attack upon some of the physical evils of the Industrial Revolution was clearly led by social reformers, such as the Chadwicks, the health professions having secondary roles such as certifying most questionably the health effects of rising damp and back-to-back houses. There was a change in the disease picture (especially the communicable diseases) but the evidence linking this to medical improvement interventions rather than to changes in the society and the environment is also questionable. The continuing decreases in incidence and mortality appear to be largely extensions of continuing trends and were not directly related, in time, to immunisation or to direct medical action'. (Mahler, 1975)

In the developed world at least there is a growing realisation that continuing improvements in health depend on the individual and the community. It is seen that health and wellbeing can be undermined by individual behaviour (e.g. smoking) and by our behaviour as a community (e.g. poverty, pollution). This is sometimes termed the lifestyle approach to health or, as Vickery (1982) puts it, 'our habits are our health'.

The most well-known and trenchant critic of the medical era has been Ivan Illich. He has gone so far as to suggest (Illich, 1976) that 'the medical establishment has become a major threat to health' and links the 'medicalisation of life' to iatrogenesis, or illness caused by medical procedures. For Illich the only possibility of the 'recovery of health' lies with the individual's capacity to understand, control and cope with his own health (and, where necessary, suffering and death). This is a provocative and stimulating (if extreme) view but one which is broadly reflected in the statements of a number of governmental and international agencies (such as the US Surgeon General and the World Health Organization). It has certainly been taken seriously as a basis for discussion within the medical establishment (McKeown, 1976), and other writers continue to point to deficiencies in health care systems and in professional practice (Kennedy, 1982).

HEALTH FOR ALL

In 1978 the World Health Organization (WHO) held the International Conference on Primary Health Care at Alma Ata in the USSR (World Health Organization 1978). The conference affirmed the paramount importance of primary care as:

... essential health care made universally accessible to individuals and families in the community, by means acceptable to them,

3

through their full participation and at a cost that the community and country can afford.

The conference was chiefly notable for the statement of the goal of 'Health for all by the year 2000' and the agreement (by 134 nations) of the Declaration of Alma Ata. The fourth point of the ten-point declaration is particularly significant.

The people have a right and duty to participate individually and collectively in the planning and implementation of their health care.

This 'right and duty' was reiterated in the report of a WHO working group on Information and health which met in Luxembourg in 1980 and concerned itself with

... the right of the patient not only to receive full information about his health status but also to have some say in decisions affecting his health (World Health Organization Regional Office for Europe, 1981).

Over the past ten years the position of the World Health Organization has consistently underlined the importance of informed self care and participation:

health science and technology have come to a point where their contribution to the further improvement of health standards can make a real impact only if the people themselves become full partners in health protection and promotion (World Health Organization 1983).

SELF CARE

We all expect and accept periods of ill health. Dunnell and Cartwright (1972) found that the majority of a population which they studied reported at least one.symptom over a two-week period. Another study of women in a new town in Scotland (Bell *et al.* 1979) found that over a three-week period 94 per cent of the group studied reported some illness. Yet this is quite compatible with a general sense of wellbeing.

Wadsworth *et alia* (1981) found as many as 95 per cent of the subjects of their study suffered from some complaint over a fortnight, yet 35 per cent described themselves as in perfect health. Obviously some ill health (acute, self-limiting conditions) is regarded as quite normal.

It is not surprising that less than one complaint in four is taken to the doctor. Over thirty years ago Drs John and Elizabeth Horder produced a celebrated diagram (Figure 1.1) showing the relative proportions of self care, primary medical care and hospital care (Horder, 1954). More recent studies have underlined the Horders' findings. Elliott-Binns (1973) found that some attempt at self treatment had been undertaken by 95 per cent of patients who came to see him as a general practitioner, while Bradshaw (1977) has estimated that 80–85 per cent of all illness in Britain is managed without resource to a doctor. Another box model (Figure 1.2) has been used by Muir Gray to show how hospital and professional community care provide less care than informal care (by family, friends and volunteers) and self care (Gray, 1983). Studies in the United States confirm a similar pattern.

When we are ill the most likely remedy is medication. On any one day it is likely that over half of us are taking some medication (Kohn, 1976). Kohn's international study showed that 27 per cent of the study population were using prescribed medicines while a further 33 per cent were taking non-prescribed, over-the-counter drugs. The most commonly taken medicines in Dunnell and Cartwright's study (1972) were analgesics (taken by 40 per cent over a two-week period) followed by cough medicines (15 per cent), skin preparations (15 per cent) and indigestion remedies (12 per cent).

Self care is such a common daily activity that its ubiquity may have obscured its existence and devalued its significance (Levin, 1981). However, when questioned on the effectiveness of self care, there is a general agreement amongst professionals that it is safe and appropriate in very many cases. Williamson and Danaher (1978) for example, found that general practitioners judged self treatment to be partially or completely effective in 75 per cent of cases and only potentially harmful in 5 per cent.

Fry (1978) sums up the role of self care as follows:

Self care is the true first level of health care and comprises numerically the major portion of the system. There are more people

5

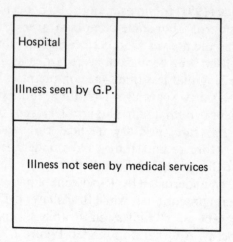

Figure 1.1
Relative proportions of illness treated by hospital care; primary care; self care.
Source: Horder, J.P. and Horder, E. (1954) 'Illness in general practice', *Practitioner*, vol. 173, pp. 177–85.

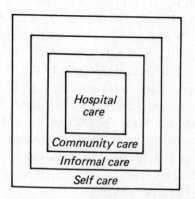

Figure 1.2
The four-box system of health care
Source: Gray J.A.M. (1983) 'Four box health care: development in a time of zero growth', *Lancet*, vol. 2, pp. 1185–6.

caring for their own complaints than there are attending health professionals. Self care taking place within the family context dictates to a degree the whole pattern of health care'.

or, putting it more passionately,

Fully 80 per cent of illness is functional and can be effectively treated by any talented healer who displays warmth, interest and compassion regardless of whether he has finished grammar school. Another 10 per cent of illness is wholly incurable. This leaves only 10 per cent in which scientific medicine – at considerable cost – has any value at all'. (Massey, 1976)

or more succinctly:

You can do more for your health than your doctor can'. (Vickery and Fries 1976).

SELF-HELP GROUPS

The ability to prevent and treat communicable and acute illness has both increased and made more apparent chronic illness and disability (Fry. 1966). This shift has been a key factor in the increase in patient participation, in the demand for information and above all in the phenomenon of the development of self-help groups for a wide variety of conditions. Chronic illnesses frequently have characteristics which make self help appropriate: they are incurable, there is a need for continuing care but there is every possibility of a viable lifestyle if rehabilitation measures are followed (McEwen *et al.* 1983). Information and the contact and support provided by fellow disabled people are important elements in the rehabilitation process.

There has been something of a boom in studies of self help in general and of self-help groups in health in particular. Many studies have concentrated on self help as a phenomenon in sociology or 'community psychology' (Gartner and Reissman, 1984). There have been a number of attempts to define what in practice self-help groups do (Caplan and Killilea, 1976; Katz and Bender, 1976). Killilea has provided a useful summary of the characteristics of self-help groups.

7

These include a membership with common experiences, offering mutual help and support; the operation of 'the helper principle' whereby the helper may benefit as much from the exchange as the recipient of the help; and the importance of an information exchange which contributes to a greater factual understanding of the problem.

Self-help groups have become a crucial part of the health care scene in the developed world over the last two decades. In the United Kingdom the self-help movement is the most recent manifestation of a long tradition of voluntary or non-statutory involvement in health and social welfare. The Wolfenden Committee on the Future of Voluntary Organisations (1978), enquiring into the role of voluntary organisations in the United Kingdom in the last quarter of the twentieth century, traces this activity back to eighteenth-century paternalism and patronage through charity. Voluntary organisations continued to act as the major provider of basic services until well into the twentieth century. For example there were many voluntary hospitals, and the care of disabled people and children relied heavily on voluntary bodies.

The Beveridge proposals and the advent of the National Health Service did not diminish the importance of the voluntary organisations but led to an adaptation of roles. In particular, from the 1950s onwards there was a reorientation of some voluntary organisations to differentiate their contribution from that of statutory services (e.g. the provision of complementary specialised services), there was the growth of pressure groups, and a flowering of self-help mutual aid organisations.

Before the Second World War almost the only organisations for people with specific handicaps or diseases were those for the blind and deaf. Then a wide range of organisations were established by and for parents of handicapped children (e.g. the Spastics Society, and the Royal Society for Mentally Handicapped Children and Adults (MEN-CAP). In turn, the 1960s and 1970s saw the boom in true self-help organisations run by disabled people themselves. There are now groups for almost every condition: 'stroke victims, epileptics, Down's Syndrome children, sufferers from Parkinson's Disease, ileostomy, spina bifida ... an endless list with branches of many of them in each health district and new ones constantly coming into existence' (Hatch, 1978).

It is almost impossible to give an accurate figure of how many

8

voluntary organisations and self-help groups there are in the United Kingdom. MacKenzie (1975) estimates that the *Directory of British Associations* includes 160 health self-help groups. This modest figure includes only the better-known national organisations. The Help for Health research project in the Wessex Regional Health Authority (Gann, 1981) identified over 1,000 national voluntary organisations in the health field and a further 1,000 local groups within Hampshire (not all of these were self-help groups in the true sense of the word, as the total includes voluntary welfare agencies such as Age Concern and the British Red Cross). In a similar information-gathering exercise on self-help groups Webb (1983) identified over 2,000 groups in London alone, while Whitehouse (1981) drew attention to at least 250 different organisations that the primary health care team might wish to use in a Manchester practice area of 21 km.

Patients, disabled people and professionals acting on their behalf may wish to contact voluntary organisations and self-help groups for a variety of types of help including assistance with financial problems, accommodation, employment, recreation, holidays, information and mutual support. But the size and ever-changing nature of the voluntary sector poses enormous information problems. The *Directory of British Associations* (1980) sums up the problem thus: 'there have been 1,100 new organisations in the past three years, nearly 800 have been disbanded, another 800 have changed their names and half the 8000 organisations have changes of address.' The Directory is concerned only with national organisations. A problem of equivalent dimensions exists at a local level, where the most important self-help activity goes on.

SELF CARE IN HISTORY

Despite recent interest in self care it is, of course, nothing new. The importance of the patient's participation in his own care was recognised by Hippocrates 2,000 years ago. 'In the art of medicine there are three factors – the disease, the patient and the doctor. The doctor is the servant of the art. The patient must cooperate in fighting the disease' (McEwen, *et al.* 1983).

Before the establishment of extensive professional medical services, health care depended largely on traditional remedies administered by relatives, friends or semi-trained wise women. In 1660 the villagers of Dry Drayton declared 'None practice physic nor professeth midwifery but charitably one neighbour helpeth another' (Elliott-Binns, 1973). Closely linked with traditional folk medicine and mutual self help was an extensive popular medical publishing business. Publications ranged from encyclopaedias to pamphlets, and covered diagnosis, treatment, convalescence, household management and 'hygiene' (Woodward and Richards, 1977). An early example of a comprehensive medical self-help guide was William Buchan's *Domestic Medicine* published in Edinburgh in 1769, and described as 'an attempt to render the Medical Art more generally useful, by shewing people what is in their own power, both with respect to the Prevention and Cure of Diseases.'

The concern with gaining information for self-care, with its associated publishing industry, was a feature of nineteenth-century American society as much as in Britain. Discussing the history of self care in America, Cassedy (1977) observes:

Wherever people have been able to obtain their own medicine or have read books about hygiene, or have had relatives, neighbours or travellers to suggest remedies, they have been ready in large numbers to rely on such sources and their own judgements rather than resort to physicians.

Many of the nineteenth-century popular medical works were related to the various contemporary moral and religious movements. For example, the Religious Tract Society published a series of *Health at Home Tracts* with the emphasis on 'the diffusion of sound information in a popular and readable form fitted to make the people sensible of their responsibility and to use all means in their power to preserve their own health and the health of those dependent upon them' (Schofield, 1890). The emphasis on sound information as the basis for personal responsibility in health has a curiously contemporary ring about it.

These movements found expression in the nineteenth-century philosophy of self help exemplified by Samuel Smiles. This notion of self help, for which there is nostalgia in certain circles today, was based on hard work, personal initiative and the overcoming of problems and adversity by one's own efforts (Smiles, 1859). Self help has in fact been claimed by a variety of political movements since the nineteenth century. 'Mutual aid', which is perhaps a better term than self help, was a key element in nineteenth-century libertarian and anarchist philosophy. Prince Kropotkin seems to have foreseen the problems of libraries and information services in the self-help field when he wrote during the 1890s: '... the countless societies, clubs and alliances which have lately grown up in such numbers that it would require many years simply to tabulate them are another manifestation of the same ever-working tendency for association and mutual support' (Kropotkin, 1914).

Self help continues to be claimed by Left and Right in the twentieth century. On the Left it is seen as a vehicle for increased control of the individual's own life, a seizure of power from the state; on the Right the call is for a dismantling of services such as the National Health Service on the grounds that a bureaucratic state has encroached on the freedom of the individual: self help here means helping oneself and letting others fend for themselves as best they can – a return to the Victorian values of Samuel Smiles (McEwen *et al.*, 1983 p. 12).

SOME DEFINITIONS

In this chapter we have started to use terms such as self care, self help and health promotion. Before going further it may be useful to look at ways in which some writers have defined these concepts.

Self care

A process whereby a lay person can function effectively on his own behalf in health promotion and prevention, and in disease detection and treatment. (Levin, 1976)

Self care refers to unorganised health activities and health-related decision making by individuals, families, neighbours, friends, colleagues at work etc.; it encompasses self-medication, self-treatment, social support in illness, first aid in a 'natural setting', i.e. the normal social context of people's everyday lives. Self-care is definitely the primary health resource in the health care system. The most important feature distinguishing it from self-help is that it does not imply purposeful organisation and is often provided on an ad hoc basis in intimate settings. (Hatch and Kickbusch, 1983)

Self-help groups

Self-help groups are voluntary, small group structures for mutual aid and the accomplishment of a special purpose. They are usually formed by peers who have come together for mutual assistance in satisfying a common need, overcoming a common handicap or life-disrupting problem, and bringing about desired social and/or personal change. (Katz and Bender, 1976)

Groups of people who feel they have a common problem and have joined together to do something about it. (Richardson and Goodman, 1983)

Health education

Strategies or learning experiences designed to bring about voluntary adjustment of behaviour conducive to health. (Green, 1978)

Health education seeks to improve or protect health through voluntary changes in behaviour as a consequence of learning opportunities. (Catford and Nutbeam, 1984)

Health promotion

Health promotion seeks to improve or protect health through behavioural, biological, socioeconomic and environmental changes. It can include health education, personal services, environmental measures, community and organisational development, economic and regulatory activities. Health promotion embraces the concepts of disease prevention as well as the notion of positive health. (Catford and Nutbeam, 1984)

Patient education

Planned combinations of learning activities designed to assist people who are having or have had experiences with illness or disease in making changes conducive to health'. (Squyres, 1980)

To sum up, *self care* is a ubiquitous everyday activity which accounts for the major proportion of health care. Important elements in self care are *health education* whereby the community is encouraged to adopt healthier lifestyles and so prevent ill health, *patient education* whereby individuals learn to cope with illness and participate in treatment and rehabilitation, and *self help* whereby individuals with common experiences come together for mutual support and advice. The provision of information on illness itself and on groups which can help is often referred to collectively as *patient information* (in the UK) or *consumer health information* (in the USA). All of these activities can be seen as part of the wider concept of *health promotion* which can include health education, patient education and self help activities, as well as other elements, in the improvement and protection of health.

ACCESS TO INFORMATION

This chapter has attempted to give a general overview of studies into self care. A more detailed picture can be gained from the reviews *Participation in Health* by McEwen, Martini and Wilkins (1983) and 'Self care responses to illnesses' in *Social Science and Medicine* (Dean, 1981). Even this brief overview, however, has made apparent just how much responsibility the individual has for his own health: responsibility for looking out for signs of ill health, carrying out basic self care measures on behalf or himself or his (or more likely her) family, deciding when to consult the doctor, coping with long-term chronic illness or disability, and making adjustments in lifestyle to improve health. All of these activities depend on information. As this book will show, the information resources which the individual needs to make decisions on health matters do exist. Vickery (1982) has reminded us of this when discussing the vast amount of information which a lay individual might need.

The bottom line is access to information. How can individuals possibly remember all of this, much less understand or use it appropriately? They cannot, just as physicians cannot remember the thousands of facts and concepts involved in highly technical decisions. Individuals can however do as physicians do by accepting responsibility for decision making and using the information resources available to them. The critical difference is that the physician's resources are well developed whereas those for the consumer lag far behind.

REFERENCES

Bell, J.M., Black, I., McEwen, J. and Pearson, J. (1979) 'Patterns of illness and use of services in a new town', *Public Health*, vol. 93, pp. 333–43.

Bradshaw, J.S. (1977) 'British barefoot doctors', *Royal Society of Health Journal*, vol. 97(4), pp. 159–64.

Buchan, W. (1769) *Domestic Medicine or the Family Physician*, Balfour, Auld and Smellie, Edinburgh.

Caplan, G. and Killilea, M. (1976), *Support systems and mutual help*, Grune and Stratton, New York.

Cassedy, J. (1977) 'Why self help? Americans alone with their diseases 1880–1950' in Risse, G., Numbers, R., and Leariff, J. *Medicine Without Doctors: Home Health Care in American History*, Science History Publications, New York.

Catford, J. and Nutbeam, D. (1984) 'Towards a definition of health education and health promotion', *Health Education Journal*, vol. 43 (2 and 3), p. 38.

Chadwick, E. (1842), *Report on the Sanitary Conditions of the Labouring Population of Great Britain*, ed. M.W. Flynn, Edinburgh University Press, 1965.

Dean, K. (1981) 'Self care responses to illness: A selected review', *Social Science and Medicine*, vol. 15A, pp. 673–87.

Department of Health and Social Security (1976), *Prevention and Health: Everybody's Business*, HMSO, London.

Directory of British Associations (1980), 6th edn., CBD Research Publications, Beckenham.

Dunnell, K. and Cartwright, A. (1972), *Medicine Takers, Prescribers and Hoarders*, Routledge and Kegan Paul, London.

Elliott-Binns, C.P., (1973) 'An analysis of lay medicine', *Journal of the*

Royal College of General Practitioners, vol. 23, pp. 255–64.

Fry, J. (1966) *Profiles of Disease*, Livingstone, London.

Fry, J. (1978) *A New Approach to Medicine: Principles and Priorities in Health Care*, MTP, Lancaster.

The Future of Voluntary Organisations: Report of the Wolfenden Committee (1978), Croom Helm, London.

Gann, R. (1981) *Help for Health: the Needs of Health Care Practitioners for Information about Voluntary Organisations in Support of Health Care*, British Library Research and Development Report 5613, Wessex Regional Library and Information Service, Southampton.

Gartner, A. and Reissman, F. (1984) *The Self Help Revolution*, Human Sciences Press, New York.

Gray, J.A.M., (1983) 'Four box health care: development in a time of zero growth', *Lancet*, vol. 2, pp. 1185–6

Green, L.W. (1978) 'Health information and health education: there's a big difference between them', *Bulletin of the American Society of Information Science*, vol. 4(4), pp. 15–16.

Hatch, S. (1978) 'The role of the volunteer in the welfare state: volunteers, mutual aid and health', *Royal Society of Health Journal*, vol. 98(5), pp. 216–19.

Hatch, S. and Kickbusch, I. (1983) *Self Help in Europe: New Approaches to Health Care*, World Health Organization Regional Office for Europe, Copenhagen.

Healthy People: the Surgeon General's Report on Health Promotion and Disease Prevention, (1980) US Department of Health and Human Services, Washington, DC.

Horder, J.P. and Horder, E. (1954) 'Illness in general practice', *Practitioner*, vol. 173, pp. 177–85.

Illich, I. (1976) *Limits to Medicine, Medical Nemesis: the Expropriation of Health*. Marion Boyars, London.

Katz, A.H. and Bender, E.I. (1976) *The Strength in us: Self Help Groups in the Modern World*, Franklin Watts, New York.

Kennedy, I. (1982) *The Unmasking of Medicine*, Allen and Unwin, London.

Kohn, R. and White, K.L. (1976) *Health Care: an International Study*, Oxford University Press, London.

Kropotkin, P. (1914) *Mutual Aid: a Factor of Evolution*, Garland, New York, 1972.

15

Levin, L.S. (1976) 'The lay person as the primary health care practitioner', *Public Health Reports*, vol. 91, pp. 206–210.

Levin, L.S. (1981) 'Self care in health: potentials and pitfalls', *World Health Forum*, vol. 2, pp. 177–84.

McEwen, J., Martini, C.J.M. and Wilkins, N. (1983), *Participation in Health*, Croom Helm, London.

MacKenzie, W.J.M. (1975) *Power and Responsibility in Health Care*, Oxford University Press, London.

McKeown, T. (1965), *Medicine in Modern Society*, George Allen and Unwin, London.

McKeown, T. (1976) *The Role of Medicine: Dream, Mirage or Nemesis?*, Nuffield Provincial Hospitals Trust, London.

Mahler, H. (1975) 'Health: a demystification of medical terminology', *Lancet*, vol. 2 (7940) pp. 829–33.

Massey, R.U. (1976), 'Educating for change: the next twenty five years', *Connecticut Medicine*, vol. 40, pp. 713–7.

Richardson, A. and Goodman, M. (1983) *Self Help and Social Care: Mutual Aid Organisations in Practice*, Policy Studies Institute, London.

Schofield, A. (1890), *Health at Home Tracts*, Religious Tract Society, London.

Smiles, S. (1859) *Self Help: with Illustrations of Conduct and Perseverance,* John Murray, London, 1958.

Squyres, W.B. (1980) *Patient Education: an Enquiry into the State of the Art*, Springer, New York.

Vickery, D.M. and Fries, J.F. (1976) *Take Care of Yourself: a Consumer's Guide to Medical Care*, Addison-Wesley, New York.

Vickery, D.M. (1982) 'The informed medical consumer: personal responsibility and decision making' in Rees, A., *Developing Consumer Health Information Services*, Bowker, New York.

Wadsworth, M.E.J., Butterfield, W.J.H., and Blaney, R. (1971) *Health and Sickness: the Choice of Treatment*, Tavistock, London.

Webb, P. (1983), 'Ready, willing but able? The self help group', *Journal of the Royal Society of Health*, vol. 103 (1), pp. 35–41.

Whitehouse, C.R. (1981) 'Organisations relevant to primary health care in two communities', *British Medical Journal*, vol. 283, pp. 701–4.

Williamson, J.D., and Danaher, K. (1978) *Self Care in Health*, Croom Helm, London.

Woodward, J. and Richards, D. (1977) *Health Care and Popular Medicine in Nineteenth Century England*, Croom Helm, London.

World Health Organization (1978) *International Conference on Primary Health Care, Alma Ata, USSR*, WHO, Geneva.

World Health Organization, (1983), *New Approaches to Health Education in Primary Care*, WHO, Geneva.

World Health Organization Regional Office for Europe (1981) *Information and Health: Report of a Working Group*, WHO Regional Office for Europe, Copenhagen.

2

The informed patient

Information to enable participation in our health is important at all stages of our lives, but never more so than when we are faced with illness and become patients.

> At a time of illness patients and their relatives need information on a number of subjects and often do not know how to go about finding it. The range of topics is wide and includes basic information about the people who provide health care, how the system operates and background information required to understand what the professional staff are saying. Because the patient's understanding of medical matters is often poor and because of stress the information given by doctors and nurses cannot always be immediately understood. Gaps in communication do occur and cause difficulties. (Tabor, 1981)

Before we can begin to cope with ill health and communicate with professional carers we need a basic understanding of our bodies, how they work and the terminology used to describe them. Many people lack this knowledge. One study (Boyle, 1970) compared 234 outpatients with 35 doctors to assess the difference between the patients' and doctors' interpretation of common medical terms. Two multiple choice questionnaires were administered, one asking for definitions of common medical terms (arthritis, heartburn, jaundice, diarrhoea, piles, flatulence) and the other the position of organs in the body. In no case did patients and doctors reach complete agreement. Although over 80 per cent of patients chose the correct definition of 'arthritis' and 'bronchitis', only 42 per cent were correct for 'flatulence' and surprisingly only 37 per cent for 'diarrhoea'. Identification of the position of organs was equally poor – half the patients did not know where the kidneys, stomach, lungs and heart are. Encouragingly doctors could select the position of organs with success.

One of the problems is a failure of basic health education. A similar project by Quiggin (1977) provides a more optimistic outlook for the new generation. This looked at children's knowledge of their internal bodily parts. The test was more difficult than that employed by Boyle in that there was no multiple choice. The children were simply asked to draw in organs on an outline of the body. Although there were some charming errors, knowledge on the whole was surprisingly good. It is interesting to note that, as in Boyle's study, there was confusion over the kidneys: 60 per cent of the girls drew only one.

Other studies (Pratt *et al.*, 1957; Dunkelman, 1979) have indicated that patients lack knowledge of basic procedures and treatments. Their reluctance to press doctors for further information when this is not offered has often given doctors a false impression of their patients' level of knowledge. A comprehensive study of general practice by Cartwright and Anderson (1980) included an examination of doctor–patient communication. Doctors generally overestimated the knowledge of the patient, while many patients were critical of the way things were explained to them. The provision of information in general practice has also been examined by Byrne and Long (1976) as part of their analysis of consultations, while Fletcher (1973) has pointed out that the most common criticism of doctors is that they fail to give adequate information. Fletcher's study indicates a further area of concern. At least a third of patients may forget information, or even deny receiving it.

PATIENTS WANT INFORMATION

There is a great deal of research evidence that patients would like more information about their condition, its treatment and management (Ley, 1979). Many patients – Ewles and Shipster (1981) suggest 35 per cent – are not satisfied with the amount and type of information given to them. In 1964 Cartwright noted that patients felt they could not obtain information easily: 44 per cent said they received no information from the hospital sister; 40 per cent had received 'a little'; while only 16 per cent felt that they had been given 'a lot' of information. It was suggested that middle-class patients communicated more easily with hospital staff and as a result received more information on their condition.

Twenty years later there does not seem to have been a great improvement. A recent survey into communication in coronary care units (Wallace *et al.*, 1985) produced the following results:

> By the time these patients were discharged, 90% of them wanted to know about the cause of their illness and 40% reported being told about it; 90% wanted to know the diagnosis and 70% reported being told their diagnosis; 90% wanted to know how long their recovery might be but only 40% reported being told; 80% of patients wanted to know about their medical treatment but only 40% reported being told about it. So it seems that most patients know their diagnosis but feel uninformed about its cause, the process of recovery and treatment.

The greatest cause of anxiety is not knowing what to expect (Franklin, 1974), and most patients believe the worst unless given a diagnosis they can understand (Skeet, 1974). The patient in hospital may have many other worries in addition to the illness itself. Hugh-Jones, Tanser and Whitby (1964) sampled medical ward patients in a London teaching hospital. Of these, 41 per cent of the men and 34 per cent of the women admitted to worries associated with being in hospital. Financial worries (39 per cent), business (25 per cent) and family responsibilities preyed on patients' minds. Many were bewildered by strange surroundings and personnel – 27 per cent did not know who had visited them in a white coat. There is a clear need for information for patients on the social aspects of ill health, financial benefits and so on, (a point underlined by Waite, 1974) and on hospital procedures and staffing.

In a revealing article, Claire Rayner has described what the lay public want to know about health issues based on an analysis of 40,000 letters received each year in her capacity as an 'agony aunt'. The health queries fall into nine main categories and are all, she suggests, inadequately met by the National Health Service. The categories are:

1 *Anatomy and physiology*: these mainly come from young people who are bewildered and frightened by changes in their bodies and emotions. This might be an indictment of education but there is also evidence of insensitivity on the part of doctors. A typical comment is 'I went to my doctor because one of my breasts is much bigger than the other and he just laughed at me'. If there is lack of knowledge of the normal healthy body can we expect early self-detection of disease and effective cooperation in treatment?

2 *Anxieties about pregnancy and childbirth*: the major demand for information here is on alternatives to the technological approach to childbirth, and interest in home confinements and Leboyer type deliveries.

3 *Birth control problems*: enquirers complain that doctors only offer the Pill, and seek information on barrier methods and IUD. One can imagine that letters expressing concern over the Pill must have increased enormously since this article was written in 1979.

4 *Child care problems*: parents seek reassurance and advice on problems with feeding, sleep, skin care, potting training. Above all they are looking for information to make an informed decision on whether to have children vaccinated for measles or whooping cough.

5 *Mental health problems*: 'Girls write in describing textbook cases of anorexia nervosa; and schizophrenia, paranoid delusions, senile dementia all loom large in the mailbag. And so does every kind of depression. Those envelop my mailbag in a miasma of misery.'

6 *Sexual problems*: 'A very large number of people seek help with frigidity, vaginismus, impotence, premature ejaculation ... Sexual distress can lead to a great deal of general distress.'

7 *Need for plastic surgery*: 'This category is one that will impress few. The women who want breasts lifted, drooped, enlarged or diminished: the men who want their bald heads recovered'. Although Claire Rayner seems to have little sympathy herself for this category she does appeal for more sympathy on the part of

21

general practitioners when dealing with such patients.

These categories of enquiry highlight a general level of concern and unmet information need in the wider community. The remaining two categories are particularly important when examining the need for information at a time of illness.

8 *Illness queries*: Many enquiries deal with illness. 'Far too many readers ask me to explain to them what the doctor meant when he said they had high blood pressure, low blood pressure, angina, fibroids, ovarian cyst, mastitis: the list is long.

Even more distressing are those who write and say the doctor has diagnosed diabetes, cholycystitis, spastic colon, or whatever and has told them to follow a particular diet and will I please provide the diet? That even a few doctors can be so offhand about their information-giving that patients feel the need to approach a newspaper or magazine for such information speaks volumes about the quality of care they are providing'.

Other letters ask for explanations of common surgical procedures, advice on activity following discharge and support following the diagnosis of a serious disorder such as multiple sclerosis.

9 *Problems of the old*: although these enquiries are grouped under the heading of problems of the old, they illustrate a more general failing – the lack of provision of information on services in the community:

What never ceases to amaze me is the number of them who are not told of the many services that are available and of the voluntary bodies who gladly help. I get too many letters from people thanking me embarrassingly effusively just because I put them in touch with their local Red Cross, or a young people's support group like Task Force. (Rayner, 1979)

Claire Rayner's article has been considered at length because it illustrates in a way more vivid than some scientific studies the unmet demands for information amongst patients and the public. In particular there is a desperate need for information to enable patients to understand and adjust to illness at a time of diagnosis, hospitalisation and discharge, and a similar requirement for up-to-date information on the maze of statutory and voluntary services available to the patient in the community.

WRITTEN INFORMATION

It is clear that patients want information and often are not given it. However there is a further problem. Patients may be given information verbally by doctors and nurses and then forget it. In a medical outpatients department 39 per cent of patients could not remember what they had been told between 10 and 80 minutes of seeing the consultant (Ley, 1977). The situation may be even worse in general practice where patients had forgotten 50 per cent of what the general practitioner had said to them within five minutes of seeing him (Ley *et al.*, 1973).

It is not difficult to see why patients fail to take in information given to them. They are in alien surroundings, perhaps in pain, almost certainly worried. The doctor may be from a different background, age, class, race and sex. The barriers have been well described in a recent book by Carolyn Faulder (1985):

> Communicating specialised knowledge to someone who is untutored in the subject is a problem in any field. Expertise generates its own jargon, and nowhere more so than in medicine. Doctors have the advantage of their skills and the clinical experience which they bring to their decision-making. Patients on the other hand are usually ignorant about the basic medical facts relating to their illness and they are further handicapped by their vulnerable emotional state. A seriously ill person is certain to be deeply worried and fearful, and is usually in no condition to absorb difficult technical information.
>
> The ugly class divisions in our society have also to be taken into account. Doctors are invariably middle class, by virtue of their education if not their origins, whereas a large number of their patients will be working class. This puts the latter at a distinct disadvantage when it comes to voicing their preferences or doubts to someone who speaks with a different accent, almost in a different language and who is surrounded by the trappings of authority.

23

One solution to this failure of communication might be the provision of printed literature which could be taken away by the patient, assimilated in his own time, shared with his relatives (who may be deeply affected by his illness) and referred to again when required.

The Royal Commission on the National Health Service (1979) recommended that all hospitals should provide explanatory booklets for patients before admission to hospital. Many hospitals do this but a survey in Bristol (Reynolds, 1978) found that 66 per cent of patients had not received the booklet which the hospital produced. The survey also revealed a general dissatisfaction with the communication of information. For example 82 per cent of patients did not know the result of their chest X-ray.

Ellis and his colleagues (1979), recognising that doctors' advice to patients may be complex and only given verbally, studied the effects of supplying supplementary written information on patients' recall and understanding. Many patients had poor understanding of verbal instructions 'which we considered we had presented with great lucidity'. The provision of brief, written information improved recall and understanding in all cases. It was recommended that all patients should leave hospital with a card giving basic advice on the illness and its treatment. This concept of take-home cards has also been examined by Seiler and Watson (1982) – this time in general practice. In order to reinforce and extend the doctor's advice, information cards were devised for 12 conditions: 4 acute problems (coughs and colds, sore throats, influenza, diarrhoea); 3 sub-chronic problems (constipation, enuresis, insomnia); and five chronic problems (heart disease, bronchitis, chronic disability, diabetes, stoma). The use of the cards was a success and the extension of the idea in primary care was suggested.

As we have seen, most general practice consultations are for minor illness which could be treated adequately using self-care measures. For children under sixteen, over half of new demands for care are for six common symptoms: stuffy nose, sore throat, coughs, vomiting, diarrhoea and minor injuries (Morrell et al., 1980). In an attempt to help parents to manage these common symptoms, a booklet was produced by Professor Morrell and his colleagues to inform them about the meaning of these symptoms, the appropriate medication, and guidance on when the doctor should be consulted. The booklet was edited by the leader writer of the *Daily Mirror* and tested for acceptability and comprehension on a group of young mothers. Study of its use confirmed a consistent change in consulting behaviour by parents who received the booklet. For five out of the six symptoms there was considerably more self care and less visits to the GP.

Later the same year the St Thomas's team looked at the use of the booklet in more detail (Anderson *et al.*, 1980). A randomised controlled trial showed that introducing the booklet led to fewer consultations for the symptoms included. However there was no increase in real knowledge of the symptoms, leading to the conclusion that 'what patients need to respond appropriately to common symptoms of illness is a simple reference manual rather than an educational programme designed to increase their knowledge about the management of illness'. Of course, another factor in the reduced consultations might be that patients interpreted the provision of the booklet as a rebuke for over-use of the GP's time and cut down visits accordingly.

The Health Education Council has since published David Morrell's booklet as *Minor Illness: How to Treat it at Home.* An earlier Health Education Council booklet *Treating Yourself* was the subject of an evaluation by Humphreys (1976). Of those who had received the booklet, 70 per cent said that it had saved them a visit to the doctor. It is estimated that this could lead to a saving of 23 per cent in GP consultations. There have been a number of other studies evaluating written information for patients (Frame, 1970), a practice booklet for parents (Pike, 1980) and the provision of self-care information through algorithms (Berg *et al.*, 1979).

UNDERSTANDING WRITTEN INFORMATION

It seems that written information can make a significant contribution to patients' understanding of advice on coping with illness and treatment. There have, however, been reservations expressed about the comprehensibility of some patient information literature.

Vivian and Robertson (1980) applied standard readability tests (Fog, SMOG and Fry) to patient information leaflets from American public foundations, pharmaceutical companies, hospitals and commercial sources. They concluded that much of the literature was potentially incomprehensible to large sections of the population. A major problem is understanding technical medical terminology. Fifteen test words were taken from a sample of printed health information sources and a group of readers were asked to give correct definitions (Cole, 1979). The words were inflame, swab, acute, endemic, antiemetic, chronic, dilated, anticoagulant, haemorrhoids, emaciation, starchy, immune system, constipation, abdomen, nutrients. All had appeared in literature designed for a lay readership. There were many problems in understanding (for example only 47 per cent knew what dilated means) particularly when the meaning was not obvious from the context.

Patient information literature on heart disease has been singled out for criticism (O'Hanrahan *et al.*, 1980; Laher *et al.*, 1981). Confusion, gaps and overlaps were evident in material from eleven different countries. Information on taking prescribed drugs was particularly poorly understood.

The use of more illustrations and, particularly cartoons, has been seen as a way of improving the readability of patient booklets. The Arthritis and Rheumatism Council (Moll *et al.*, 1977) considered increasing the number of cartoons in a booklet on gout, but it was concluded that this did not significantly increase the value of the material as a communication aid.

A recent cooperative study between the Departments of Child Health and Education at the University of Nottingham (Nicoll and Harrison, 1984) is particularly significant, bearing in mind the type of literature available to patients in the UK. A total of 109 booklets were examined, including 'baby booklets' given at antenatal clinics, commercial pamphlets and literature from the Health Education Council, Department of Health and Social Security and specialist voluntary organisations. These represent the main sources of health information for a lay readership in the UK. Flesch readability scores were computed for the booklets and the reading levels compared with national newspapers. Many of the booklets were far less readable than might be hoped, the most comprehensible being those produced by the Health Education Council, commercial organisations and the baby books. Some DHSS leaflets on the other hand required a reading level higher than that required for *The Times*.

A major cause for concern is how difficult many of the voluntary organisation booklets were to read. Frequently these represent the only source of information for patients on a wide range of chronic disorders and disabilities. Health education services have the ability to produce readable literature but in the past have strayed infrequently beyond the bounds of preventive health and have produced little on coping with illness and disability. Voluntary organisations have an unrivalled knowledge of how their members cope with illness and disability but often lack the resources and skills to put this information over effectively. There is a strong case for a closer partnership.

Even if material is comprehensible there are other pitfalls. The 'baby books' examined in the Nottingham study are an important source of information for parents: 99 per cent of mothers attending antenatal clinics in York received copies of the British Medical Association's *You and Your Baby* while only 47 per cent attended antenatal classes. These booklets, as Nicoll and Harrison found, are readable but the quality of information is often suspect and sometimes inaccurate (Perkins, 1981). In particular, they may confuse unnecessary advice with essential information: 'the idiocy of advising women to have their hair done with the same seriousness as advising them to sterilise baby feeding bottles'. At worst, these booklets can be patronising, inducing guilt and feelings of social inferiority, authoritarian rather than authoritative. In her examination of 'baby books' Perkins appeals for professionals and parents to have a wider choice of material than that available in many hospitals and clinics.

Despite the necessary reservations shown in the studies above there is a good deal of valuable material available, and library and information services can make an enormous contribution to patient education by identifying this material and making it available for use. Guidelines for librarians to use in selecting information materials for patients have been produced by the Community Health Information Network in Cambridge, Massachusetts (Dalton and Gartenfeld, 1981). Eight major selection criteria have been identified: accuracy, currency, point of view, audience level, scope of coverage, organisation, style and format. To be really effective, the material needs to be provided in the right circumstances, taking full account of environment, social background, educational level and so on. It is a fallacy to assume that simply providing health information will lead to healthy actions (Green, 1978). In examining the role of the library Marshall and Haynes (1983) have pointed out that the provision of information materials can be effective in changing health behaviour in the short term, but to have a long-term effect the material should be part of a wider educational strategy.

PATIENT EDUCATION ACTIVITIES

There is now an increasing interest in patient education activities, particularly in nursing, stimulated by the introduction of the 'nursing process' in the USA and UK. The 'nursing process' involves an approach to nursing where the needs of the whole patient – social, emotional and educational as well as medical – are taken into account. A recent issue of *Topics in Clinical Nursing* was devoted entirely to education for self care (1980) and contained the statement 'we must conclude that nursing is heading away from a strict medical disease model of patient submission, to actively promoting the self care movement'. Ten years earlier *Nursing Clinics of North America* had an issue containing a symposium on patient teaching (1971). As an extensive review by Cohen (1981) shows, patient education is now a major topic in nursing. Of the many books now available on the topic most are American (Megenity and Megenity, 1982; Rankin and Duffy, 1983; Redman, 1981; Squyres, 1981; Woldrum, 1985) with the notable exception of Jenifer Wilson-Barnett's *Patient Teaching* (1983). Most publications concentrate on a total educational approach but the provision of information materials is a key element of this.

Two conditions, diabetes and hypertension, have been the subject of particularly large numbers of studies in patient education. In both cases relatively cheap home testing equipment provides the opportunity for patients to be closely involved in monitoring their own health and treatment. In diabetes, simple blood glucose monitoring apparatus can give patients regular and detailed information on their blood sugar level. They can then alter their medication, diet and exercise accordingly. The importance of information for diabetic patients on how to monitor their condition and detect potential problems has been noted in a *Nursing Clinics* symposium on diabetes: patient education and care (1977), while Delbridge (1975) is one of a number of authors to look at the importance of education of children for the management of their own diabetes.

Hypertension is unlike diabetes in that the effects of a lack of patient understanding and incorrect treatment are not immediately obvious. However, simple home blood pressure monitoring kits provide similar opportunities for patients to participate in their own care (Wilkinson and Rafferty, 1978). A full explanation of the disease, its long-term nature and possible serious consequences has been found to be crucial to effective management.

Numerous studies have been made on patient education approaches to specific conditions, including arthritis (Stross, 1977), asthma (Maiman, 1979), back pain (Kvien, 1981), cancer (Grant and Davison, 1975), heart disease (Boggs, 1978), kidney disease (Wolf, 1976) and stoma care (Lawson, 1978). Further studies have been reviewed by Tabor (1981) and McEwen, Martini and Wilkins (1983). The Wessex Regional Library and Information Service has produced an extensive bibliography of reports of patient education activities entitled *Patient Progress* (1984).

INFORMATION AND THE REDUCTION OF STRESS

Entering hospital, particularly for surgery, is a stressful event. Patients experience fear of the unknown, fear of pain, fear of mutilation and of death. This fear and anxiety is not only distressing in itself but may have a profound effect on the recovery process. Janis (1958) conducted a series of interviews with patients undergoing surgery and made observations about levels of pre-operative anxiety and post-operative recovery. He found that extreme anxiety before the operation heralded a stormy recovery. Absence of any feelings of apprehension or fear was also not conducive to a smooth rehabilitation. The ideal state was a realistic degree of anxiety – an informed apprehension.

Since then, there have been a number of studies assessing the effect of giving information to patients pre-operatively. One of the first (Egbert *et al.*, 1964) found that the length of post-operative hospital stay was shorter for those patients who had been given information, and that they required fewer analgesics. Hayward (1975) compared a group of patients who had received information about anaesthesia, operative techniques, sensations following the operation and exercises, with a control group who did not receive information. The informed patients required fewer drugs, and those who had not received information reported more pain.

In addition to experiencing less pain and consuming less drugs it seems that informed patients also have fewer complications. Boore (1976) found that patients given a detailed account of their care and expected progress had fewer post-operative infections. Boore also found (1977) that information on exercises reduced post-operative breathing complications and lessened the length of hospital stay. Clearly, personality factors may prevent the assimilation and use of information. It is nevertheless interesting to note that in one trial (Andrew, 1967) patients who had been given information experienced less anxiety even if they could remember nothing of the information!

The provision of information to patients has been found to have a beneficial effect on stress in situations other than surgery. Elms and Leonard (1966) examined the provision of information on hospital routines, facilities and procedures and found that information on these reduced anxiety on admission to hospital. Patients also need advice and help on discharge, where inadequate preparation can lead to anxiety. A major study by Skeet (1970) found that 37 per cent of patients were discharged with less than 24 hours' warning, 19 per cent needed practical help at home and often did not know how this need would be met and 59 per cent received no advice other than 'take care of yourself'.

Medical tests and procedures are also a cause of anxiety. In her excellent book *Stress in Hospital*, Wilson-Barnett (1979) examines in some detail patients' experiences of a special test – a barium X-ray. There is a clear message in this book that providing information to patients leads to reduced anxiety. We are, however, reminded of the problems associated with the recall and understanding of information and the importance of its provision in the right setting. Hawkins (1979) has commented that patients may receive more information about complex or unusual tests than about routine ones like venepuncture or barium meal, probably because staff assume patients already understand everyday procedures. He makes an appeal for more literature for patients to reinforce doctors' advice and to dispel myths.

INFORMATION AND COMPLIANCE WITH TREATMENT

As we have seen the most likely remedy for ill health is medication. As many as one in four people are taking prescribed medicines at any one time. The doctor prescribes the medicine, the pharmacist dispenses it, but its application, successful or otherwise, depends on the patient. Yet research has shown that between 30 per cent and 50 per cent of patients do not take drugs properly (Blackwell, 1973). This can cause grave problems in conditions which depend on long-term medication. It has been estimated (Haynes, *et al.*, 1979) that less than 30 per cent of hypertensive patients benefit from their treatment. The other 70 per cent do not comply with treatment advice.

When the patient is in hospital nurses check and administer drugs. Then the patient is discharged and, overnight, he has to take responsibility for his own drug therapy. This lack of supervision can be a major factor in non-adherence to treatment. For instance, in a study on diabetics' adherence to insulin and diet regimes at home, it was found that 80 per cent of patients failed to administer their insulin properly, 50 per cent tested their urine in a way which would distort results and 73 per cent had unacceptable meals with unacceptable spacing (Watkins, 1967).

The term 'compliance' suggests a state of subservience to the medical model ('acquiescence, obedience, docility, pliability' *Roget's Thesaurus*) but failure to adhere to medical treatment is not just irrational behaviour for which the patient must be blamed (Stimson, 1974). In a classic study Haynes and Sackett (1976) identified more than 250 factors relating to compliance. These range from the weather (Badgley and Furnal, 1961) to safety-lock pill dispensers (Lane *et al.*, 1971). Haynes and his colleagues drew particular attention to the importance of a stable family life and absence of side effects in ensuring that patients take prescribed medicines. There is also evidence to suggest that non-compliers with treatment differ in ways independent of the effect of the treatment. For example men who did not take a placebo in a trial of preventive therapies for coronary heart disease died at twice the rate of those who complied with taking the placebo (Coronary Drug Project Research Group, 1980).

One of the major factors in non-compliance has consistently been found to be lack of information (Ley and Spelman, 1967). In one hospital study, 30 per cent of patients were wrong when questioned as to how often they took at least one of their drugs, only one in sixty knew the names of the drugs being taken, and 75 per cent were wrong about the part of the body affected by the drug (Marks and Clarke,

1972). More worrying was the fact that over half assumed they understood their drugs and only 5 per cent asked for doctor for clarification. It is not surprising then that Stewart and Cluff (1972), in their review of a number of investigations, reported that 25–59 per cent of patients made errors in self medication and up to 35 per cent of patients made errors which could pose serious threats to their health. Their conclusion was that 'in our society better instructions are given when purchasing a new camera or automobile than when the patient receives a life saving antibiotic or cardiac drug'.

The desire and need for information on prescribed medication is demonstrated in a letter to the *British Medical Journal* following a radio phone in programme (Faunch, 1979)

> I was surprised at the number of people who were worried about the long-term effects of drugs and the possibility of their becoming 'addicted', particularly as the drugs most mentioned were minor tranquillisers and analgesics. More disturbing was the fact that many patients had no idea why they should still be having to get repeat prescriptions for these items after several months, if not years. The overwhelming flood of response I received was an indication not only of the interest the subject provoked but also of what appears to be a genuine gap in patient care somewhere along the line.
>
> Callers were generally shy to go back to their GP and not always able to get to the retail chemist. It does seem a shame that there is nobody to give a few minutes' advice or reassurance that could make all the difference between a successful recovery or a worrying course of treatment.

A number of studies have shown that clear information does indeed promote adherence to drug taking. Colcher and Bass (1972) found that, when patients had information on antibiotics, they did on the whole complete the ten-day course. The provision of information was as effective as giving long-acting intramuscular injections of penicillin. Studies by Sharpe and Mikael (1974) and Linkewich and colleagues (1974) confirmed these findings. Research currently taking place in Southampton indicates that the provision of patient information leaflets on penicillin and anti-inflammatory analgesics increases patient satisfaction, makes patients more likely to complete the course of treatment and significantly increases their knowledge of side effects (George *et al.*, 1983).

The problem of providing simple accurate information on drugs was discussed at a meeting of the Medico Pharmaceutical Forum in 1980 and described in a leading article 'Drug information for patients: keep it simple' in the *British Medical Journal* (1980). Representatives from the medical, pharmaceutical and information professions, as well as consumer bodies and voluntary organisations, met again under the same auspices in 1985. At this meeting several different opportunities were identified for informing patients about medicines. These might occur before the consultation (health education), during the consultation with the doctor (information on benefits and risks of the treatment, and the treatment plan), at the dispensing point by the pharmacist (dosage, how to take the drug and how to store it) and after starting to take the medicine (what effects to expect and when, possible side effects and interactions, what to do if they recur) (Herxheimer and Davies, 1982).

The move towards original pack dispensing offers a great opportunity for the inclusion of patient package inserts in all prescribed medicines. These inserts should give patients information on dosage, frequency of dose, duration of treatment, whether the drug should be taken before, during, or after meals, whether alcohol, driving or operating heavy machinery should be avoided, and whether there are any adverse effects requiring prompt attention (Hermann *et al.*, 1978).

The same caution applies to the readability of patient drug information leaflets, package inserts and medicine labels as it does to other patient literature. Herxheimer and Davies (1982) have made an appeal for information from the prescriber, the pharmacist and the manufacturer to be harmonised so as to complement, not contradict, one another. There have been attempts to produce medicine labels with symbols for those with literacy problems (Adult Literacy Support Services, 1980). A recent call for plain English to be used on medicines has been made by Raynor (1985). Among his suggestions are:

'To be instilled' is widely misunderstood. Why not use 'One drop into each ...'?

'Complete the prescribed dose' was misunderstood by 40% of those asked. Why not use 'Keep taking the tablets until finished'?

33

'Use sparingly' was misunderstood by a third of patients, one of whom thought it meant 'Slap it on'. Why not use 'Apply a thin layer to the affected area only'?

'This medicine may colour the urine or stools'. 44% misunderstood 'stools'. Unfortunately an acceptable and understandable alternative is not immediately obvious!

COST-EFFECTIVE INFORMATION

It is indisputable that the provision of information to patients can have significant effects on health care. Clear, readable, accurate information can help patients to manage minor illness themselves and to know when it is really necessary to consult the general practitioner. The informed patient experiences less stress and anxiety in hospital, requires fewer painkilling drugs and shorter hospital stays. Information improves patient compliance with drug regimes, preventing costly and potentially dangerous errors in taking medicines, and allowing early detection of harmful side effects. Information on organisations, services and benefits is essential if patients are to be cared for in the community.

In an article back in 1968 Healy drew attention to the cost-effectiveness of information provision, and indicated the growing number of studies which show that giving information to patients improves recovery, reduces the number of days in hospital and the number of outpatient visits and lowers the likelihood of re-admission to hospital. Since then many more studies have corroborated this view. Green (1976) has suggested that patient education programmes control costs by better use of health resources and the increased capacity of patients for self care.

A recent article entitled 'Cost effective advice' (Slack, 1985) combines the professional perspective of the nurse with the personal experience of the relative in underlining the importance of information and suggests some ways in which the patient's needs might be met. She gives a clear message for library and information services and for the authorities who fund them.

Some time ago my mother suffered a severe stroke. During her hospital stay I spent many hours waiting for doctors, nurses, news,

34

standing in the corridor with nothing to do, frustrated because I wanted to know how to care for my mother and how to help her. The staff were of little help to me and there was no written information. I ferretted about in libraries, wrote to the Chest, Heart & Stroke Association and searched for information that should have been in the ward. I noticed that the ward had a high readmission rate – hardly surprising as patients and relatives had no instruction about aftercare and community back-up was over-stretched and poor.

Most of the patients in the ward had one of about five diagnoses. It should be easy and would be helpful to have a range of appropriate leaflets and booklets in the waiting room. A video giving information, showing the home nursing care that might be needed or giving instruction on how to help the patient in hospital would enlist cooperation from the patients and relatives. If the hospital cannot provide the money it could be raised by a league of hospital friends, the community health council or even by selling tea to visitors. Indeed it would not be difficult to justify the cost to management. A library search will reveal a variety of evidence that patients with more information about their care recover more quickly and go home sooner.

Hospital nurses are in an ideal position to teach successfully and most patients want information desperately. But there is a long way to go before patient education becomes standard practice.

ETHICS AND INFORMED CONSENT

It is perfectly possible to make a case for the informed patient in hard cash terms, but there is also an ethical and humanitarian case. In a recent and crucial book Faulder (1985) links the patient's right to information to the broader rights of man ethic originated by eighteenth-century philosophers like Locke, Hume and Rousseau. The fundamental ideal remains the same today – that by virtue of our humanity we all possess an equal and undisputed claim to basic rights like life, liberty and the free expression of ideas. Health care and the rights of patients are the latest entrants into the rights arena.

The concept of informed consent is fundamental to traditional medical ethics.

Those in health professions acknowledge the individual's right to bodily integrity. When a medical intrusion on a person is advisable, the patient (or his representative) ordinarily has the authority to accept or decline the treatment proposed. By exercising this right, the patient has entered into a contractual relationship with those clinicians who are responsible for making judgements and decisions concerning the patient's care. For this relationship to be effective, the patient must accept responsibility for his own judgement rather than relinquish his right to the assumed authorities. He must find a viable system in which he can communicate his ideas as well as receive information about his illness. (Carpenter and Langsner, (1975))

The basic premise is that every human being has the right to determine what shall be done to his own body. In essence this should mean that the doctor has a duty to educate his patient so that he can make decisions for himself.

Shannon (1977) has asked 'What should the patient be told?' to enable genuine informed consent and suggests that, for an acceptable consent to be arrived at, the doctor must disclose to his patient all the information he has concerning the purpose, possibilities, uses and values of the treatment as well as the risks, present and possible. Barkes (1979) also emphasises the duty to explain the alternative forms of treatment which are available. In cancer, for example, this would include the possibility of radiotherapy, chemotherapy or surgery, or a combination of these. Of equal importance is the patient's right to remain uninformed.

Practically speaking there are two problems in informed consent: inadequate informing and inadequate consenting.

The patient who is in physical and/or emotional stress is unable to listen, query and ascertain facts in order to make a rational decision about consent. The physician while making rational judgements based on the facts at hand often fails to communicate the necessary information to the.patient on which informed consent could be based. (Carpenter and Langsner, 1975)

In reality informed consent is often a fiction (Laforet, 1976), a theoretical concept rather than 'a process for true patient participation in clinical decisions' (Carpenter, 1974). It is often argued that there can never be true informed consent because patients' understanding of their medical situation will always be markedly inferior to the knowledge of the doctor. The patient, however, has an unrivalled perception of the personal implications of treatment. 'This does not prevent her understanding perfectly adequately its direct significance for her providing of course that it has been properly explained' (Faulder, 1985).

In the United States, the law states that the final choice of therapy rests with the patient and not the doctor. The patient must have free access to all he needs to know in order to decide for himself on a particular procedure or treatment. The doctor must rarely, if ever, withhold information or pressurise the patient, irrespective of scientific, medical or personal factors. In the United Kingdom there is no such principle, despite a High Court judge's laudable statement that 'no amount of professional skill can justify the substitution of the will of the surgeon for that of his patient' (Gwynne, 1978). Lord Justice Edmund Davis (1973) has outlined the common law precedents in Britain which suggest that there is no precedent which places on the medical profession a responsibility to give information to the patient. However, there has recently been an important test case in England dealing with the issue of informed consent: *Sidaway v the Board of Governors of Bethlem Hospital* (reported in *The Times* February 22nd 1985). Mrs Sidaway had a history of severe pain and, in 1974, had an operation on her neck to relieve this. The doctor whom she described as 'a man of very very few words' did not tell her that there was a 1–2 per cent risk that her spinal cord might be damaged. In the event it was damaged, leaving Mrs Sidaway disabled. The grounds for her action were that the doctor had not disclosed the risk and, had she known of it, she would not have consented to the operation. The House of Lords dismissed Mrs Sidaway's case on the grounds that deciding what information to give a patient was 'as much an exercise of professional skill and judgement as any other part of the doctor's comprehensive duty of care to the individual patient' (Lord Diplock). There are interesting features in this case in that various expressions in the judgement seem to suggest that surgeons are expected to disclose more information than others because of the invasive procedures involved, and that more information is expected in an elective procedure than in an emergency one (Carson, 1985).

However, the essential judgement remains that informed consent has no place in English law.

The patient's right to information is much more clearly established in the United States (Annas, 1975). The Accreditation Manual for Hospitals issued by the Joint Commission on Accreditation of Hospitals (1980) states that the patient should receive 'adequate information concerning the nature and extent of his medical problem' and 'instruction in self care'. In 1972 the American Hospital Association produced a Patients' Bill of Rights. Although this has no legal standing, it has been used as a model by several government bodies in North America which have adopted legally binding bills of rights. In January 1984 the European Parliament tabled a resolution inviting the Commission to submit as soon as possible a proposal for a European Charter on the Rights of Patients. In both declarations, the right to information is an essential feature.

American Hospital Association – a Patient's Bill of Rights [*Extract*]

The American Hospital Association presents a Patient's Bill of Rights with the expectation that observance of these rights will contribute to more effective patient care and greater satisfaction for the patient, his physician, and the hospital organization. Further, the Association presents these rights in the expectation that they will be supported by the hospital on behalf of its patients, as an integral part of the healing process. It is recognized that a personal relationship between the physician and the patient is essential for the provision of proper medical care. The traditional physician–patient relationship takes on a new dimension when care is rendered within an organizational structure. Legal precedent has established that the institution itself also has a responsibility to the patient. It is in recognition of these factors that these rights are affirmed.

1. The patient has a right to considerate and respectful care.
2. The patient has the right to obtain from his physician complete current information concerning his diagnosis, treatment and prognosis in terms the patient can be reasonably expected to understand. When it is not medically advisable to give such information to the patient, the

information should be made available to an appropriate person on his behalf. He has the right to know, by name, the physician responsible for coordinating his care.

3. The patient has the right to receive from his physician information necessary to give informed consent prior to the start of any procedure and/or treatment. Except in emergencies, such information for informed consent should include but not necessarily be limited to the specific procedure and/or treatment, the medically significant risks involved, and the probable duration of incapacitation. Where medically significant alternatives for care or treatment exist, or when the patient requests information concerning medical alternatives, the patient has the right to know the name of the person responsible for the procedures and/or treatment . . . .

. . . No catalog of rights can guarantee for the patient the kind of treatment he has a right to expect. A hospital has many functions to perform, including the prevention and treatment of disease, the education of both health professionals and patients, and the conduct of clinical research. All these activities must be conducted with an overriding concern for the patient and, above all, the recognition of his dignity as a human being. Success in achieving this recognition assures success in the defense of the rights of the patient.

[Extract from Resolution approved by the American Hospital Association of Delegates, 6 February 1973]

Resolution on a European Charter on the Rights of Patients
[*Extract*]

a) the right to available treatment and care appropriate to the illness
b) the right to prompt treatment
c) the right to adequate social security cover to allow the rights set out in a) to be exercised
d) the right to free choice of medical practitioner and health-care establishment
e) the right of access to hospital services within a reasonable travelling distance
f) the right to information concerning diagnosis, therapy and prognosis, the patient's right of access to his own medical

data, and the patient's right to give his consent or to refuse the treatment proposed.

g) the right to medical confidentiality, the only possible exceptions to which should be on a limited number of serious and well-defined grounds, having due regard for the integrity of the human person

h) the patient's right to lift the obligation of confidentiality completely or in part as regards his own medical records

i) the right to complain based on 'damage to the interests of the patient'

j) the right to an appeal procedure before the courts

k) the rights and duties of medical practitioners

l) the patient's right to be represented by independent associations and organisations

m) the definition of the legal status of the patient in a health-care establishment

n) the right to respect for private life and for religious and philosophical convictions

o) the right to a dignified death.

[Extract from Resolution tabled by the European Parliament on 19 January 1984]

REFERENCES

Adult Literacy Support Services (1980) *Understanding Labels: Problems for Poorer Readers*, ALSS, London.

Anderson, J.E., Morrell, D.C., Avery, A.J., and Watkins, C.J. (1980) 'Evaluation of a patient education manual', *British Medical Journal*, vol. 281, pp. 924–6.

Andrew, J.M. (1967) *Coping Styles: Stress Relevant Learning and Recovery from Surgery*, PhD dissertation, University of Los Angeles, California.

Annas, G.J. (1975) *The Rights of Hospital Patients*, Avon, New York.

Badgley, R.F. and Furnal, M.A. (1961) 'Appointment breaking in a paediatric clinic', *Yale Journal of Biology and Medicine*, vol. 34, pp. 117–23.

Barkes, P. (1979) 'Bioethics and informed consent in American health care delivery', *Journal of Advanced Nursing*, vol. 4, pp. 23–38.

Berg, A. and Logerfo, J. (1979) 'Potential effect of self care algorithms on the number of physician visits', *New England Journal of Medicine*, vol. 300, pp. 535–7.

Blackwell, B. (1973) 'Drug therapy patient compliance', *New England Journal of Medicine*, vol. 289, p. 249.

Blackwell, B. (1976) 'Treatment adherence', *British Journal of Psychiatry*, vol. 129, pp. 513–31.

Boggs, B. (1978) 'A coronary teaching program in a community hospital', *Nursing Clinics of North America*, vol. 13(3), pp. 457–72.

Boore, J.R.P. (1976) '*An Investigation into the Effects of Some Aspects of Preoperative Preparation of Patients on Postoperative Stress and Recovery*, PhD thesis, University of Manchester.

Boore, J.R.P. (1977) 'Preoperative care of patients', *Nursing Times*, vol. 73(12), pp. 409–11.

Boyle, C.M. (1970) 'Difference between patients' and doctors' interpretation of some common medical terms', *British Medical Journal*, vol. 2, pp. 286–9.

Byrne, P.S. and Long, B.E.L. (1976) *Doctors Talking to Patients*, HMSO, London.

Carpenter, W.T. (1974) 'A new setting for informed consent', *Lancet* vol. 1, pp. 500–1.

Carpenter, W.T. and Langsner, C.A. (1975) 'The nurse's role in informed consent', *Nursing Times*, vol. 71, pp. 1049–51.

Carson, D. (1985) 'The patient's right to know', *Health and Social Services Journal*, vol. 95, p. 278.

Cartwright, A. (1964) *Human Relations and Hospital Care*, Routledge and Kegan Paul, London.

Cartwright, A. and Anderson, R. (1980) *Patients and Their Doctors*, Journal of the Royal College of General Practitioners Occasional Paper 8.

Cohen, S.A. (1981) 'Patient education: a review of the literature', (76 references), *Journal of Advanced Nursing*, vol. 6, pp. 11–18.

Colcher, I.S. and Bass, J.W. (1972) 'Penicillin treatment of streptococcal pharyngitis: a comparison of schedules and the role of specific counselling'. *JAMA*, vol. 222, pp. 657–9.

Cole, R. (1979) 'The understanding of medical terminology used in printed health education materials', *Health Education Journal*, vol. 38 (4), pp. 111–21.

Coronary Drug Project Research Group (1980) 'Influence of

adherence to treatment and response of cholesterol on mortality in the Coronary Drug Project', *New England Journal of Medicine*, vol. 303, pp. 1,038–41.

Dalton, L. and Gartenfeld, E. (1981) 'Evaluating printed health information for consumers', *Bulletin of the Medical Library Association*, vol. 69(3), pp. 322–4.

Davis, Lord Justice Edmund, (1973) 'The patient's right to know the truth', *Proceedings of the Royal Society of Medicine*, vol. 66, pp. 533–8.

Delbridge, L. (1975) 'Educational and psychological factors in the management of diabetes in children', *Medical Journal of Australia*, vol. 2, pp. 737–9.

'Drug information for patients: keep it simple' (1980) leading article, *British Medical Journal*, vol. 281, p. 1,393.

Dunkelman, H. (1979) 'Patients' knowledge of their own treatment: how it might be improved', *British Medical Journal*, vol. 2, pp. 311–14.

'Education for self care' (1980) Issue, *Topics in Clinical Nursing*, vol. 2.

Egbert, L.D., Battit, G.E., Welch, C.E. and Bartlett, M.K. (1964) 'Reduction of postoperative pain by encouragement and instruction of patient', *New England Journal of Medicine*, vol. 270, pp. 825–7.

Ellis, D.A., Hopkin, J.M., Leitch, A.G. and Crofton, J. (1979) 'Doctors orders: a controlled trial of supplementary written information for patients', *British Medical Journal*, vol. 1, p. 456.

Elms, R.R. and Leonard, R.C. (1966) 'Effects of nursing approaches during admission', *Nursing Research*, vol. 15, pp. 39–48.

Ewles, L. and Shipster, P. (1981) *One to One: A Handbook for the Health Educator*, East Sussex Area Health Authority, Lewes.

Faulder, C. (1985) *Whose Body is it? The Troubled Issue of Informed Consent.* Virago, London.

Faunch, R. (1979) 'What the public wants to know', *British Medical Journal*, vol. 1, p. 1,627.

Fletcher, C.M. (1973) *Communication in Medicine*, Nuffield Provincial Hospital Trust, London.

Frame, A. (1970) 'An evaluation of an information booklet for patients', *Health Bulletin*, vol. 28(4), pp. 39–43.

Franklin, B.L. (1974) *Patient Anxiety on Admission to Hospital*, Royal College of Nursing, London.

George, C.F., Waters, W.E. and Nicholas, J.A. (1983) 'Prescription information leaflets: a pilot study in general practice', *British Medical Journal*, vol. 287, pp. 1,193–6.

Grant, A.S. and Davison, R.L. (1975) 'Questions behind the answers: what people really want to know about cancer', *International Journal of Health Education*, vol. 18(2), pp. 109–18.

Green, L.W. (1976) 'The potential of health education includes cost effectiveness', *Hospitals*, vol. 50, pp. 57–61.

Green, L.W. (1978) 'Health information and health education: there's a big difference between them', *Bulletin of the American Society of Information Science*, vol. 4 (4), pp. 15–16.

Gwynne, A.L. (1978) 'The patient's consent', *Journal of Maternal and Child Health*, vol. 3, pp. 275–7.

Hawkins, C. (1979) 'Patients' reactions to their investigations: a study of 504 patients', *British Medical Journal*, vol. 2, pp. 638–40.

Haynes, R.B. and Sackett, D.L. (1976) *Compliance with Therapeutic Regimens*, Johns Hopkins University Press, Baltimore.

Haynes, R.B., Sackett, D.L. and Taylor, D.W. (1979) 'Practical management of low compliance with anti-hypertensive therapy: a guide for the busy practitioner', *Clinical and Investigative Medicine*, vol. 1, pp. 175–80.

Hayward, J. (1975) *Information: A Prescription Against Pain*, Royal College of Nursing, London.

Health Education Council (1976) *Treating Yourself*, H.E.C., London.

Health Education Council (1984) *Minor Illness: How to Treat it at Home*, H.E.C., London.

Healy, K.J. (1968) 'Does preoperative instruction really make a difference?', *American Journal of Nursing*, vol. 68, pp. 62–7.

Hermann, F., Herxheimer, A. and Lionel, N.D.W. (1978) 'Package inserts for prescribed medicines: what minimum information do patients need?', *British Medical Journal*, vol. 2 pp. 1,132–5.

Herxheimer, A. and Davis, C. (1982) 'Drug information for patients: bringing together the messages from prescriber, pharmacist and manufacturer', *Journal of the Royal College of General Practitioners*, vol. 32, pp. 93–7.

Hobbs, P., Eardley, A. and Thornton, M. (1977) 'Health education with patients in hospital', *Health Education Journal*, vol. 36, pp. 35–41.

Hugh-Jones, P., Tanser, A.R. and Whitby, C. (1964) 'Patients' view of admission to a London teaching hospital', *British Medical Journal*, vol. 2, pp. 660–4.

Humphreys, L. (1976), *Self Responsibility in Health Care: An Evaluation of the Health Education Council Booklet 'Treating yourself'*, MA Thesis, University of Reading.

Janis, I.L. (1958) *Psychological Stress*, Wiley, New York.

Joint Commission on Accreditation of Hospitals (1980) *Accreditation Manual for Hospitals*, Joint Commission, USA.

Kvien, T.K. (1981) 'Education and self care of patients with low back pain', *Scandinavian Journal of Rheumatology*, vol. 10, pp. 318–20.

Laforet, E.G. (1976) 'The fiction of informed consent', *JAMA*, vol. 235 (15), pp. 1,579–85.

Laher, M. and O'Malley, K. (1981) 'Educational value of printed information for patients with hypertension', *British Medical Journal*, vol. 1, pp. 1,360–1.

Lane, M.F., Barbarite, R.V., Bergner, L. and Harris, D. (1971) 'Child resistant medical containers', *American Journal of Public Health*, vol. 61, pp. 1,861–8.

Lawson, A.L. (1978) 'The stoma therapist and the urinary diversion patient', *Nursing Times*, vol. 74, pp. 1,938–9.

Ley, P. and Spelman, M. (1967) *Communicating with the Patient*, Staples Press, St Albans.

Ley, P., Bradshaw, P.W., Eaves, D. and Walker, C.M. (1973) 'A method for increasing patients' recall of information presented by doctors', *Psychological Medicine*, vol. 3, pp. 217–20.

Ley, P. (1977), 'Psychological studies of doctor–patient communication' in Rachman, S. (ed.) *Contributions to Medical Psychology*, Pergamon, Oxford.

Ley, P. (1979), 'Improving clinical communication' in Oborne, D., Gruneberg, M.M. and Eiser, J.R., *Research in Psychology and Medicine*, Academic Press, London.

Linkewich, J.A., Catalano, R.B. and Flack, H.L. (1974) 'The effect of packaging and instruction on outpatient compliance with medication regimens'. *Drug Intelligence and Clinical Pharmacy*, vol. 8, pp. 10–15.

McEwne, J., Martini, C.J.M. and Wilkins, N. (1983) *Participation in Health*, Croom Helm, London.

Maiman, L.A. (1979) 'Education for self treatment by adult asthmatics', *JAMA*, vol. 241(18), pp. 1,919–22.

Marks, J. and Clarke, M. (1972) 'The hospital patient and his knowledge of the drugs he is receiving', *International Nursing Review*, vol. 19, (1) pp. 41–51.

Marshall, J.G. and Haynes, R.B. (1983) 'Patient education and health outcomes; implications for library service', *Bulletin of the Medical Library Association*, vol. 71(3), pp. 259–62.

Megenity, J. and Megenity, J. (1982), *Patient Teaching: Theories, Techniques and Strategies*, R.J. Brady, Maryland.

Moll, J.M.H., Wright, V., Jeffrey, M.R., Goode, J.D. and Humberstone, P.M. (1977) 'The cartoon in doctor–patient communication', *Annals of the Rheumatic Diseases*, vol. 36, pp. 225–31.

Morrell, D.C., Avery, A.J., and Watkins, C.J. (1980) 'Management of minor illness', *British Medical Journal*, vol. 1, pp. 769–71.

Mullen, P.D. and Green, L.W. (1984) *Measuring Patient Drug Information Transfer*, Pharmaceutical Manufacturers Association, Washington, DC.

Nicoll, A. and Harrison, C. (1984) 'The readability of health care literature', *Developmental Medicine and Child Neurology*, vol. 26, pp. 596–600.

O'Hanrahan, M., O'Malley, K. and O'Brien, E.T. (1980) 'Printed information for the lay public on cardiovascular disease', *British Medical Journal*, vol. 281, pp. 597–9.

Perkins, E.R. (1981) 'Clinic booklets: a help or hindrance in patient education?', *Nursing Times*, vol. 77, pp. 781–3.

Pike, L.A. (1980) 'Teaching parents about child health using a practice booklet', *Journal of the Royal College of General Practitioners*, vol. 30, pp. 517–9.

Pratt, L., Seligman, A. and Reader, G. (1957) 'Physician views on the level of medical information among patients', *American Journal of Public Health*, vol. 47, pp. 1,277–83.

Quiggin, V. (1977), 'Children's knowledge of their internal body parts', *Nursing Times*, vol. 73, pp. 1,146–51.

Rankin, S.H. and Duffy, K.L. (1983) *Patient education: issues, principles and guidelines*, Lippincott, Philadelphia.

Rayner, C. (1979) 'Reality and expectation of the British National Health Service consumer', *Journal of Advanced Nursing*, vol. 4, pp. 69–77.

Raynor, D. (1985) 'Labels on medicines: do patients understand them?' *Self Health*, no. 7, pp. 11–12.

Redman, B.K. (1980) *The Process of Patient Teaching*, Mosby, St Louis.

Redman, B.K. (1981) *Issues and Concepts in Patient Education*, Appleton, Century, Crofts, New York.

Reynolds, M. (1978) 'No news is bad news: patients' views about communication in hospitals', *British Medical Journal*, vol. 1, pp. 1673–6.

Royal Commission on the National Health Service, (1979) HMSO, London, Para. 10.29.

Seiler, E.R. and Watson, L.M. (1982) 'Illness specific cards: a feasibility study', *Journal of the Royal College of General Practitioners*, vol. 32, pp. 435–9.

Shannon, T.A. (1977) 'What should the patient be told?', *New England Journal of Medicine*, vol. 296(9), p. 517.

Sharpe, T.R. and Mikeal, R.L. (1974) Patient compliance with antibiotic regimens', *American Journal of Hospital Pharmacy*, vol. 31, pp. 479–84.

'Sidaway v. the Board of Governors of Bethlem Hospital', *The Times*, 22 February 1985.

Skeet, M. (1970), *Home from Hospital*, Dan Mason Nursing Research Committee, London.

Skeet, M. (1974) 'Over to them', *Royal Society of Health Journal*, vol. 4, pp. 179–82.

Slack, P. (1985) 'Cost effective advice', *Nursing Times*, vol. 81 (14), p. 26.

Squyres, W.B. (1981) *Patient Education: An Enquiry into the State of the Art*, Springer, New York.

Stewart, R.B. and Cluff, L.E. (1972) 'A review of medication errors and compliance in ambulant patients', *Clinical Pharmacology and Therapeutics*, vol. 13(4), pp. 463–8.

Stimson, G.V. (1974) 'Obeying doctor's orders: a view from the other side', *Social Science and Medicine*, vol. 8, pp. 97–104.

Stokes, J.B., Payne, G.H. and Cooper, T. (1973) 'Hypertension control: the challenge of patient education', *New England Journal of Medicine*, vol. 289, pp. 1,369–70.

Stross, J.K. (1977) 'Educating patients with osteoarthritis', *Journal of Rheumatology*, vol. 4 (3), pp. 313–6.

'Symposium on diabetes: patient education and care' (1977) *Nursing*

Clinics of North America, vol. 12(3), pp. 361–445.

'Symposium on teaching patients' (1971) *Nursing Clinics of North America*, vol. 6 (4), pp. 571–690.

Tabor, R.B. (1981) 'Information for health: informing patients and public' in Carmel, M., *Medical Librarianship*, Library Association, London.

Vivian, A.S. and Robertson, E.J. (1980) 'Readability of patient education materials', *Clinical Therapeutics*, vol. 3 (2), pp. 129–36.

Waite, M. (1974) 'Patient concern', *Health and Social Service Journal*, vol. 84 (2), pp. 2,482–3.

Wallace, L., Wingett, C., Joshi, M. and Spellman, D. (1985) 'Heart to heart', *Nursing Times*, vol. 81, pp. 45–7.

Watkins, J.D. (1967) 'Observations of medication errors made by diabetic patients in the home', *Diabetes*, vol. 16 (12), pp. 882–5.

Wessex Regional Library and Information Service (1984) *Patient Progress: a Bibliography of Patient Education Activities*, W.R.L.I.S., Southampton.

Wilkinson, P.R. and Rafferty, E.B. (1978) 'Patients' attitudes to measuring their own blood pressure', *British Medical Journal*, vol. 1, p. 824.

Wilson-Barnett, J. (1979) *Stress in Hospital: Patients' Psychological Reactions to Illness and Health Care*, Churchill Livingstone, Edinburgh.

Wilson-Barnett, J. (1983) *Patient Teaching*, Churchill Livingstone, Edinburgh.

Woldrum, K.M. (1985) *Patient Education: Tools for Practice*, Aspen, New York.

Wolf, Z.R. (1976) 'What patients awaiting kidney transplants want to know', *American Journal of Nursing*, vol. 76 (1), pp. 92–4.

3

Health Information in the UK

There is no right to health information in the United Kingdom. As the National Consumer Council guide *Patients' Rights* (1983) indicates, the position in the UK is:

> ... if patients specifically ask for information their questions should be answered fully and truthfully. The fact remains though that patients have no absolute legal right to information about their case, and the information varies a lot from doctor to doctor.

The importance of the provision of information on voluntary organisations to parents of handicapped children has been recognised in one piece of legislation, the 1981 Education Act. This suggests that local health authorities have a statutory duty to provide information to parents.

> If the Authority are of the opinion that a particular voluntary organisation is likely to be able to give the parent advice or assistance with any special educational needs that the child may have, they shall inform the parent accordingly.

This Act refers to a very specific field, the special educational needs of handicapped children, and the phrase 'if the Authority are of the opinion' leaves it open to a good deal of discretionary interpretation. For other patients and parents there is not even this degree of legal support for the right to information.

The stimulus for health information provision in the UK has come not from legislation but from developments in health care policy and the vociferously articulated views of health care consumers. During the 1980s, policies for the National Health Service (NHS) have stressed the importance of care in the community and the prevention of illness and disability, rather than a high-cost, high-technology, hospital-based curative approach. In 1981 the Department of Health and Social Security published its handbook of policies and priorities. Amongst the priorities in this report called *Care in Action* are the following:

> ... creating awareness by voluntary, community and commercial organisations of the need to harmonise their efforts to ensure that the community has a positive approach to health promotion and preventive medicine ....
> ... identifying the resources in the informal and organized voluntary sectors, the private sector and the statutory services and enabling them to operate together in a concerted way ....
> ... giving people the information they need to make sensible decisions about personal health and encourage in the community a responsible attitude to health matters.

There are two clear messages here. The individual needs information to enable sensible decision-making in health. But the health authorities also need up-to-date information on resources available from the voluntary sector to ensure a cooperative and concerted approach to health care.

CONSUMERISM IN THE NHS

During 1984 the National Health Service was subjected to a management enquiry conducted by Sir Roy Griffiths of Sainsbury's. Quality assurance and the acceptability of services to consumers were recognised by Griffiths as being as important within the public sector as in the commercial marketplace. The Griffiths report argued 'Businessmen have a keen sense of how well they are looking after their customers. Whether the NHS is meeting the needs of the patient, and the community, and can prove that it is doing so, is open to question' (Ham, 1985).

In fact, rather more is known about how well the NHS is performing from the 'customer's' perspective than is suggested in the Griffiths report. A variety of mechanisms exist through which health care consumers can articulate their views and through which information is available about the social acceptability of the NHS. Health authorities are made up of part-time appointed members drawn from the local community, bringing a lay perspective to the NHS. These members are appointed as individuals rather than representatives and this necessarily limits the extent to which they can act as a vehicle for local needs and preferences. Alongside the health authorities the Community Health Councils (CHCs) have the job of representing the needs of the public in the NHS. Although their role and impact varies from district to district, they have, on the whole, been a valuable channel for public views. CHCs draw one-third of their membership from voluntary organisations and these are a further means of consumer involvement in the health service.

Many voluntary organisations act as pressure groups. Organisations such as MIND (National Association for Mental Health), NAWCH (National Association for the Welfare of Children in Hospital), and the NCT (National Childbirth Trust) have, on a number of occasions, provided valuable information on how well existing services are performing and areas in which improvements are needed. On a local level, a number of health centres and general practices now have patient participation groups. One of their major functions is to express the views of users of the health centre or practice. Nationally, bodies like the Patients Association and the College of Health have successfully influenced government and policy makers, often through skilful use of the media.

Despite these mechanisms one does not have to be Ian Kennedy, let alone Ivan Illich, to see that consumer satisfaction is often low and that public participation is not as effective as it ought to be (Maxwell and Weaver, 1984). One positive suggestion made in the Griffiths report was that market research techniques should be employed 'to ascertain how well the service is being delivered at local level'. The closest approximation to market research in the NHS is the survey work carried out by large numbers of CHCs to test local perception of the health services, expressed needs and satisfaction (Farrell and Adams, 1981). A large number of surveys about health and health services have been summarised by Cartwright (1983). In some areas a great deal of work has been undertaken – accessibility of primary care services (Simpson, 1979), attitudes to hospital services (Gregory, 1978), maternity services (Kitzinger, 1979).

A recent Marplan survey commissioned by the National Association of Health Authorities (Halpern, 1985) showed a high level of consumer satisfaction. Asked for their overall opinion of the NHS, 36 per cent of the sample said they thought it was 'extremely good' or 'very good', and a further 41 per cent thought the NHS was 'fairly good'. So 77 per cent had a positive opinion of the NHS. The areas of concern were dissatisfaction with waiting times, treatment following discharge – and, confirming a number of earlier studies, information provided. Indeed, 27 per cent said they had been given too little information, compared with 68 per cent who felt they had received 'about the right amount' and 1 per cent too much. It is interesting to note that patients least satisfied with information provision came from London and the North of England.

SOURCES OF HEALTH INFORMATION

Information is a two-way process. The individual health care consumer needs information in order to participate in his own health care and use health care resources. In return he can feed information on his needs and preferences back to the health care providers using some or all of the channels outlined above. In the United Kingdom there are many sources for the information he needs. Studies have shown that family, friends and neighbours are primary sources of information (Beal, 1979). A large-scale study of the information needs of elderly people (Epstein, 1983) showed that 30 per cent turned to their family for advice and 14 per cent to neighbours, compared with 12 per cent to the general practitioner and only 2 per cent to advice centres like Citizens' Advice Bureaux. The most pervasive source of information is the media. The individual is bombarded with messages from television, radio, newspapers and magazines – although many of these messages are not from what may be described as health enhancing forces (Jacobson and Amos, 1985). Health education forms part of basic education in schools and may be a continuing influence using the power of the media. Health information is also available in the high street where the pharmacist is, for many, the first and most frequent contact with a health professional.

As the individual enters the formal health care system he encounters a number of health professionals in particular the general practitioner and the health visitor, for whom information – and advice-giving is an important role. If he has to enter hospital, he may be fortunate enough to encounter nursing and medical staff skilled in communication with patients, or may find an information and advice centre within the hospital. In the wider community, a range of information and advice services are available, from the generalist (e.g. public libraries, Citizens' Advice Bureaux) to the specialist services in the areas of health and disability (e.g. Community Health Councils, DIALs – Disablement Information and Advice Lines). And of course there are the many hundreds of voluntary organisations and self-help groups who see the provision of information to their members as a central activity. In this chapter we will look at each of these sources of health information in turn.

THE MEDIA

The relationship between medicine and the media has become closer and more constructive since the early years of the century when William Osler could write:

> In the life of every successful physician there comes the temptation to toy with the Delilah of the Press – daily and otherwise. There are times when she may be courted with satisfaction, but beware: sooner or later she is sure to play the harlot and she has left many a man shorn of his strength and the confidence of his professional brethren (Osler, 1932).

Although there is still some mistrust of the influence of the media (a postal survey of 1,300 GPs described in *British Medicine* in 1979 found that 66 per cent saw newspapers and radio and television programmes as a hindrance to their work), there is a growing understanding of the separate but related responsibility of doctors and journalists (Bedford, 1979 and Dolman, 1981). Eastwood and Smith (1973) have drawn attention to this.

Doctors and journalists belong to professions which have intimate contact with the public. Doctors are constrained to further the public good by considering the wellbeing of the individual. Journalists, conversely, often use the individual to increase public interest which when aroused can frequently improve the wellbeing of the community.

The distinguished doctor and journalist, C.M. Fletcher, has seen the problem from both sides. 'Doctors have to come to terms with this conflict in attitudes and learn to appreciate that journalists and broadcasters are no less responsible than they are themselves and just as concerned with the good of the public' (Fletcher, 1973).

The increased responsibility of the media in its portrayal of disability has been remarked on by Wendy Greengross (1981) in an article on the media and International Year of Disabled People. She writes:

The media have accepted their role in this with enthusiasm and alacrity, examining the needs of disabled people and generally bringing them out of the closet and forcing upon viewers and listeners some realisation that there are many severely disabled people around who are capable of speaking for themselves as intelligently, as movingly, and as wittily as anyone else, and that inside twisted, even grotesque, bodies there are ordinary people who are as nice or as nasty as anyone else. Quite a change from a few years ago when the editor of a well-known women's magazine refused a series on the emotional problems of the disabled, saying with some distaste 'My readers don't want to know anything about that'. The much-maligned 'Crossroads' with Sandy in his wheelchair since 1972, has considerably changed attitudes to spinal cord injuries and created an acceptance of wheelchairs and their occupants, but without much examination of the emotional problem of being surrounded in an iron cage, or the physical problems of access.

Newspapers and magazines

Newspapers are read by millions of people each day and they have the advantage over radio and television in that the reader has a permanent record of the information on the printed page. A Canadian study (Richardson, 1969) found that a weekly dental column in a newspaper had a much greater effect than a weekly radio broadcast. Medical journalists are usually responsible and well informed and aim to present information in an attractive and memorable form. Ronald Bedford, the science editor of the *Daily Mirror*, has reminded us (1979) that respected medical journals such as the *British Medical Journal* and the *Lancet* make their latest issue available, at least a day before publication, to the medical correspondents of the national newspapers, BBC, ITV and the Press Association. This explains why a patient can be in possession of medical information in a potted form before the GP has the authorised version. Meditel, a closed user group for doctors, on the British public viewdata system, Prestel, aims to give doctors warning of what patients will be asking them by listing medical features on television, radio and in the newspapers that week.

The 'agony' columns of newspapers and weekly magazines are read avidly by millions (Smith, 1983). Even Sherlock Holmes confessed that he read 'nothing except the criminal news and the agony column. The latter is always instructive' (*The Noble Bachelor* quoted in Williamson and Danaher, 1978). As described in more detail in the previous chapter, Claire Rayner (1979) has analysed the 40,000 letters she receives each year as a medical journalist. Agony columns are found in magazines from many countries. At a recent conference, Dr Kim Solstad (1985) traced the history of question and answer columns in Danish magazines. Although answers have appeared in personal columns in Danish magazines since the 1930s, these tended to be inscrutable (K. Keep in the shade and rub them with lemons). A major advance in the value of agony columns as a tool for health education came in the 1950s with the inclusion of the questions as well as the answers. Dr Solstad commended the potential of weekly magazines for conveying health information. In Denmark these magazines are read by 55 per cent of women and 35 per cent of men over the age of 15.

Radio and television

Over the years, radio and television have produced many features on all aspects of health and disease. The *Dictionary of Social Action Programmes* produced by the Volunteer Centre's Media Project is published twice a year and attempts to identify national and local television and radio programmes, or regular features which are likely to be of interest, to social welfare agencies. The current issue lists 34 programmes or features on disability, 14 for the blind, 19 for the deaf and hard of hearing, 10 for the elderly, 55 in the field of health information and health education (including radio doctors), and a further 88 general advice shows which often have a health content. Television programmes such as *Wellbeing* (Channel 4) and *Where There's Life* (Yorkshire) are widely viewed. *Open Space* and *Grapevine* (BBC) have given self-help groups the opportunity to participate in programmes and present a case or give information on the air. On radio, *Medicine Now* (Radio 4) is a magazine programme on new treatments and research, *Does he take sugar?* (Radio 4) is highly regarded for its combination of practical information and advice and challenging features on disability, and *In Touch* (Radio 4) provides similar news and facts for blind people. A more directly educational role is undertaken by the Open University in conjunction with the media. In addition to formal academic modules the Open University has designed courses aimed at the more general audience such as 'The Pre-School Child', 'The First Years of Life' and 'Health Choices'.

Phone-in programmes are becoming increasingly popular on local and national radio. These programmes give people the opportunity to seek help from experts without entering into the personal relationship implied in, for example, visiting the general practitioner. There have been a number of studies of the use and effectiveness of phone-ins. Adrian Rogers (1980) an Exeter GP has analysed the problems presented by 158 callers to a regular medical open-line programme on Plymouth Sound. Not surprisingly, as the programme was broadcast between 2.00–4.00 p.m., 88.7 per cent (140 callers) were women. The average age was 44 years, and the most common type of problem was skin disorders, followed by emotional problems and gynaecological disorders. The most unusual calls concerned Gilbert's Disease and Duchenne's Disease. Three callers were advised to take urgent action as, for example, one caller who complained of a bleeding mole which was potentially malignant. Ninety-six callers were referred back to their general practitioners.

Some of the most detailed research into the use of local radio was carried out by Penny Webb when Area Health Education Officer for

Merton, Sutton and Wandsworth. In 1981 she answered an off-air advice line at BBC Radio London for three hours every Wednesday afternoon for one year. The analysis of these 244 calls makes an interesting case study (Webb, 1981). The value of off-air advice lines is that enquirers can ring up in confidence and that far more problems can be dealt with than individually on the programme itself. As in Roger's study, Webb's research showed that most callers were women and this was reflected in the preponderance of women's health problems. She observes that the most consistent piece of advice seen in magazine health columns or on radio phone-ins is that enquirers should talk to their doctor. This research indicates that most people had already seen their doctor and that this had failed to meet their expectations. It could be that radio listeners need more information on how to communicate with their doctor.

During May 1982 Penny Webb went on to participate in a two-week phone-in project on London Broadcasting Company (LBC). The project's aim was to investigate the use and abuse of drugs in the family. Queries covered solvent abuse, prescription drugs (particularly tranquillisers), over-the-counter drugs, slimming drugs, hormones, alcohol and illegal drugs. (Webb, 1982). Tranquillisers accounted for the largest number of calls (899 or 61 per cent).

Television companies have carried our their own research into the impact and effectiveness of their programmes. A detailed examination of the BBC's medical programmes and their effect on lay audiences was made by the BBC's General Advisory Council in 1976. This examined a range of specific medical programmes as well as programmes like *Horizon* which featured a health topic on a regular basis. Despite a general public squeamishness (43 per cent were disturbed by operations on television and 7 per cent by people even looking ill) medical programmes were as popular in 1976 as they are ten years later.

The most comprehensive recent evaluation has been of the Channel 4 series *Wellbeing* by the Centre for Mass Communication Research at Leicester University (McCron and Dean, 1983). The report looks in great detail at the audience size, the educational impact of the series, and the operation of the follow-up service whereby Broadcasting Support Services (BSS) distributed leaflets and operated a telephone feedback service. The overall impression from the research was that *Wellbeing* was, in television terms, a successful programme attracting a considerable audience and a high level of audience appreciation. Most importantly, it showed that health programmes need not follow a 'doctor knows best' approach. Health programmes presented, at least in part, from the perspective of the public can make exciting television which encourages people to think for themselves.

PUBLICATIONS

Popular medical publishing is a boom area and it is impossible to begin to describe the range of publications available.* There is a long tradition of medical encyclopaedias, and modern versions of these remain popular (*the Penguin Medical Encyclopaedia* and the *Pears Medical Encyclopaedia* for example). A more innovative approach based on the flow chart can be found in Vickery and Fries's *Take Care of Yourself* (1980). Originally published in America, the book uses flow charts to indicate possibilities for self treatment and to indicate when professional help should be sought. Other general guides for the lay reader include dictionaries of operations (Delvin, 1981; Stanway, 1981) and the excellent popular pharmacopoeia, *Medicines: A Guide for Everybody* (Parish, 1984). H. Winter Griffith's *Instructions for Patients* (1982) is a major American aid to patient education. It is a looseleaf compilation of 350 instruction sheets of general information, treatment and warning signs on a wide variety of conditions. The sheets can be removed for photocopying and a copy given to the patient. Other important kinds of general guides are the source books of organisations, aids, benefits and services such as the indispensable *Directory for disabled people* (Darnbrough and Kinrade, 1984) and directories of voluntary organisations and self-help groups, of which a number are available.

For specific health topics, several publishers have impressive lists of titles. The Oxford University Press *The Facts* series is written by leading consultants and gives authoritative descriptions of major conditions for the lay person. Titles cover topics such as *Back Pain, Breast Cancer, Coronary Heart Disease, Multiple Sclerosis.* Churchill Livingstone publish a series of slim *Patients' Handbooks* ranging from

*A core list of publications is given in Chapter 5.

Help with Bedwetting to *Epilepsy Explained*. A series of *Pocket Health Guides* is available from Hamlyn while Martin Dunitz publishes the well-received *Positive Health Guides*. Sheldon Press has produced an excellent series *Overcoming Common Problems* with an emphasis on psychological problems.

Other important publishers of books on health for patients and the public are the Consumer's Association, the Souvenir Press *Human Horizons* series and Penguin Books who, with titles like *Our Bodies Ourselves* provide a stimulating antidote to a sometimes conservative field. Typical of the latter is the British Medical Association's *Family Doctor* series of 40 booklets for a lay readership, available through chemists' shops.

The Health Education Council and Scottish Health Education Group are responsible for a wide range of booklets, leaflets and posters on topics related to the promotion of good health. Most specialist patient organisations produce booklets on coping with specific handicaps and illnesses. Examples of these are the British Diabetic Association, the Chest, Heart and Stroke Association, the Association for Spina Bifida and Hydrocephalus, the Spastics' Society, MENCAP and MIND.

A number of magazines are devoted to health for the lay person. *Doctors Answers* (Marshall Cavendish) appeared over a two-year period as an alphabetical guide to health and illness. The weekly parts were designed to cumulate into a home medical encyclopaedia. Magazine publishers are becoming aware of the market for glossy publications based on current interest in diet and fitness. One of the most successful of these is *New Health* (Haymarket) which combines a positive health message with an emphasis on alternative, and particularly herbal, cures. *Handicapped Living* (A.E. Morgan) has broken new ground by presenting advice on the practical aspects of living with disability in a popular format which appears on ordinary bookstalls. It has been described as 'the disability *Autocar*'. The College of Health's quarterly *Self Health* is more comparable to *Which* or *New Society*. It offers a stimulating combination of investigative reporting and well documented factual and news items in a setting free from advertising.

Many voluntary organisations and self-help groups publish journals, or at least newsletters, which give details of new advances in treatment and research, practical advice on self care and notification of new publications, useful addresses and so on. These range from the professionally produced journal of the large national organisations (for example *New Generation* from the National Childbirth Trust and *Open Mind* from MIND, the National Association for Mental Health) to typed and duplicated newsletters from small self-help groups. The quality of production is not necessarily an indication of the value of the information content. One of the most valuable sources of shared advice and contacts for parents of handicapped children is the *In Touch Newsletter* typed and distributed by Mrs Ann Worthington from her home in Cheshire.

Publications and information sources on health for the lay public have been reviewed in *Information sources in the medical sciences* (Tabor and Gann, 1984).

AUDIOVISUAL MATERIALS

Audiotapes

Since the development of the convenient and widely used audio-cassette there has been much experimentation in its use for educational purposes. Patient education is no exception. Midgley and Macrae (1971) have demonstrated that the use of audiotapes can significantly increase patients' understanding of their condition. A number of studies have examined the use, in the home, of audiotapes for patients with conditions such as chronic bronchitis, hypertension, epilepsy and diabetes (Fry and Meyrick, 1984). Patients can borrow tapes and play them at home on compatible popular equipment. The recording can be listened to by all the family and has the advantage of involving relatives in what is, after all, a family problem. In the United States (TelMed), Australia, and now in the UK (Healthline), another way of listening to tapes at home is over the telephone. Members of the public can telephone a publicised local number and request a pre-recorded tape on the topic of their choice which is then played to them over the telephone.

A number of hospitals have used audiotapes to prepare patients for surgery and hospital procedures. When the daycare unit at Kingston Hospital was opened in 1979 an educational cassette tape was developed to prepare patients for a hernia repair operation. At the patient's first visit a date is fixed for the operation and an audiocassette tape, of approximately 20 minutes duration, is lent. This contains an explanation of what a hernia is, and how it is repaired surgically, an account of pre-operative and post-operative procedures, and some advice to patients about exercise, lifting and so on. Use of the tape by 119 patients over a nine-month period was monitored by Baskerville and colleagues (1985). The availability of cassette players was widespread, with 84 per cent of the patients owning one. Of the remaining 18 people most could borrow one from family or friends. Only two patients were unable to listen to the tape. Few patients listened to the tape alone. Most people (75 per cent) listened with their spouse and in 32 per cent of households other members of the family also listened. A significant minority (15 per cent) brought in friends and neighbours! The majority of patients (90 per cent) found the information on the tape adequate. Of those who did not, most wanted even more detailed information. More importantly, when questioned after the operation 94 per cent wrote that the recording accurately described the events on the day of the operation and afterwards. Patients suggested that tapes should be made available prior to any surgical operation; other popular suggestions were pregnancy, heart disease, and hypertension.

Audiotapes for patients have also been used to put over more general health education messages in the doctor's waiting room. In 1976 a South East London general practice experimented with the introduction of a 'dial access' tape system for patients within the surgery (Clarke *et al.*, 1976). Five telephones were installed and spaced out between the seats in the waiting room. Patients selected tapes from a leaflet and picked up the telephone. The receptionist answered it and set the selected tape in motion. Twenty tapes, varying in length from 90–240 seconds were chosen and prepared. Leaflets were distributed in the waiting room and a display stand drew attention to the service. In the 7½ months of operation 350 tapes were played. In spite of renewed publicity during the course of the project, this amounted to only 2.5 per cent of the 14,000 who came to the surgery. The authors conclude that a dial access tape system is probably not the best way to put over health messages to patients in the waiting room.

Display machines

The tape–telephone project described above was not a great success probably because the medium was unfamiliar to the patients waiting for an appointment. Patients waiting to see the doctor have certain expectations. They expect to sit in one place, to find an atmosphere of 'hushed reverence', to hear conversation, if it exists at all, take place in whispers, to find a few old magazines behind which they can hide, and to answer their call by self-consciously tiptoeing away. In other words, they expect to be able to merge discreetly into the background and are not prepared to take any action which would upset the status quo (Clarke *et al.*, 1977). It was hoped that the tape–telephones would not disturb this equilibrium, but inbuilt conservatism proved stronger.

As a follow-up to this experiment a different approach was tried, this time using a Showmatic display machine. This is simply a device to display a sequence of posters. All too often posters, like calendars, become an unseen unnoticed part of the general background. The display machine has an important feature which negates this effect – the posters move. The machine can hold a sequence of up to 30 posters which are displayed two at a time, and there is a movement which constantly attracts the eye. This second experiment adopted an advertising approach: short messages for a mass audience with frequent repetition and the addition of humour (Clarke, 1980).

The machine proved to be a cheap and effective medium. It ran for several thousand hours with no maintenance or servicing. Compared with tape–slide machines which are prone to bulb failure, jamming slides and focusing problems, it was very convenient. Evaluation of the project showed that, although detailed information could not be transmitted, it was very effective for health education messages in a situation where there is a captive audience for short periods of time. Many patients were stimulated to ask their doctor further questions and there were instances of patients saying 'I don't need to see you now doctor. I have just seen the answer outside'. Similar experiments have been carried out using the Rotabine technique of moving display panels (Brown and Watson, 1984).

The multiple choice quiz board is another-relatively low-cost device which can be left with the minimum of supervision over fairly long periods of use. Battery-operated quiz boards were developed some time ago by the Scottish Health Education Group and covered topics such as smoking and heart disease, and smoking and pregnancy (Paton *et al.*, 1980). The boards were made from preprinted card with an aluminium foil conductive circuit. A 'pen' is attached by a wire to one terminal of a dry cell battery and the other terminal is connected via a light to the board. When the correct answer, from several alternatives is touched by a pen, the circuit is completed and the bulb lights up. It is evident that people enjoy the quiz board and the element of competition increases interest.

Television and video

Moving from low-cost techniques to those requiring a larger capital investment, we come to television and, more specifically, to the use of videotapes for health and patient education. In a useful article, Bonfield (1983) has described the advantages of television as a medium:

> Inherent in the nature of the medium are several traits that make television an ideal vehicle for patient education. It is a dynamic visual medium, capable of relaying a large quantity of information in an interesting and concise manner. It provides continuity and uniformity of material presented so the health care provider knows exactly what each patient has been exposed to. Subjects which patients may be embarrassed to ask about or which individual staff members may prefer to avoid, may be openly addressed on television. Patients may watch televised programmes more than once and arrange their own viewing to coincide with times when they are receptive to the information. Family members and friends can view programmes as well, allowing the educational experience, with the understanding and support resulting from it, to reach beyond the hospitalized individual. This approach relieves staff of rote teaching responsibilities, allowing them to focus on individual needs. They are provided with the means of presenting the same information several times without talking down to the audience.

Early televisual developments for patient education were through the medium of closed-circuit television. Since 1976, the Massachusetts General Hospital in the USA has been operating a closed-circuit television channel which transmits information directly to patients' bedside televisions. The Fairview General Hospital in Cleveland, Ohio, installed closed-circuit television for patients in the early 1970s and shows tapes on getting to know the hospital, special diets, and

62

what to expect in the X-ray department (Ballantyne, 1974). In Australia patients at the Flinders Medical Centre, South Australia, have access to three internally generated health information channels in addition to the normal broadcast channels (Turner and Larcombe, 1983).

The widespread use of videotapes, particularly in the home, has given a boost to television as a medium over the last few years (Tattersall and Marinker, 1983). In 1982 The Economic Intelligence Unit reported that 15 per cent of UK households owned a video recorder. This figure is now 24 per cent (*New Society*, January 1986). Video may be a particularly attractive medium for those who would not readily read printed material. Like audiotapes, they can be used at leisure in the home and shared with the family.

In the hospital setting videos have been used to entertain and inform patients in waiting areas. The accident and emergency department at Northampton General Hospital is like most others in that patients often experience long waiting times. This is especially true for people with relatively minor injuries whose wait will be prolonged as more serious cases take priority. Liable to become increasingly bored, anxious and frightened they have traditionally had little to entertain them. The nursing staff at Northampton observed that the same information is frequently given to patients individually – for example, the correct procedure for self certification or the need for precautions against tetanus. This information is often given during or after treatment when the patient is least receptive. The notion of reinforcing this information by use of video prompted the Northampton staff to make information films of their own (Gillespie and Orton, 1985). The prototype tape which includes local material dispersed with general health education messages has been well received. Some patients are so absorbed they miss having their name called out. There are plans to introduce new topics, including films directed at children.

Through its Video Unit, Northampton Health Authority is one of the health authorities actively involved in producing videos for its own staff, for social services departments and for local voluntary organisations such as MIND, and the National Society for the Prevention of Cruelty to Children. Videos produced by the Unit at the Department of Community Medicine, 39 Billing Road, Northampton, cover health education topics such as exercise, smoking and heart disease, documentaries on the work of professionals like chiropodists, and operating department assistants, and patient education topics including diabetes, radiotherapy, and aids for disabled people.

The Forth Valley Health Board in Scotland has been a pioneer of video-recorded health education programmes. During 1979, 1980 and 1981 a research project involving the production and evaluation of videos was carried out in conjunction with the Scottish Health Education Unit (Graham, 1980). The first two programmes covered care of the sick child at home and infant feeding. Evaluation of the infant feeding tape indicated that the videotapes made the mothers more aware of important aspects of infant feeding, for example, sterilisation of bottles and teats, and action to be taken in sickness or diarrhoea. The project went on to produce tapes on constipation and diabetes, in association with the University of Stirling, and these too have been evaluated. However, because most research depends on written questionnaires or verbal replies, this may put the evaluation of videotapes at a disadvantage since those who learn most effectively from audiovisual media are the less literate and articulate. Nevertheless, evaluation did show that many younger people in particular wanted back-up information in booklet form. In fact the booklet accompanying the constipation video was so well received that it called into question the value of producing the video at all! Video programmes currently available from Forth Valley Health Board, 33 Spittal Street, Stirling include those described above plus tapes on injecting insulin, vasectomy, leg ulcers, asthma in childhood, and back pain. A microcomputer program for diabetes education has also been produced on cassette and disk for the BBC micro.

The most ambitious schemes for the use of new technology have come from the South Western Regional Health Authority. Here the problems of communication in a region stretching from Gloucester to the tip of Cornwall, and beyond to the Scilly Isles prompted consideration of techniques including facsimile transmission, teleconferencing, office technology and the development of a series of video programmes aimed at patients with particular conditions, and the wider public (Stroud, 1985). A consultant dermatologist in Exeter cooperated with the video team in producing a film about psoriasis which is shown to patients and relatives. *Sailing too Close to the Wind* encourages patients to avoid a second heart attack and also tells the public how to avoid a first one. *I Hope You are Well* introduces the patient to a general practice, tells them who does what and hopefully tells them how to make the best use of the available resources. The policy in Devon is to close its mental handicap hospital at Starcross, and a series of videos for the public and parents of mentally handicapped children have been produced to help smooth the way to community care. These have been extremely successful and illustrate the power of television to change attitudes. South Western Region has now set up a central collection of video programmes based at the library of the Torbay Postgraduate Medical Centre, Torquay, Devon.

In the Wessex Region, Project Icarus, a registered charity, has produced video programmes on topics including smoking, drug abuse and alcoholism as well as documentaries on life in a unit for mentally handicapped children, and the effects of burns injuries. Project Icarus, based at 4 Clarence Parade, Southsea, Hants., is also the publisher of the acclaimed biography of Neil Slatter entitled *Lucky Break*? (Hurley, 1983). Neil broke his neck in a motorcycle accident and the book describes his experiences as a patient in a spinal injuries unit and how he coped on discharge. *Lucky Break*? is an excellent example of the contribution which personal accounts can make to a deeper understanding of the experience of illness and disability.

Cable television may be an important medium in the future, although it has not been taken up to any great extent in the UK. In the United States many homes have access to cable channels and hospitals and health organisations have joined together to form the Pittsburgh Health Cable Coalition which acquires and produces programmes for the city's Health Services channel. Today the channel offers several hours of health programmes each day with a billboard message service when programmes are not being broadcast. Early in 1982 the Coalition also began to produce a magazine programme called Healthline Pittsburgh (Horvath, 1983). By the end of the decade we can look forward to the establishment of this kind of 'community cable' in the UK. A number of voluntary organisations are now meeting as a forum entitled Cable in the Community to discuss these issues (c/o Community Service Volunteers, 237 Pentonville Road, London, N1).

Computer-assisted learning

The latest developments in new technology which have implications for patient information are in the area of computer-assisted learning (CAL). Because of the interactive manner in which they operate CAL programs offer the possibility not for dehumanised or mechanised learning but for a personalised, tailor-made approach which can be undertaken at the user's own pace. Patients are beginning to be faced with computers in medical practice for screening and diagnosis and, in most cases, they have not found the technology stressful (Pringle, *et al.*, 1985). At St James Hospital, Leeds, a computerised questionnaire has been introduced for routine antenatal interviewing, and has proved widely acceptable. When questioned, 70 per cent of expectant mothers said they liked the computer, with only four disliking the technique. Indeed, computerised interviewing seemed to have a relaxing effect on many women. Women from ethnic minority groups in particular appreciated the unlimited time they had to answer questions. It is hoped to develop the technique further for antenatal health education on topics such as diet in pregnancy (Morgan, 1984).

CAL programs have been available for some time in the United States and seem to be well accepted. A microcomputer-based CAL project has been running for several years at the University of Minnesota Health Centre (Ellis, *et al.*, 1982). Here, an Apple microcomputer was placed in the waiting area with a poster inviting people to try health awareness games. Evaluation showed a high rate of acceptance, with over 70 per cent of clinic users having used the system. While some interest was undoubtedly due to novelty, the fact that 10 users a day could be sustained over a 9-month period indicates the persistent attraction of the medium. When the microcomputer was made available at the Minnesota Health Fair in the town centre people queued for half an hour to use the programs.

In the UK, CAL is already well established in medical and nursing education, and now we are beginning to see a number of its applications in the health field. Such programs as there are for the public tend, like the other audio visual media described above, to be in the field of preventive health education rather than patient education to assist in coping with specific illnesses. Many of the CAL programs which have been developed in the UK have been rather amateurish and are often written for one type of microcomputer and are hence incompatible with other machines. They also tend to be written by enthusiastic medical personnel with only a basic grounding in programming. There is of course a danger that a computer specialist could design an imaginative program that was good on colour, graphics and so on, but poor on health education (Morgan, 1984).

There are currently plans to develop a British version of the American Body Awareness Resource Network (BARN) by the London School of Economics. BARN (or Barny to its friends) is designed as a confidential, non-judgemental source of health information for adolescents (Morgan, 1985). The topics offered as programs include alcohol and smoking education, communication skills, human sexuality, and stress management. The program runs on an Apple II computer and is in use in health centres, schools and youth clubs in Wisconsin. BARN is a new concept in the field of health information, offering games and interactive interviewing. It tries to teach skills needed to cope with real life situations like giving up smoking. Most of the BARN programs end with local names, addresses and telephone numbers for further advice and help. It may well prove an interesting and imaginative program to use in the UK, although it would require a good deal of modification for use in the British cultural setting. BARN lacks the sophistication of the interactive computer games now commercially available and which are highly popular in the home market.

The SOFTPHASE project for the Health Education Council at Chelsea College is making a listing of all CAL health education software packages currently available in the UK. For example, *Dietmaster*, a dietary analysis program for the Spectrum is now being marketed. Diet and exercise programs are becoming common, with a marketing strategy aimed at female home computer users. *Watch your Weight*, published by the Consumers Association and running on the BBC micro, guides the user through recipes for slimming meals with the assistance of a calorie calculator. *PACE* (Personally Analysed Computer Eating) for the BBC and Commodore also suggest a daily calorie intake and meal ideas. An alcohol education quiz for the Sinclair QL has been developed by the Department of Community Medicine at King's College, London, while the Department of Paediatrics at St Thomas's Hospital has produced an interactive computer game for young diabetics for the Sinclair ZX Spectrum. Many teenage diabetics appear resistant to instructional material and so the St Thomas's program is designed to incorporate graphics and a competitive game (Clayden, 1985).

A promising area is the use of computer graphics to teach anatomy and physiology. Jonathan Miller's pop-up book *The Human Body* is now available as *Bodyworks*, a package for the Spectrum 48K, with seven programs to illustrate cells, digestion, respiration, circulation, nerves and muscles.

As 'expert' systems develop over the next few years the home computer field is surely one which will be more fully exploited as a channel for health information and education. Expert systems are computer programs which encapsulate human expert knowledge of a particular subject, usually in a network of rules or probabilities. A user can consult the system as he would a human expert by telling it what the problem is and answering questions to clarify the details. The system will then make the required analysis, diagnosis, or recommendation. Since the first serious expert system – Mycin – was written at Stanford in the mid-1970s to help doctors to diagnose meningitis, expert systems have been developed to give advice on a wide range of topics. However, the medical field continues to attract a lot of attention and there is growing recognition among doctors that expert systems can be extremely useful as diagnostic aids. In November 1985 the *Guardian* reported the development of the first medical expert system for home computers (Anderson and Watson, 1985). The system *Your Health*, is available on the Sinclair Spectrum and Amstrad microcomputers. It uses a simple expert system to diagnose dietary imbalance, and allows a user to calculate his recommended daily allowance of various nutrients and compare them with his actual food intake. The ability of the program to give advice tailored to each individual user is what gives a system like *Your Health* an enormous advantage over conventional printed material.

PRESTEL

Prestel is the British public viewdata system. The thinking behind Prestel began in 1970 when a Post Office research team considering how the telephone network might be put to more profitable use outside normal office hours, came up with the idea of a community information system. The Post Office would provide the computer and telephone network and then sell space to anyone wishing to put information on the system. The system was originally called Viewdata, which has now become a generic term, and the Post Office has changed the name to Prestel. Since its launch in 1978, libraries and information services have been involved as users and information providers (Andrew and Horsnell, 1980).

When Prestel started, expectations were high. Here was an information system based on familiar technology, the telephone and television, presenting information in an attractive colourful way through an easy-to-use menu. The system seemed to hold particular promise for those whose access to other information services was limited; disabled people, the deaf, the housebound. But the public did not take the new child to its bosom (Drummond, 1980), and it was realised that there was little genuine public demand for Prestel and that 'technology push has triumphed over demand pull' (Cawkell, 1980). At its launch, the Post Office had predicted 100,000 users by the end of 1980 with exponential growth after that. Seven years later it is still only halfway to target. And, of the 50,000 users, less than half are in the domestic market. Prestel is not alone in this failure to capture the public imagination. The German system Bildschirmtext has been similarly unsuccessful. The Irish have recently set up their public viewdata system, Cognotec, and have learned from the experiences of Prestel. Realistically it has been designed as a commercial information system from the outset and community information developments have followed from this. In an attempt to attract information providers, Cognotec is charging a comparatively cheap rate for IPs (£2,500 p.a. with no page charges). This compares favourably with Prestel, where high IP charges have deterred smaller organisations, while the cost of using the system (and the necessity for a telephone and an adapted television) have been prohibitive for the disadvantaged groups for whom it has the most potential.

One of the earliest experiments in public use of the system was in Birmingham Reference Library. Here, the library approached the local Community Health Council to provide information on doctors' waiting lists, lists of local hospitals, late opening hours of chemists, bus services to hospitals etc. (Drummond, 1980). However, there were problems with the laborious procedure for updating and the cumbersome indexing structure, and the project indicated a number of basic flaws in the system. There have been further studies of the public use of Prestel (Maynes, 1982; Redfearn, 1983; Kania, 1985).

A number of national organisations have quite large databases on

Prestel. The Department of Health and Social Security has over 600 pages of information currently available, including 200 on social security benefits, 100 on help for disabled people, a 70-page guide to the National Health Service and 300 pages of health information for people going abroad. The Health Education Council pages include information about the HEC itself, basic health advice and the facility for ordering HEC publications. Some voluntary organisations have been involved with Prestel since its inception and have made use of the facility which allows users to donate money to the organisation at the touch of a button. The Royal National Institute for the Deaf has been particularly aware of the value of a soundless information medium and has a number of pages describing the resources and services of the RNID. Other relevant databases include those provided by the Ministry of Agriculture (food additives) and professional bodies such as the Royal College of General Practitioners (publications, RCGP Information Service, diary of events). Self-diagnosis charts are available from the information providers, Macmillan.

One of the growth areas has been in closed user groups: databases only available to certain users in possession of a password. A number of pharmaceutical companies offer this service to medical practitioners. Meditel is an extensive information provider in the medical field and provides classified advertisements, details of courses and conferences, information on practice management, and medical telesoftware on a closed user group basis. The very useful *Medicine in the News* which gives details of health-related features in the press, radio and television is also available through Meditel. This service has been developed in conjunction with the Medical Information Research Unit at Leeds Polytechnic.

Despite reservations there is still a future for Prestel. The basic Prestel standard is now in use throughout most of the world offering the opportunity of international networking. Microcomputers are having an enormous impact, and Prestel's recent improvement in the home market can partly be ascribed to Micronet 800, the telesoftware and micronews service accessible by home computer (Yeates, 1984). All the popular home and business microcomputers can now access Prestel since suitable software packages and modems have become widely and cheaply available. The real advance, however, is in the move away from reliance on the relatively crude menu-driven public Prestel system towards relatively cheap but powerful private viewdata systems which are now available even for microcomputers (Yeates, 1982; Strickland-Hodge, 1985). Many systems can now integrate private viewdata with conventional databases, and we can look forward to improved graphics and the incorporation of video images in the near future.

HEALTH EDUCATION AND HEALTH PROMOTION

The development of health education services stems in part from the Public Health Acts of 1925 and 1936, which made provision for the publication and dissemination of health information. It was, however, the Cohen Report (1964) which provided the framework for current health education services. Powers to undertake health education were given to local authorities by the 1946 National Health Services Act. The 1974 reorganisation of the National Health Service placed the responsibility for health education services with the Area Health Authorities and, with the removal of the area tier of NHS management, provision was made at district level. Most, but not all, district health authorities provide a health education service staffed by qualified health education staff.

Health education officers have been recruited from a variety of backgrounds, with nursing and teaching predominating (Smail, 1983). In the past many health education officers took no further specific training although a diploma in health education was available at London University in the 1960s. Subsequently a postgraduate course designed specifically for the training of health education officers was set up at Leeds Polytechnic in 1972, followed by courses at the Polytechnic of the South Bank, London, and Bristol Polytechnic.

The work of local health education units varies enormously, reflecting local needs and level of financial support and expertise available (Parish, 1983). The greater part of the work of the local health education unit is done not directly with the public but through a variety of health care professionals and other statutory and voluntary agencies. The role of the nurse as health educator has been described in some detail by Strehlow (1983). Health education is an essential element of the practice of health visiting, school nursing, district nursing, family planning nursing and midwifery. Other important health educators are general practitioners, environmental

71

health officers, teachers, social workers, youth leaders and voluntary agencies (Sutherland, 1979).

Most district health education units maintain a resource centre from which teaching and learning aids can be supplied to professionals and organisations in the District Health Authority. Leaflets and posters produced by the Health Education Council or local health education unit are also supplied. Following the recommendation of a joint Health Education Council/Department of Health and Social Security report (*The Recruitment, Training and Development of Health Education Officers*, 1981) many health education units now have a library. In 1982 Croydon Health Education Department appointed a full-time qualified librarian to a health education officer post. The librarian has an important role in providing library and information services to health educators and undertaking health education activities through libraries and other community outlets (Kempson, 1984).

On a national level, the Health Education Council has an extensive Resource Centre consisting of an information section, a lending library and a large reference collection of audiovisual materials. A service is provided for officers and members of the HEC, for all involved in formal or informal health education, and for the public. Resource lists are produced on 22 topics and there are monthly lists of recent additions to stock and journal articles of interest. The HEC and, in particular its Resource Centre, is enthusiastically embracing new technology. The Council is an information provider on Prestel and publications can be ordered by this means. A closed user group is also operated for health education units with Prestel sets or micro-computers. A network of microcomputers (the Hi-Net system) has been installed which will enable automation of the journal articles database, the library catalogue and leaflet collection. The HEC is also a pioneer of interactive video experimentation (Sharp, 1985). Excellent libraries are also maintained by the Scottish Health Education Group in Edinburgh and the Irish Health Education Bureau in Dublin.

There is a growing realisation that the educational approach is only one aspect of the health education process. Environmental, economic, political and social factors are equally important. Increasingly the more all-embracing term 'health promotion' is being used in preference to the narrower 'health education'. In Bath District Health

Authority, for example, the Health Education Unit has been redesignated the Health Promotion Unit. This is not to denigrate the educational approach to positive health, rather it is to say that there is more to health promotion than providing leaflets, posters and films, and organising talks. The new emphasis is on public relations, marketing and community development (South East Thames Regional Health Promotion Group, 1984). There is also increased interest in the promotion of maximum wellbeing amongst those with chronic disorders and long-term disabilities. For example, a project at Leeds Polytechnic has been examining health education with spinal cord injury patients (Lawes, 1984).

Large-scale innovative projects have adopted this broader definition of health promotion. In Liverpool a Travelling Health project has used adapted buses to provide basic fitness tests and healthy lifestyle assessment. The Health Buses have been staffed by 126 previously unemployed people under the Manpower Services Community Programme. A major feature of the project has been the building up of this cadre of informal health educators. Large numbers of people who might otherwise miss health education messages have been reached, and a root cause of ill health, unemployment, has been tackled by providing healthy, albeit temporary, employment opportunities. Health fairs and other promotional events have been linked to the International Garden Festival and the Tall Ships Race, and well-known figures such as the Liverpool football team have lent their support to campaigns (Ashton and Seymour, 1985).

In Wales a major prevention programme has been launched to reduce the rate of deaths from heart disease, which is the highest in Europe, (the equivalent of a jumbo jet crashing every fortnight). Heartbeat Wales is funded by the Health Education Council and the Welsh Office and will run for five years. The project began with the largest health survey ever conducted, involving 30,000 people who were asked to monitor their diet, exercise, smoking habits and blood pressure. The programme will continue with a range of approaches involving education in schools, the involvement of industry and agriculture, community and mass media activities, and further market research (Davies, 1985). The philosophy behind the Heartbeat Wales programme places great emphasis on working with people not against them, on participation not passivity, and on increasing self confidence and self empowerment. These are very much the themes of health promotion today.

A recent development in health promotion has been the establishment of 'health shops' where information and advice can be provided in a non-clinical high street setting. One of the first examples of this approach was the Women's Health Shop which operated in Edinburgh during 1983 and 1984 (Robinson and Roberts, 1985). The shop was situated centrally in the High Street and was well served by public transport. Inside, the overall impression was 'comfortable but not smart'. The staff consisted of two health visitors, two clerical assistants, and a community worker all of whom worked on a part-time basis. The shop was open for three and a half days a week, at a total yearly cost of £22,000 including staff, rent and rates. A wide range of materials was on display including books, leaflets, factsheets, a video and an exhibition which changed its theme every few weeks. Any woman making a medical or personal enquiry was seen by the nurse in a private room. Over the 16-month period of operation over 5,600 women visited the shop as well as 400 men (an average of 24 people each day). Almost 30,000 leaflets and factsheets were distributed, the most popular being on 'women's problems'. A total of 955 women (17%) had a discussion with the nurse, many of whom were referred to self-help groups and other helping agencies. The shop undoubtedly provided an attractive method of health education and health promotion, mainly on a one-to-one basis. By calling it a shop, women were encouraged to come as equals. It may be that the health shop is a more effective way of altering behaviour than mass education campaigns, and this approach is now being tried elsewhere.

PRIMARY CARE

The general practitioner is the first point of contact with the formal health care services, and acts as the gateway to the rest of the system. The GP is just one member of a primary health care team which usually includes the health visitor, the district nurse, and often other community-based staff such as the physiotherapist, occupational therapist, midwife and social worker. The primary care setting offers many opportunities for information provision (Fry and Meyrick, 1984), and many primary care professionals are involved in general health education as a major part of their work (Tyser, 1975; Fowler,

1985). Some practices have gone further and actively involved patients as participants in the activities of the surgery. The first real example of the participation of lay people in primary care was the Peckham Experiment of the 1930s. This began with a small group of lay people who were aware of the importance of the social environment to health and illness. A Family Health Club was established which provided general health checks and, in particular, concentrated on the care of infants and children. The concept was realised in the years 1935–39 with the founding of the Pioneer Health Centre in Peckham. It reopened in 1946 after the war but faded with the introduction of the National Health Service in 1948 (Pearse, 1979).

In the 1980s an attempt has been made to set up a new experimental centre along the same principles as the original Peckham project. The new Peckham Health Project was run by a committee drawn from local residents of four high density housing estates. Activities included discussion groups and the production of leaflets on common health topics (for example, children's illnesses, breastfeeding), and a video on doctor–patient relationships. Although the project ended after four years because of changes of key personalities and lack of long-term funding, it was, however, successful in giving people more information about health and illness, and in demystifying some of the workings of the Health Service. The project workers concluded, 'We learnt that giving people information about health is not sufficient – people need the confidence and encouragement to use it' (Fisher and Cochrane, 1982).

Patient participation groups have become increasingly common since the 1970s. The first successful patient participation group was formed in 1972 in Berinsfield, Oxford, with the general objective of allowing the views of patients to be heard directly by the general practitioners. The Berinsfield Group was closely followed in 1973 by the Aberdare Patients Committee in Glamorgan and the Bristol Practice Association. Each of these is described in a Royal College of General Practitioners Occasional Paper *Patient Participation in General Practice* (Pritchard, 1981). There is now a considerable amount of literature on the operation of patient participation groups. Dr Peter Pritchard, the founder of the Berinsfield Group has been responsible for a number of interesting papers including a practical guide to starting a group (Pritchard, 1983).

A survey published in 1982 (Paine, 1982) reported 37 active patient participation groups. There are now more than 60 and a National Association of Patient Participation Groups has been established. As more groups have formed, an increasing proportion have also foundered. A failure rate of 25 per cent has been reported (Mann, 1985). In an attempt to avoid the failure which had befallen other groups, the Patient Participation Group at Collingham Health Centre, Nottinghamshire undertook a survey to find out what patients wanted from the group (Hutton and Robins, 1985). There was a clear lack of knowledge about the functions of the group but the evidence suggested that if activities such as transport, self-help groups, first aid classes were arranged and publicised they would be well attended. In particular it was felt that a change of name might increase interest in the patient participation movement as a whole. The term 'patient' with its implications of 'sick person' may put off people who pride themselves on never needing the doctor. The Collingham Group has now adopted the name 'Village Care' to overcome this.

The 1982 survey showed that groups vary enormously in their role but about half are providing information, usually in the form of newsletters or directories of local health care facilities. For example, The Kentish Town Health Centre Users' Group has produced a *Health Centre Users' Handbook*, while the Birley Moor Health Group in Sheffield has issued a number of publications including a booklet about the group and basic leaflets on health problems such as high blood pressure. An Occupational Health Project based at Birley Moor Health Centre has provided an information service on hazards at work and legal advice on compensation. The use of a practice brochure by 262 new and established patients in Norton Medical Centre, a group practice in Stockton-on-Tees, has been evaluated (Marsh, 1980), and the most interesting finding of this study was that use of the brochure led to greater use by patients of members of the primary care team other than the GP.

Some practices are now setting up practice libraries for patients. The Dib Lane surgery in Leeds has established, in its waiting room, a lending library for patients comprising 500 books and a collection of audiotapes on health-related topics. Analysis of the first year's use (Varnavides *et al.*, 1984) showed 703 borrowings. Borrowers ranged across the spectrum of social class and educational status, but women predominated. The most popular book has been *Breast is Best* by P. and A. Stanway. Many of the borrowers admitted that they seldom read books. Most borrowings were opportunistic although a few were recommended by health care staff. A similar library has been established by a West Midlands general practice. In this case some of the books have been provided by the public library (Purposive private library, 1984).

Other general practices are exploiting information technology to bring information to patients. Many people do not receive the welfare benefits to which they are entitled. As roughly two-thirds of the population consult their general practitioner at least once a year, the GP is ideally placed to detect those suffering financial hardship and to advise them on their benefit entitlement. However, the complex system of social security benefits makes it difficult for the GP to give accurate advice. At Lisson Grove Health Centre in London a welfare benefits assessment program has been written which runs on a Hewlett Packard HP85B computer. It is being rewritten for use on other microcomputers and should be available in 1985. A local social security officer uses the program to advise patients (Jarman, 1985).

The idea of general practice patients keeping their own medical records has been supported by a number of writers (Metcalfe, 1980). There are practical and administrative reasons for them doing so. Every thousand records take up 17 feet of shelf space and 10 per cent of patient records cannot be found when the patient attends the surgery. The use of cooperation cards is well established in the care of pregnant women and there is no evidence that women lose them. By keeping the record card at the patient's home all members of the primary care team could see the record on home visits, communication between the various professionals would be improved, and going through the record would be an excellent basis for the patient to discuss the illness with the professional.

The special use of the health visitor as the professional with a key responsibility for linking patients with sources of help and information in the community was recognised by the Snowdon Report *Integrating the Disabled* (1976):

... the health visitor should be the person who acts as the referral point for the disabled person, and be responsible for coordinating whatever action is needed for all types of disability under the general direction of the general practitioner, and that her training should equip her for this role.

The report also makes clear the need for a reliable source of information for professional and patient alike:

> there should be a resource centre in each area from which a health visitor with special responsibility for the disabled would function. The centre would not only be available to all members of the primary health care team and the voluntary organisations for disabled people and the disabled people themselves, but should also concern itself with arousing the interests of the general community in disablement problems.

Use of the Wessex Regional Health Authority's Help for Health Information Service indicates that health visitors do indeed have this key role in information provision. Almost one in five enquiries come from health visitors, far more than any other group. An evaluation of Help for Health has indicated that the existence of the service has led to increased contact between health visitors and self-help groups (Bell, 1983).

A fascinating project carried out by the Community Nursing Service in Paddington and North Kensington has examined how the health visitor can work with community groups to promote awareness of health issues (Drennan, 1984). The project worker worked closely with 23 local community groups from mother and toddler groups and youth clubs to active pensioner associations. Health courses for women and pensioners were set up and new support groups established. The project worker became a source of information for people with whom the health services may have little contact. Just as importantly, she could also feed information about these people's needs and expectations back to the health service providers.

THE PHARMACIST

Of all the professional groups working in the field of health care the community pharmacist is the most accessible, and arguably the least appreciated, according to the *Pharmacist's Charter* (1984). He is available throughout the working day, he can be consulted without appointment and without charge, and has a role extending far beyond the dispensing of prescriptions and sale of toiletries. In the pharmacist

78

the public has a ready source of health care advice and guidance to supplement that provided by medical practitioners (Harris, 1984).

The *Pharmacist's Charter* is a statement by the Pharmaceutical Services Negotiating Committee on extending the role of the pharmacist in the provision of health care to the community. The Committee believes that the information, advisory and counselling role of the community pharmacist should be extended and that this would result in significant savings in medical consultation time and drug costs. The familiar retail environment of the chemist's shop could even be more conducive to discussion than the formalised atmosphere of a surgery consulting room. In many ways the pharmacist can provide a 'safety net' on which general practitioners depend; interpreting and reinforcing the doctor's advice and acting as a link between the public and the medical profession by advising patients to consult their doctor when appropriate.

The extended role of the pharmacist has received a cautious welcome from bodies such as the British Medical Association ('Expanding role for pharmacists', 1978) although as casual eavesdropping in any chemist's shop will show, the information and advice role of the pharmacist is already a well established reality. In 1967 20 retail chemists in eight towns in England were contacted and agreed to keep records relating to customers requesting medical advice (Whitfield, 1968). Over a two-day period there were 616 requests for medical advice. The customers who asked for advice were predominantly women, the majority of whom were under 40 years of age. The most common enquiries dealt with respiratory symptoms, followed by skin problems, gastro-intestinal disorders and 'tonics'. In 35 instances patients were referred to a doctor but, in most cases, advice from the pharmacist and/or the provision of an over-the-counter remedy was adequate. The study concluded that pharmacists will have 'to cast off the mantle of their artisan predecessors and take a more active part in providing information and advice about the medicines which they handle' (Office of Health Economics, 1964).

Further evidence of the range of enquiries taken to the pharmacist can be found in an article in *Health Education Journal* (Pilkington, 1979) where a general practice pharmacist records how over a ten-day period she received 43 requests for advice. These varied in complexity from simple coughs and colds to advice on weaning, a child who swallowed a plastic pen lid, and treatment for a knock-kneed horse!

A recent survey in *Which* is less sanguine about the advice given by pharmacists to the public ('Advice given across the chemist's counter', 1985). Consumers' Association 'patients' visited 200 chemists' shops. The 'patients' described four minor symptoms which they claimed to have themselves (mild headache; sore throat; indigestion; constipation) and four more serious problems belonging to the researcher's 'father' (bad headache lasting a week; sore throat and cough; indigestion lasting a month; diarrhoea for three days). The Consumers' Association expressed concern that a large proportion of enquiries, even for the potentially serious disorders, were answered by unqualified counter assistants. For the serious symptoms one in four pharmacists said the patient must see a doctor; a further one in two mentioned this; around one in four gave no advice to see a doctor and, in most cases, sold a medicine instead. In spite of the Pharmaceutical Society's positive feelings about the informal retail surroundings of the shop, the Consumers Association was also concerned about the lack of privacy. If private consulting areas are available, the CA suggests, the shops should display prominent signs advertising the fact. The findings of this survey form part of the Consumers' Association's evidence to the Nuffield Inquiry into the role of pharmacists.

Pilkington (1979) has suggested a role for the pharmacist which includes drug consultant, guardian of public safety, reducer of the national drug bill and general health adviser, but she is realistic in suggesting that this potential can only be fully exploited if the pharmacist is given the official recognition and status that the role demands. As the retail pharmacy is a commercial business, the recognition given to health education activities needs to be expressed in financial terms. In a survey by Harris (1982) retail pharmacists were asked if it was possible to extend the health education part of the services provided on their premises. Sixty seven per cent said yes and, when presented with a list of suggestions on how this could be achieved, 'giving financial recognition to this aspect of retail pharmacy' was ranked first.

INFORMATION AND ADVICE SERVICES

Locally-based information and advice services have become essential to many of us but it is only in the last 40 years – significantly since the beginning of the Second World War – that such services have been introduced. That they developed at all and continued to expand has largely been due to the initiative of voluntary organisations such as the National Association of Citizens' Advice Bureaux and the National Council for Voluntary Organisations. The National Consumer Council is another body which has contributed to this movement. The NCC believes that the right to information and advice is a right of citizenship and that this right can only be fulfilled by comprehensive provision of reliable local information and advice services. Beginning with *The Fourth Right of Citizenship* (1977), a review of advice agencies, the NCC has gone on to produce reports on the role of the Post Office as a source of information (*Post Office, Special Agent*, 1979); practical guides on publicity about information and advice centres (*Publicity Please*, 1982) and the use of information technology (*Computer Benefits*, 1982); and an investigative report *Advice Agencies: What They Are and Who Uses Them* (1982). The latter is a detailed review of services from generalist and specialist agencies. We will concentrate here on information and advice services of direct relevance to health, illness and disability.

COMMUNITY HEALTH COUNCILS

Community Health Councils were set up as part of the major reorganisation of the National Health Service in 1974 and were charged with the duty of representing the local community's interests in the health services to those responsible for managing them. In Scotland this function is undertaken by local Health Councils. The NHS reorganisation circular HRC (74) 4 indicated that the new CHCs might like to direct their attention to the effectiveness of services and their adequacy in relation to health care needs; to comment on standards and facilities for patients; and to advise people on how to make complaints. Roberts (1978) has described some functions which are common to all CHCs – visiting NHS premises, consultation in health service planning, taking up complaints – but there is wide variance in the work patterns of individual CHCs.

The creation of the CHCs as consumer bodies has been seen by some (Rosen, 1979; Levitt, 1980) as the one significant and important innovation of the 1974 reorganisation. Others have questioned whether the CHCs have enough power to make any real impact on the NHS – are they watchdogs or lapdogs? (Orriss, 1974; Langridge, 1977). The influence of the CHC has been hampered by problems of access to information about health services and a defensiveness on the part of the health authorities (Griffiths, 1982). There have also been problems in ascertaining what the public wants from its health service. Community Health Councils are made up of a panel of lay members with, in most cases, a paid secretary and assistant. There has been a tendency for some CHCs to regard their membership as a representative group of the population being served and therefore to assume that the views expressed by members will do as a public response. Certainly there is a good deal of variety in CHC membership although this has been characterised as predominantly middle-aged and middle-class. What the membership does tend to exclude is the people who do not get involved in the kinds of organisations which can nominate members to the CHCs – local authorities, political parties, trades councils and voluntary bodies (Levitt, 1980).

Many CHCs have tried to rectify this imbalance by carrying out surveys of the local population to determine their experiences, perceptions and expectations of local health services. Many are involved in a wide range of activities to do with the collection and dissemination of information – public meetings, 'surgeries' where complaints can be heard and advice given, press releases, the production of guides to services, door-to-door leafletting and other publicity exercises using, among other things, beermats and carrier bags (Burkeman, 1980).

Despite these activities the CHCs do not seem to be widely known. A survey into the public's information needs carried out by the Centre for Research into User Studies at the Sheffield School of Librarianship (Beal, 1979) confirms this. Only 30 per cent of the sample knew what CHCs were, and only 20 per cent had seen any publicity about them. This report draws attention to the potential of the CHC as an advice and information centre on health and the health services. The CHC for St Thomas's Health District in South London, for example, has run an information and advice service from shopfront premises since 1976, as well as providing back-up and support to other agencies including voluntary organisations and other local information services (Kempson, 1984).

82

Community Health Councils are increasingly becoming involved in health promotion activities. They can identify local issues and needs, advise on health promotion from a consumer point of view, transmit information through membership and contacts, help stage local events, and use surveys and monitoring techniques to provide feedback on the successfulness of campaigns. Other examples of CHC activities in health promotion have included setting up Well Women Clinics, awarding prizes to supermarkets for healthy food practices (Stockport), good practices in mental health projects, children's health clubs and the appointment of health information workers (Newcastle) (*Health Promotion: The Challenge for CHCs*, 1983).

CITIZENS' ADVICE BUREAUX

The Citizens' Advice Bureau (CAB) service was the result of inspired forward planning by a group of voluntary organisations which came together at the time of the Munich crisis in 1938. Since war seemed unavoidable it was felt that a new service would be required to answer the flood of queries which would inevitably arise about rationing, evacuation, conscription and so forth. The day after war was declared a network of CABs opened throughout the country (Rowland, 1973). Bureaux services became even more necessary once bombing raids began. When the Blitz struck Coventry the Bureau there worked in the open high street outside the city hall. With the ending of the war the need for the Citizens' Advice Bureau service was still urgent. The shortage of housing was a serious problem, as were employment and training difficulties. Subsequently, the emergence of the welfare state and the complex structure of social security benefits brought its own host of problems and needs for information (Blackford, 1981).

Today there are over 900 Citizens' Advice Bureaux, largely staffed by volunteers. There are 14,000 voluntary advice workers who undergo a basic training course and continuous in-service training, which includes information handling and interviewing techniques. Each volunteer is expected to work at least one session a week after undergoing the ten-week basic training course. The voluntary worker is the cornerstone of the CAB service, and a further 8,000 volunteers are involved as members of management committees, honorary treasurers etc. Paid organisers number less than 2,000 and are more common in inner city areas because of pressure of work and difficulties in finding volunteers. Although the running costs of a Citizens' Advice Bureau are met largely by local authority grants, the service is entirely independent.

There is a national office, the National Association of Citizens' Advice Bureaux, which provides a comprehensive and detailed information service to local Bureaux. Each month all Bureaux are sent a package covering new legislation, regulations, organisations and administrative procedures. This national information is augmented by local information added by the Bureaux themselves. All advice workers are trained in the use of the information system. The NACAB Information Service is so highly regarded that its adoption by a wider range of organisations has often been urged. The National Council for Social Service's review of advice services in rural areas *The Right to Know* (1978) recommended that NACAB make their files more readily available, and that small purpose-built information packs might be provided for mobile libraries, information vans, and key individuals like the clergy and the postmistress. More recently, the Northumberland Rural Citizens Advice Bureau has carried out a project to set up village contact schemes and develop information packs and training programmes for use by other agencies (Elliott, 1984). Since 1984 a basic information pack has been available. The pack is designed for community information services, rural advice schemes and such like, and not for experienced Citizens' Advice Bureau workers. Included is a section of basic health information ('How the NHS works'; 'Changing your doctor'; 'Making a complaint': 'Services and organisations for particular problems').

As a generalist advice service the CAB is a key first point of contact for the member of the public, or the health worker who is uncertain where to turn to for information (Little, 1980; Ricketts, 1980). Although enquiries which might be categorised as health-related do not form as large a proportion of total enquiries as, for example, social security, employment, housing, or consumer affairs, the CAB is still a significant source of health information for the public. The generalist nature of the service is its strength in that problems relating to housing, employment, income etc., which may be the cause or the outcome of health difficulties can be advised on within the same service. The enquirer can be referred to a more specialist agency when the need arises.

84

A major study of who uses Citizens' Advice Bureaux, and why, has been published by the Greater London Citizens' Advice Bureaux Service. The report *Citizens' Advice* (Greater London Citizens' Advice Bureaux Service, 1985) examines who uses London Bureaux, the problems they experience and the service they receive, and recommends some ways in which the service could be improved. The overwhelming majority of clients in London are poor. Almost 90 per cent had below average weekly incomes, 74 per cent lived on less than two-thirds of the average income and 35 per cent had less than one-third of average income. Bureaux see above-average proportions of unemployed, disabled, single parents and ethnic minorities. There are more enquiries about social security, housing, and consumer problems than other subjects. The Report shows that Bureaux are seriously overworked and under-resourced. There is a need for more Bureaux located in the right places, more staff and more resources and the establishment of local specialist units to deal with more complicated queries, such as tax and immigration.

At a local level a Bureau has enormous freedom of action. Rowland (1973) quotes a number of initiatives. York CAB was the first to cooperate with the Child Poverty Action Group in the establishment of a welfare rights stall; Paddington CAB was the first to be integrated with a neighbourhood law centre; Kensington CAB the first to appoint a West Indian community worker. The information and advice needs of members of ethnic minority groups have recently been examined by a project in Kirklees (National Association of Citizens' Advice Bureaux, 1984).

Chapeltown Citizens' Advice Bureau in Leeds has addressed itself specifically to the information needs of disabled people. Over the years there was a growing awareness that the Citizens' Advice Bureau was not fulfilling its duties to local disabled people. The CAB premises were inaccessible to wheelchairs, while many people had difficulty getting out of home at all to visit the Bureau. Although enquiries could be made over the telephone, this was far from ideal when dealing, for example, with complex benefit problems. There were not enough volunteers or paid staff to make home visits, and no staff had any particular expertise in dealing with disabled clients or in services and benefits for disabled people. The Chapeltown Bureau was not of course unusual in its lack of provision for disabled people. It just had the imagination to look into the problems and try to find some solutions.

In September 1979 funding was given by Manpower Services Commission (under the Special Temporary Employment Programme) to employ two workers for one year. The workers were used to identify disabled people in the area, carry out a survey of their needs and to follow this up with welfare rights advice. The use of Manpower Services Commission funding (now usually through the Community Programme) has over the last two or three years become a widely used method of employing extra workers in information and advice projects. The Chapeltown questionnaire, case studies and proposals for improving services to disabled people (access surveys of CAB premises, recruitment of disabled volunteers, home visits etc.) may be found in the *Chapeltown CAB Disability Project Report* (National Association of Citizens' Advice Bureaux, 1980).

HOSPITAL-BASED ADVICE SERVICES

When in hospital, patients and families may have a wide range of information needs, covering not only the illness itself but also the social and economic problems which ill health and hospitalisation can bring. But those patients can be distinctly disadvantaged in attempting to obtain advice. The problems are particularly acute for those in long-stay and mental hospitals. Some patients are unable to contact advice centres because they are in a locked ward, for others it is simply that years of institutionalised living has made them unable to step beyond the walls of the hospital. To meet these needs a number of advice centres have opened on hospital premises. In most cases these have been satellites of local Citizens' Advice Bureaux.

Brent Citizens' Advice Bureau had already developed a reputation for bringing information and advice to the public through its mobile CAB, when in 1979 it was approached by the social work department of the Central Middlesex Hospital, Acton, to discuss providing a service within the hospital. Based on the mobile CAB in the hospital carpark this became the first ever bedside service for patients who would not otherwise get to a CAB. CAB volunteers visited wards with trolleys loaded with a basic collection of information leaflets. It was decided from the outset that certain wards should be excluded from the visits – maternity, because patients stayed for too short a time; paediatric, because the patients themselves were too young to be clients and their parents had access to outside services; neurosurgery, because many patients were unconscious or unable to carry on a conversation; and psychological medicine, where it was considered therapeutic for patients to make the journey to an outside CAB if necessary. During the first four months of the project over 600 enquiries were answered including a number from hospital staff.

It is interesting to compare the experiences of the Brent project with two other CAB hospital projects in London – at Northwick Park, Harrow, and St Bartholomew's Hospital. Both of these were part-time services and there were no ward visits; in the case of Northwick Park because of the CAB's unwillingness and in the case of St Bartholomew's because of opposition from medical staff. The success of the Central Middlesex experiment rested very much on the provision of a full-time service with close contact with patients on the wards (Fears, 1980).

The first CAB to be set up in a mental hospital was at Middlewood Hospital, Sheffield (Phillips, 1976). One of the main reasons for introducing the service was to reduce institutional dependence among the patients. As the principal social worker at Middlewood commented 'There's always a tendency to do things for people in institutions. It's far better if you make patients aware that there's a housing department or legal advice outside and encourage them to seek their own solutions.' The room, telephone and stationery were provided by the hospital and twice-weekly afternoon sessions provided by volunteers.

The need for an impartial advice service in the psychiatric hospital was also recognised at Tooting Bec Hospital. In 1980 staff at a local law centre approached Lambeth CAB to arrange advice sessions within Tooting Bec Hospital. The two afternoon sessions were used by patients, relatives and, to a lesser extent, staff. The most common areas of work were: social security benefits; debt counselling; immigration rights; divorce, custody and maintenance; and patients' rights which often involved mediating with outside bodies such as Community Health Councils and MIND (Grimshaw, 1985). In 1982 an application was made to the Greater London Council for funding to set up an independent Citizens' Advice Bureau at Tooting Bec Hospital, running regular advice sessions for patients, relatives and staff, offering ward visits and producing a range of bulletins, news sheets and leaflets. The advice service was also in an ideal position to monitor complaints and feed these back to the hospital with a view to changing hospital policy and practice. The application was successful and project staff were appointed in June 1983. Staff salaries and running costs are provided by the GLC until May 1986 at a level of approximately £27,000. The project is currently involved in discussions with West Lambeth Health Authority regarding continuation of the project beyond May 1986.

Each of the hospital advice services described so far has developed through the Citizens' Advice Bureau service. The Advice and Legal Representation Project at Springfield Hospital in Wandsworth, South London is slightly different in that it is a sub-office of the Wandsworth Legal Resource. The Advice and Legal Representation Project provides the 900-bed psychiatric hospital with the on-site services of a solicitor and advice worker who give free consultation to patients and, on a limited basis, to their relatives and hospital staff. The project works as an autonomous unit within the hospital and is subject to solicitors' rules regarding confidentiality and procedure. This can sometimes cause problems. The advice worker Jenny Rogers explains:

> There is the difficulty of working in the hospital without being part of a clinical or medical team. Our codes of practice are different from those of the hospital. We are here to act on patients' instructions and without patients' permission we can't talk to others about that individual's problems. It is sometimes difficult for hospital staff to understand this. (Klein, 1984)

Despite the inherent complexities of an independent project based within a hospital, it seems to be working well and hospital administrators have spoken enthusiastically about the constructive support given to patients, and the way it has relieved social workers' workload. A detailed report of the first year's work is available from the project (*Advice and Legal Representation Project,* 1983).

DIAL: DISABLEMENT INFORMATION AND ADVICE LINES

The first DIAL began in a cloakroom in a residential centre for disabled people in Alfreton, Derbyshire. In the mid-1970s there was a growing feeling that, although existing advice services could provide accurate and up-to-date information, what they so often lacked was direct experience of disability. DIAL Derbyshire was set up to provide an information service based on an empathetic understanding of the experience of disability and first-hand knowledge of the reality of local facilities for disabled people. Information was provided for disabled people by disabled people. The idea took off and soon DIALs were opening in Newcastle, Liverpool, Norwich, Rugby and Portsmouth. It was soon apparent that what they needed was an umbrella body, on the same principle as the National Association of Citizens' Advice Bureaux, through which they could assist each other to provide a more effective service. In 1977 Ken Davis, the founder of DIAL Derbyshire, set up a steering committee to consider such a body. The outcome was a network of 25 local groups with a head office in Derbyshire known as DIAL UK (Whitehouse, 1982). Today there are over 60 DIALs and new ones are opening all the time.

Most DIALs are autonomous, self-governing and self-financed from local sources. There will probably be a management committee drawn from local voluntary organisations and representatives of the statutory services. DIALs have a diversity of staffing arrangements, some having full-time paid workers (often funded by Manpower Services schemes), others relying totally on volunteers. DIAL UK has produced guidance on the training of DIAL workers though most DIALs organise their own training programmes. For example, as long ago as 1977, one of the first DIAL-type services, the Disabled Advice Service in Wandsworth, ran a training programme which involved speakers from the Department of Health and Social Security, Home Help Service, Housing Department, Neighbourhood Law Centre, Consumer Advice Centre, and Welfare Rights Service (Beazley, 1978). Most DIALs maintain a close contact with their local library and Citizens' Advice Bureau.

About a third of the problems presented to DIALs relate to social security benefits (Saunders, 1983; Burgess, 1985). DIALs will often accompany a disabled person to a Supplementary Benefit or National Insurance tribunal, or attend at their home if they are being assessed for Attendance Allowance, Mobility Allowance or some forms of equipment. There are also frequent enquiries on community services, housing, car adaptations, equipment, holidays, travel, sport, sex and personal relationships.

One of the most successful DIALs in the country has been DIAL

Portsmouth, founded by Pat Saunders, a well-known disabled journalist. Established five years ago it now operates from a Disabled Living Centre, which in addition to DIAL contains an aids demonstration centre, meeting rooms, and a drop-in snack bar. There are eighteen staff most of whom are disabled, and are employed under Manpower Services Commission schemes or on a voluntary basis. In 1984 an Apricot Xi microcomputer was installed to handle a database of addresses of national and local voluntary organisations and services. Having established a substantial clientele amongst disabled people living in the Portsmouth community, DIAL is now turning its attention to the many newly disabled people who leave hospital with no information on how to cope with their new circumstances.

As Pat Saunders has made clear, the majority of patients who return to the community after a long period in hospital involving a permanent disability receive no written or printed information, and such verbal advice as they may have is minimal, casual and negative.

> Taking as an example the physically disabled person facing the rest of his life in a wheelchair, the transition from the safe, caring hospital environment to a hostile community is traumatic both for him and his family. He arrives home into the hands of a totally untrained, apprehensive, caring relative without a single word about self-management. He knows nothing of the potential problems of bowels, bladder, diet, lack of exercise, circulation and pressure sores. Important decisions may have to be made about pensions, benefits, income tax, housing, mobility and equipment. Some decisions have to be made immediately, others can wait – he does not know which. This is the time when the disabled person and the caring relative need calm, unhurried, unbiased advice from a hospital information clinic. (Saunders, 1980).

To meet some of these needs DIAL Portsmouth has set up an information and advice clinic in a room in the hospital foyer at Queen Alexandra Hospital, Portsmouth. The clinic is open on Monday from 2–6 pm to coincide with visiting hours. Ward sisters make referrals to administration who send a collective timed list to the DIAL office each Wednesday. Normally each patient attends twice – first, about three weeks before departure, a brief interview to determine the client's needs; then, in the final week a longer interview which is really a briefing for disability. To take care of personal problems, the DIAL team is always one male and one female. Each patient is given a 'Starter's Kit' – a large envelope with appropriate leaflets and some typed material appropriate to the individual. A small set of books is available for sale. A firm date is made for the client to visit DIAL some six weeks later. Clients with any disability or of any age are interviewed with or without the caring relative. It is for the patient to decide whether he wishes to attend the clinic.

INFORMATION ON AIDS FOR DISABLED PEOPLE

The consumer of aids and equipment does not at present have the same rights of choice, representation and information enjoyed by consumers of other products. This is because little information is primarily directed at the user of aids and choice tends to be exercised by the professional advisers employed by the agencies supplying them. There are few places where aids can be seen and compared. Usually the consumer is dealing with unfamiliar equipment and has no past experience to use as a guide. There are few direct links between the manufacturer and the people who use his products. These points are made strongly in an extensive survey *Aids for People with Disabilities: A Review of Information Services* carried out by the Research Institute for Consumer Affairs (1984) as one of a number of reports to mark the Consumers' Association's Silver Jubilee. The RICA report discusses the need for information on aids, the existing information network and the ways in which information is collected and distributed to disabled people and professionals working with them.

The Disabled Living Foundation provides information on every aspect of disability, except medical matters. It is recognised as the foremost centre for information about aids and equipment. Information about aids is collected from manufacturers, reference to research, special investigations, and regular contact (through formal committees and continuous informal contact) with the range of professional staff, organisations and individuals concerned with aids. Basic information about aids on the market is distributed to subscribers on a set of 22 information sheets, which are updated annually. Information is also given by the DLF advice service, at the London Aids Centre, through books, teaching packs and contact with the media.

The Royal Association for Disability and Rehabilitation is an umbrella organisation which has many interests including mobility, legislation, housing and holidays. RADAR have a mobile aids centre, organise local panels of people who make 'one-off' aids, have set up (with the DHSS) six Communication Aids Centres and are coordinating an international project on communication aids. Information is published through books and two regular magazines, *Contact* and *Bulletin*.

Other national information sources on aids are the Spastics' Society which has an advice service, a permanent display of equipment for children, and a visiting aids centre; Disablement Electronic Aids Reference Service (DEARS) which exists primarily to put professionals with similar interests in touch with one another; and the Handicapped Persons Research Unit at Newcastle Polytechnic which carries out postgraduate research and consultancy on various aspects of disability including evaluation of aids. Numerous other organisations concerned with disability generally (for example Disablement Income Group) or with specific disabilities may carry out evaluation of aids and publish information through their magazines and newsletters.

In most regions there are Aids Centres which have permanent exhibitions of equipment, extensive collections of literature, manufacturers, catalogues etc., and permanent or visiting professional staff who can give advice. Aids Centres are funded by various sources (through NHS, social services or voluntary organisations) and are therefore autonomous although matters of common concern are discussed through a Joint Aid Centres Council. In addition there are specialist Communication Aids Centres and Special Microelectronics Resource Centres which give assessments, advice and help. Details of these are given in the *Directory for Disabled People* (Darnbrough and Kinrade, 1984).

LIBRARIES

Community information

Medicine, along with law, has been a subject which, in the past, public libraries have approached with caution. However, there has been a significant shift in attitude with the development of community

92

information services over the last ten years. In a paper to the Info 85 Conference in Bournemouth the County Librarian of Derbyshire, Peter Gratton, considered the scope of 'community information':

> In terms of subject range, 'community information' covers jobs, housing, money matters, individual rights, family matters, welfare benefits, how to tackle bereavement, drug problems, living with asthma and rheumatism, how to report suspected child battering, age-related problems, dealing with VAT, animal welfare organisations, race relations and discrimination, consumer advice, voluntary groups, pensions, how to deal with a notice to quit and so on and so on – the whole range of 'I should like to know' or 'I need to know' information. (Gratton, 1985)

It would be possible to make a case for all of these subjects to be also regarded as health information – not only the obvious ones like living with asthma and rheumatism, or the housing and money problems associated with long-term illness or disability, but also consumer advice on orthopaedic beds or cold cures, the welfare of pets when people are admitted to hospital, and dealing with VAT for voluntary groups.

One of the earliest, most successful and most influential community information services was set up at the Bretton Library in Peterborough in 1977 (Bunch, 1979). From the outset it was intended that this new purpose-built library should act as a dissemination point for information from local voluntary and statutory agencies, and should offer the opportunity for special advisers to be available to give help with particular problems – legal, housing, health etc. An interview room was incorporated in the library and sessions were provided by the Citizens' Advice Bureau and the Community Health Council. A community file of local organisations and a self-help collection of books, periodicals and packs was developed. Not all libraries have found shared arrangements with other information agencies successful and, even at Bretton, there were differences of approach between the library and Citizens' Advice Bureau. But today most larger public libraries provide community information collections as an extension of their traditional reference services, and these usually contain a good deal of health related material. Alan Bunch who was responsible for the Bretton service has produced an excellent overview of *Community*

93

Information Services: Their Origin, Scope and Development (Bunch, 1982) and, more recently, a practical guide to establishing and running community information services, *The Basics of Information Work* (Bunch, 1984).

In 1977 the Library Association appointed a research officer for community information, Elaine Kempson. As a result of many requests for guidance on the practical aspects of setting up community information services in public libraries, a working party was set up to use the experiences of this research project to prepare guidelines for librarians. The resulting publication *Community Information: What Libraries Can Do* (Library Association, 1980) draws on the practical experiences of a variety of public libraries to show just how libraries can provide problem-solving information to the public, often in cooperation with other agencies. The Community Information Project was also responsible for a first-class bibliography on rights literature *Know How to Find Out Your Rights* (Morby, 1982) which contains a section on health information, with an emphasis on mental health. The report of the first five years of the Community Information Project makes fascinating reading (Community Information Project, 1982).

The Community Information Project continues today on an independent basis, and has developed a particular expertise in the use of information technology for advice centres. Guidelines for local information and advice centres on the use of computers (Ottley and Kempson, 1982) have been followed by a state-of-the-art review of agencies now using computers to give local community information (Community Information Project, 1985). The most valuable feature of the survey is a summary table of 34 projects with details of systems and names and addresses of contacts. The Community Information Project's newsletter *Computanews* is a continuing source of lively and up-to-date information on computers for advice services.

An interesting example of the use of information technology to provide community information is the PIRATE (Public Information in Rural Areas Technology Experiment) in Devon. Building on the experiences of the community information project carried out in South Molton, this British Library-funded project is examining the use of microcomputers for information in rural areas. The most original aspect of the project is the use of ALS Browser terminals with a touch-sensitive screen to provide a simple to use access point to the database which is stored on a Torch CH 520 microcomputer. Users

94

select the information they require from a menu which includes a range of health topics (Creber, 1985; Moore, 1985). The Torch micro-computer is also used in Cambridge where the Cambridgeshire Library and Information Service and the Eastern Area of the National Association of Citizens' Advice Bureaux are creating a joint database of local information. Links have been established with the county's mainframe computer and some files are about to be output to a compatible machine at the District Health Education Unit (Heaton, 1985).

Hospital libraries

Two types of library tend to be found in hospitals – the medical or health care library for staff, and the recreational library for patients. Although there are multidisciplinary libraries combining both elements for patients and professionals, it is fair to say that the two types of service are regarded as very distinct. The merging of the Medical Libraries Section and the Hospital Libraries Group of the Library Association in 1978 to form the Medical Health and Welfare Libraries Group was regarded by some as a shotgun wedding. Patient or health information services have been seen as an area of common ground between the medical and welfare librarians and a means to weld the two elements of the profession together. Despite this hope, the standard textbook, *Hospital Libraries and Work with the Disabled in the Community* (Going, 1981), devoted only a few paragraphs to information for patients, as recently as 1981, and for their part, medical librarians in some areas have not always been ready to make their services available to consumers as well as professional providers of health care. Emphasis has tended to be on reading as an escape rather than as a source of information to help in facing and coping with problems, although concurrently there has been a great deal of interesting work done on the value of reading as therapy (Rubin, 1978). A Reading Therapy sub-group of the Library Association Medical Health and Welfare Libraries Group (LA/MHWLG) has now been established.

Information for patients has now become a live issue in the medical, health and welfare library world. Papers on the topic are now common at study days and conferences organised by the LA/MHWLG. The Group's journal *Health Libraries Review* features regular articles on health information. An excellent overview entitled 'Consumer health information services' (Kempson, 1984) appeared in one of the first issues and has made the task of compiling this chapter much easier. A regular column 'Patient information' is edited by Robert Gann and gives details of new developments, publications and organisations in the field.

It is interesting to note that even university libraries are now becoming involved in health information for the public. Mike Lewis, Assistant Librarian at the University of Sussex, was seconded to Brighton Health Authority and East Sussex Social Services for two months in 1984 to set up a library in the Community Mental Handicap Team room at Foredown Hospital, Portslade. One of the unusual elements of the project was that the library should be available not just to professional staff but also to parents and other carers. The core collection consists of about 130 books on most aspects of mental handicap, and there are subscriptions to 30 journals (Lewis, 1985).

The increased interest in information services for patients has been due in no small measure to the practical example of two successful hospital-based services; the Health Information Service at the Lister Hospital, Stevenage, and the Wessex Region's Help for Health Information Service based at Southampton General Hospital.

Lister health information service

The Health Information Service at the Lister Hospital has grown chiefly as a result of the interest and enthusiasm of the librarian, Sally Knight. Sally is very much a pioneer of health information services. For six years now she has produced *Popular Medical Index*, a unique publication which lists medical articles in the general press. Through this work she has developed contacts with medical and health columnists in women's magazines. She has also produced a directory of voluntary organisations in the health field, *Help! I Need Somebody* (Knight, 1980).

In 1982 the public library service provided funding for a temporary part-time library assistant post specifically to develop the health information service to the general public. They were especially fortunate in that there was a state enrolled nurse already working as a full-time library assistant in the public library. Julie Mackenzie was appointed to work for a part of her time at the Lister Hospital and, because of her skills, has been responsible for most of the day-to-day development of the service. The first six months of her appointment were primarily concerned with developing the information collection. This is now one of the most extensive collections in the country of general medical information written for the lay person. It consists of booklets and leaflets from voluntary organisations, but especially of articles from medical, nursing and popular magazines. These files are supplemented by a small collection of reference books, and the library maintains indexes both of self-help groups and of books, including novels, which relate to specific illnesses or disabilities and are available through the public library system. From April 1983 detailed records have been kept of enquiries which were received. At that time about 10 enquiries were referred each month from public libraries. In addition there were about four telephone enquiries, two personal callers and one enquiry by letter. Over the period since April 1983 use of the service has increased dramatically so that in January 1984, 43 enquiries were referred by public libraries, about four telephone enquiries were received each day, 10 people visited the service personally and there were 10 enquiries made by letter. In other words, in nine months, the total number of enquiries had increased from 17 to 143 a month – more than an eight-fold increase (Kempson, 1984).

About 90 per cent of these enquiries are made by the general public and about a third of them through a public library. Whilst the number of enquiries received through public libraries has increased considerably, by far the greatest increase has occurred in enquiries received direct from the general public; by telephone, post and, most surprisingly, by personal callers. No systematic attempt has been made to identify how users had found out about the service but it is clear that, with limited publicity, word of mouth and personal recommendation must be the major means.

Not only has the number of enquiries grown but the enquiries received have become increasingly complex over the nine months that the service has been developed. Few enquiries are for details of self-help groups: that has never been the main focus of the Lister Health Information Service. Most relate to specific complaints where the enquirers want to understand their illness, how it will affect their lives and details of self-care possibilities to enhance the medical care they are receiving. Others usually relate to major operations like hysterectomy or mastectomy.

Frequently the Health Information Service is contacted by people suffering from severe complaints with very bad prognoses, who have received insufficient information from the doctors treating them. In all such cases, and any others where there is cause for concern, the information assistant will contact the patient's doctor. This is done with the patient's consent, and the doctor is asked to look at the information before it is given to the patient. Ideally, the doctor would agree to give the patient the information direct.

By April 1985 enquiries were running at 200 a month. Of these, perhaps 10 per cent could not be answered from existing resources and a major feature of the Lister service has been the production of custom-made literature for the enquirer. The Health Information Service has recently received richly deserved recognition in the form of the Silver Jubilee Award of the Consumers' Association. The Award will be spent on further development of the service, particularly in the areas of evaluation and publicity. Leaflets publicising the service are being distributed to all public libraries in Hertfordshire inviting the public to contact HIS through their local library.

Help for health information service

Help for Health has developed in a slightly different way from the Lister Health Information Service, in that there has always been a stronger emphasis on self-help groups and their publications, and more use by professionals as well as the public. This is partly due to the origins of the service.

The Help for Health project began in 1979 when the Wessex Regional Library and Information Service received a grant from the British Library to investigate needs for information about self-help groups and ways in which this information could be made available. Research confirmed that tracing relevant voluntary and self-help groups was a major need, particularly for community-based health professionals such as general practitioners, community nurses, health visitors and social workers.

In 1980 the final report of the British Library Help for Health project was prepared (Gann, 1981). The report drew attention to the wealth of self-care resources available and the lack of an effective mechanism for communicating this information. The report recommended the establishment of an information unit to identify self-help groups and publications, keep this information up-to-date and make it available to health care professionals and the public. Five years later Help for Health is, with Regional Health Authority funding, providing the most comprehensive information service on self care in the UK.

Help for Health operates from an information unit at Southampton General Hospital and is staffed by one information officer (a librarian) and one information assistant. Running costs of the service in 1985 were £27,000 per annum, consisting of staffing costs, travel and subsistence, printing of information and publicity materials, subscriptions to self-help groups, and purchase of books, leaflets and other information materials. The collection consists of a database of 1,000 national and 2,000 local self-help groups; a library of directories of organisations and services, and popular medical books; a collection of several thousand self-care booklets and leaflets principally originating from self-help groups; and subscriptions to over 100 self-help journals. Each month 500–600 enquiries are answered. The most frequent users are health visitors, followed by members of the public. Most enquiries are received over the telephone, although there are also personal visits and letters. It is interesting to note that, while professionals are happy to contact the information service by telephone, the majority of letters come from members of the public. Perhaps it is easier to express a personal problem in a letter. Requests for addresses of groups can usually be answered immediately over the telephone. Others are met by sending self-help leaflets, photocopies of articles or factsheets in the post. There is no charge for any aspect of the enquiry service. There is, in addition, an active self-financing publications programme through which guides to self-care literature and organisations in particular subject areas are nationally available (the *Communication* series). A major bibliography of biographical and fictional accounts of illness and disability has also been produced (Tabor, 1983).

The database of organisations is stored on a Commodore 8096 microcomputer using Silicon Office software (Gann, 1983). A standard format for each organisation records name of organisation, address, postcode, telephone number, brief details of activities, date of last contact, and a series of subject keywords. The keywords are based on the Medical Subject Headings (MeSH) thesaurus developed by the National Library of Medicine, with the introduction of British

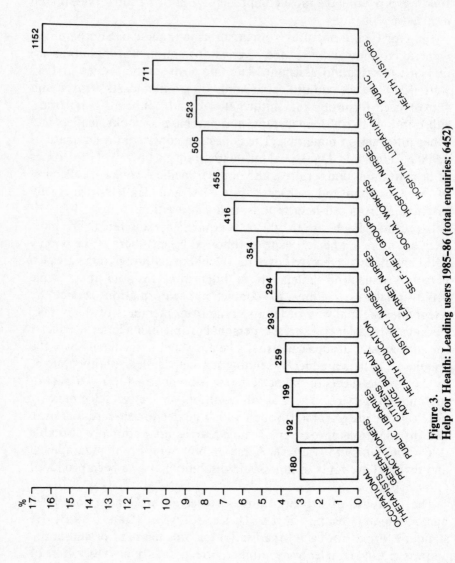

Figure 3.
Help for Health: Leading users 1985–86 (total enquiries: 6452)

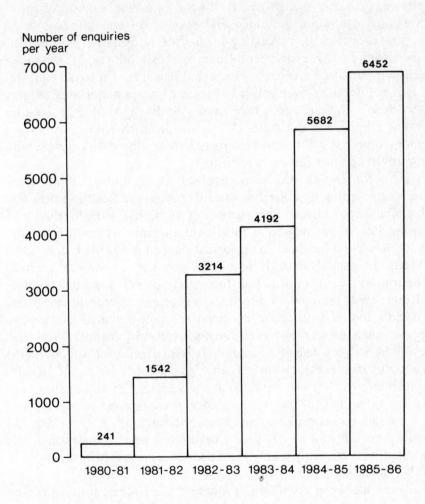

Number of enquiries per year

Figure 3.2
Help for Health: Growth in enquiries 1985–86

concepts and spellings. In response to enquiries received by the information service, the database can be searched for organisations dealing with a particular disease or disability, offering a particular service, or based in a particular town – or a combination of these. Standard letters are generated and sent on an annual basis, to all organisations listed, requesting up-to-date information on contacts and activities. An experimental database of bibliographic details of self-help literature has been set up, and it is intended to develop this further. Literature from self-help groups forms a major area of 'grey literature', difficult to trace and rarely appearing in major bibliographies and databases. It is anticipated that the Commodore microcomputer will be replaced in 1986 with a hard disk system with improved communication capabilities.

Help for Health has been involved in a number of 'outreach' activities, setting up collections of information in health centres and hospital departments. The success of these has varied, usually in proportion to the degree of local commitment and involvement. A notable success has been the Information Centre for the Elderly at St Martin's Hospital, Bath. Here a consultant with an unusual grasp of the importance of information for elderly people and their relatives (Rowe, 1984) initiated an information centre in a geriatric unit where patients and relatives could take away specially prepared information packs on a variety of topics (bowel problems, bladder problems, eyesight, stroke). The assistance of Help for Health was sought on the content and presentation of the packs and Help for Health information sheets are available at the Centre. The scheme has been successful because of the expressed local need, the keen involvement of an enlightened consultant, and the seriousness of intent which has gained funding for a part-time worker to supervise the project. An evaluation is currently taking place and the scheme is to be extended to other hospitals in the district.

There has been considerable interest from other authorities and agencies in the establishment of schemes on the Help for Health model. In 1982 an information package, containing advice on a core collection of material, and ways of storing and indexing the collection, was produced to give guidance to those planning similar services (Gann, 1982). This is now out of print. A report on the first five years of the service (Gann, 1984) summarises the background, resources, operations and funding of Help for Health. Interest has not been

102

confined to the UK and an advisory visit was made to the World Health Organization Regional Office for Europe in 1983. The contribution to the WHO's philosophy of participation in health continues to be recognised (Gann, 1985 and 1986).

A subject which once aroused a certain amount of controversy has now become widely accepted amongst health care librarians. It is gratifying to see the amount of serious attention given to information for patients and the public in the discussions of the joint DHSS/Regional Librarians Group working party on district library services (evidence of the contribution made to the working party by Roy Tabor, the Regional Librarian of Wessex, who was responsible for many of the early discussions on patient information and who established the Help for Health project). The proposals arising from this working party have been published as part of the King's Fund's Körner documentation (*Providing a District Library Service,* 1985), and include the following recommendations:

3.19 Library provision for health consumers, who include patients or clients, their relatives and the general public, is not well developed at present. To promote awareness of the NHS and an informed approach to health, information should be readily available which
a) indicates the range of statutory and voluntary services available, and how they operate; and
b) increases understanding of the professional advice offered, improves cooperation with treatment and helps to alleviate fears.
3.20 A district library service, in providing a service to the consumer, will have to liaise closely with health education staff, the public library network and voluntary organisations. Information may be provided directly to the consumer or through a health care professional.

COMMUNITY HEALTH PROJECTS

Many community health projects have the provision of information as one of their main focuses. Community health projects are neighbourhood-based schemes which have been initiated or are directed by local people. A community worker may be employed to work on health issues which are relevant to the whole local community or to specific groups within it (Rosenthal, 1983). Community health projects tend to be based within deprived urban areas and are one response to the inequalities in health highlighted by the Black Report (Black, 1982).

One of the earliest community health projects was the Waterloo Health Project set up in South London in 1977. Its aims are to encourage individuals and groups to participate more in their own treatment through the development of their own knowledge and self confidence; to develop mutual support groups and informal support networks; and to encourage action on local health issues. The Project provides an information and advice centre as part of the Waterloo Action Centre. As well as providing help to individuals, the work on information provision can act as an indicator of particular health issues which need to be taken up more widely. For example, the need for a self-help group on the menopause was identified after several women had visited the Action Centre for information and advice (Kempson, 1984).

Another interesting example is the Albany Health Project based in Deptford. Deptford is part of London's docklands and suffers from urban decay. Many of the jobs in the area have disappeared and today one in five is unemployed. Back in 1894 the Albany Centre was set up to help the working people of the area, and it was here in 1977 that a community health project was established to try and tackle some of the health issues which contemporary local people felt were important to them. The report of the first five years of the project (Albany Health Project, 1983) provides a fascinating insight into the activities of a community health project, which, in Deptford, have included a women's health group, young people's and pensioners' health clubs, an estate newsletter, acupuncture sessions, and arranging for groups of local people to take Open University Community Education courses such as 'Health Choices' and 'The First Years of Life'. An information stall in Deptford market was a regular feature at the beginning of the Project until enthusiasm ran out.

Bath may seem a long way from the London docklands, but the Whiteway Estate exhibits some of the same problems. Begun in the 1930s it was the first concentration of council housing development in Bath. The area consists mainly of housing unrelieved by meeting places or focal points. There is only one shop for a population of nearly 3,000, there are few public telephones and public transport is poor and relatively expensive. Approximately 23 per cent of the economically active in Whiteway are unemployed. Educational welfare figures indicate that 90 per cent of children living in Whiteway come from low-income families, and 21 per cent of the families on the Child Abuse Register covering all of Bath live in Whiteway. As a response to these problems a community health worker was employed with funding made available jointly from the health and local authorities, and a semi-detached house was made available on the estate as the project base. The report of the first year of this project is now available (Whiteway Health Project, 1985), describing the establishment of groups for mothers and toddlers, an unemployment and health group, and a discussion group on choices in childbirth.

The philosophy of the Whiteway Health Project has been to increase people's self confidence and to enhance, rather than undermine, the contribution of local people. It was felt that the limited resources of the Project should be directed towards supporting the very important information and advice role already filled by key local people, rather than establishing an information service which might be seen as an alternative to established, if informal, channels. Accordingly, from March 1985, monthly sessions have been held at the Project to provide up-to-date information on welfare benefits to those best placed to improve take up of benefits – local GPs, health visitors and other relevant professionals, and local people who are used by members of the community as sources of information, advice and help. The Whiteway Project is interesting not only for its activities, but for a clearly articulated philosophy which says that the establishment of formal information services is not always in the best interests of the local community.

Nationally, community health initiatives have been monitored by the Community Health Initiatives Resource Unit based at the National Council for Voluntary Organisations. CHIRU aims to promote and support community health projects by assisting existing ones and by stimulating the formation and helping the development of fledgling schemes. The project has collected information on initiatives throughout the country by writing to community health councils, councils for voluntary service, health education units, and voluntary organisations. As the development officer, Alison Watt, put it 'We're talking about 10,000 community health initiatives – local people organising around a common health issue. Not many of us know about the number of people out there beavering away making a statement about the NHS's failure adequately to meet people's needs' (Klein, 1984). CHIRU has organised a number of workshops and conferences, including one entitled *Community Development in Health: Addressing the Confusions* which was held at the King's Fund Centre in London in 1984. The report of this conference provides a useful overview of the community development approach to health, and includes a list of 28 community health projects with details of activities (Somerville, 1985). The National Council for Voluntary Organisations has also produced a handbook of community health initiatives which describes some projects and gives practical advice on funding (Smith, 1982).

RESOURCE CENTRES AND CLEARING HOUSES

There are now a number of 'resource centres' for community organisations and self-help groups. The most extensive network, although not always referred to by that name, are Councils for Voluntary Service. These are non-profit making, non-governmental organisations concerned to promote voluntary activity in local areas. There are currently around 200 CVSs throughout England. Names vary from area to area and you may also find Councils of Social Service, Councils of Community Service, Guilds of Voluntary Service etc. There is a national coordinating body called Councils for Voluntary Service – National Association, which is based at the National Council for Voluntary Organisations. CVSs function not only as local umbrella groups and focal points for voluntary activity, but also aim to act as a link between voluntary organisations and statutory authorities. The National Council for Voluntary Organisations has published an extremely useful booklet *Working with Self Help Groups* (Richardson, 1984) which describes the ways in which self-help groups can be assisted in a practical way by Councils for Voluntary Service and others.

Councils for Voluntary Service do not exist primarily to meet the information needs of the public, but many individuals do go to the CVS for information about local voluntary groups. More central to the function of a CVS is the information it holds for, and about, local groups: information about how they can constitute and fund

106

themselves, how they can go about finding premises, transport etc., how they can contact existing groups working in similar areas. The resource centre for community groups might be responsible for the production of newsletters and directories, maintaining a library or information room, running training courses, providing meeting rooms for groups, use of office equipment, and assistance with publicity and printing. Two useful guides have been produced which give case studies on services provided by some resource centres and practical guidance ('CVS in Action', 1981; Taylor, 1983).

The Nottingham Self Help Team is a model for support systems directed specifically at self-help groups. Set up in 1982, through joint financing by the local health authority, it functions in association with the Nottingham Council for Voluntary Service. The Team is there to enable fledgling groups to talk to someone who knows and understands their situation. Resources offered to local groups include office services, a place to hold meetings, air time on local radio, printing facilities and training courses (Wilson, 1982 and 1983). A directory of self-help groups has been produced and the local newspaper runs a monthly column drawing attention to particular groups. A *Self Help Group Starterpack* has been developed for people wanting to set up new groups. This is an indispensible guide, and not only for people from the Nottingham area (Wilson, 1983).

Another form of resource centre is the computerised information bank of organisations within a given area. The Wessex Help for Health service is an example of this, though working from within the statutory sector. The Community Council for Wiltshire has established a county-wide voluntary organisations database as part of its Home Office funded WIRE (Wiltshire Information Resource Exchange) project. WIRE uses a Shelton SIGNET hard disk microcomputer with Superfile software to store a database of over 8,000 Wiltshire-based groups. Copies of the database on floppy disk have been made available to Councils for Voluntary Service, addresses have been printed onto adhesive labels for use by smaller specialist organisations, and major information providers such as libraries and Citizens' Advice Bureaux have been provided with alphabetical printouts with geographical and subject indexes (WIRE, 1985).

A scheme to establish a National Self Help Support Centre has recently been launched by the NCVO and the Volunteer Centre. It hopes to become a forum for all interested in self help, a contact point for the media, and to offer information, training and consultancy. In addition, the Department of Health and Social Security has set up a fund of £1.6 million to establish 18 three-year projects looking at ways of supporting local self-help initiatives. The staff, who are based at local resource centres and councils for voluntary service, started work in December 1985.

The term 'clearing house' has not yet gained wide popularity in Britain. A clearing house is an information centre on self-help groups, often on a national or international basis. In principle, it functions like the local resource centres described above, but in practice, with a national centre, the information function becomes paramount. It should have a library of practical and more academic works and up-to-date directories of groups and be able to deal with enquiries from professionals, the general public and self-help groups (Richardson, 1984). The concept of the clearing house originated in the United States where there are examples in operation in a large number of cities, and has more recently been extended to Europe. The World Health Organization has set up an Information Centre on Research into Self Help, initially in Hamburg and more recently (from 1984) in Leuven, Belgium.

Many national organisations in Britain have clearing house functions. The head offices of the major voluntary organisations generally have information departments*. For example, MIND has developed an extensive information service which maintains files of addresses of organisations in the mental health field and a substantial cuttings service and journal collection (Drake, 1980). Unfortunately financial restraints have curtailed some of the services which MIND would like to offer. A recent issue of *Assignation*, the Aslib Social Sciences Information Group Newsletter (*3*(1)October 1985) has reviewed national information centres in the field of ageing. In the area of child health, the information service of the National Children's Bureau is particularly up-to-date and helpful. Contact a Family, an organisation concerned to promote self-help among families with handicapped children provides an information service which can link parents with others in the same position. The Women's Health Information Centre is a national information and resource centre for

* A directory of major information sources is given in Chapter 5.

108

women's health issues, maintaining a library and register of women's health groups and campaigns, and producing a newsletter and broadsheets. The Community Health Group for Ethnic Minorities is a national voluntary organisation operating an information and resource centre. Material is collected in the languages of the main ethnic minority groups and an 'ethnic switchboard' gives advice to individuals in their own language on medical, legal and social problems.

Two national information services are worth mentioning in more detail: the Cancer Information Service of BACUP (British Association of Cancer United Patients) and the College of Health.

CANCER INFORMATION

The importance of information, both in prevention and early detection, and in enabling the patient to adjust and cope with cancer is well recognised. However, the provision of accurate and sympathetic information has not always matched the need. Patient education nurses are common in the United States but so far only one has been appointed in this country. This is at the Royal Marsden Hospital in London.

The patient education work at the Royal Marsden Hospital, a specialist cancer hospital, has been developed for two reasons. First, there has been a growing demand from consumers for this type of help. Patients were expressing a need to understand what was likely to happen to them as their illness progressed so that they could have more control over their lives. Many had a feeling of helplessness. Coupled with this, one of the senior nurses had a growing conviction that there was a gap in the care of patients. Patients need far more information about the nature of their complaint, its treatment and how to cope with a chronic illness. This conviction has grown through extended clinical contact with patients and has been confirmed by discussions with other nurses. As a consequence the senior nurse, Pat Webb, has made study tours to the United States where, not only is patient health literature prolific, but almost every hospital has a patient educator.

Subsequently, the Royal Marsden Hospital has agreed to fund an innovative post of senior nurse to develop patient education services, supported by a research assistant. There are three components to this work: research, professional teaching and the establishment of a resource centre. Interviews with patients have been used, firstly to identify the needs for information and secondly to evaluate materials written to meet those needs. The Royal Marsden runs courses for qualified nursing staff from hospitals throughout Britain as well as from overseas. These courses include sessions on providing information for patients and also on the interpersonal skills needed for such work. A resource centre has been set up for use by health care professionals and by patients and the general public. This has involved collecting together consumer health information materials and, following the research with patients, writing booklets to fill gaps in provision. The salary of the senior nurse is met by the hospital, the research is currently funded by the Cancer Research Campaign and the publications by donations from drug companies. Although the primary focus of the work of the Royal Marsden Hospital is cancer nursing, the results of the research and development there will have a much wider applicability to health information services generally (Kempson, 1984).

Some Regional Health Authorities now have Regional Cancer Organisations. The first of these (North Western; Yorkshire; Wessex; and South West Thames) were established on a trial basis by the Department of Health and Social Security in the early 1970s. The RCOs were intended to coordinate all activities relating to cancer, from prevention, diagnosis, treatment, care and research to education of the health care professions and the public. Each has developed a different organisation and pattern of activities but . all have a commitment to wider dissemination of information.

In some areas self-help cancer information services are now being started. A telephone helpline for cancer sufferers and their relatives has been set up in Manchester. The Cancer Aid and Listening Line (CALL) opened in 1983 and is operated by trained volunteers all of whom have had personal experience of cancer. The service is advertised in GPs' surgeries, hospitals, Citizens' Advice Bureaux and the local press. Volunteers offer support and information to callers seven nights a week in complete confidence (Eardley and Brown, 1985). A more comprehensive nationally-based service has been established by CancerLink. CancerLink grew out of the perceptions of a group of people with personal and professional experience of cancer, that although most of the medical needs of cancer patients were being catered for, there was not enough emotional and practical support. CancerLink saw that this gap could be bridged most effectively by providing an information service linked to a network of self help groups. CancerLink provides training courses for groups in communication skills, running group sessions and basic knowledge of cancer. In the words of Petra Griffiths, one of the founding members of CancerLink 'When I had cancer I found that the medical services provided were excellent but that there was a desperate need for someone to listen when I needed to get things off my chest.' CancerLink was started in 1982 and now provides a full-time daily information service staffed by workers with nursing and advice service experience (CancerLink, 1985). CancerLink is working closely with CALL to establish regular meetings of cancer support groups.

In October 1985 the most wide-ranging service of all was established – BACUP (British Association of Cancer United Patients, their families and friends). BACUP was founded by Dr Vicky Clement-Jones, an endocrinologist whose career was interrupted by ovarian cancer at the age of 35 (Clement-Jones, 1985). Despite being a practising doctor when her own cancer was diagnosed, she felt – as many patients do – ill-equipped to cope. There was, she discovered, a crying need for more knowledge about treatment, support services and financial help. Like the Royal Marsden patient education service, BACUP is based closely on American experiences. The National Cancer Institute of the US Department of Health and Human Services provides a 'phone-in Cancer Information Service for the general public. BACUP works along similar lines. Enquiries are answered by experienced cancer nurses who have undergone further training in counselling and telephone communication skills. A database has been created of services available to cancer sufferers including screening, treatment and research centres, transport services, cancer patient support groups, financial assistance and home nursing services. In addition to answering specific questions, BACUP provides, in response to individual requests, a series of written information booklets, leaflets and sheets and some audiovisual materials. Some selected literature produced by other cancer organisations is also distributed. BACUP also produces its own newspaper for cancer patients and their families, which discusses such issues as communication problems for cancer patients, the work of other cancer charities, coping with hair loss following chemotherapy, and self-help groups. The ultimate goal is to involve as many cancer patients as possible in describing their ways of coping with cancer (Morris, 1985).

The BACUP Information service is very closely monitored. At the end of each enquiry a record form is filled in describing the nature of the call, age and occupation of caller, how she or he found out about BACUP, and what material was provided. Each caller is then sent a questionnaire to find out what they thought of the service and the information provided. A telephone monitoring system has been installed to check how long callers wait, how many ring off etc. The result of this detailed evaluation should be enormously useful to other information services.

COLLEGE OF HEALTH

One of the most significant recent developments in consumer participation in health has been the College of Health. The College of Health was established in 1983 by Michael Young, whose impressive list of achievements includes the Consumers' Association. Like the Consumers' Association, the College of Health is a non-profit-making body funded by members' subscriptions. Writing in the first issue of the College's journal *Self Health* Michael Young outlines the philosophy of the new organisation as follows:

The health of the nation is promoted by a number of Colleges already, such as the College of Surgeons, Physicians, General Practitioners, and Nursing. Why should yet another, the College of Health, be set up alongside them, specifically for patients?

The reason for establishing the College of Health to be run as a non-profit making charity lies in the present imbalance between medical professionals and their patients. The former have power, the latter do not. This is not just due to the emotional dependence which many sick people cannot avoid. It is also due to the large gap between the knowledge and information of the two parties. Information (as always) is power. The best way of putting professionals and patients on more level terms is therefore to endow

112

patients with more of it. So the main purpose of the new College is the same as that of the other colleges, that is to improve education, in our case the education of lay people. (Young, 1983)

To be more specific, the main concern of the College of Health is with information to serve four main purposes: prevention, treatment, self care, and building bridges between conventional and alternative medicine. Information is provided through a number of channels. An information service is provided for members, based on an extensive database of self-help groups established through the cooperation of the Wessex Help for Health Information Service. A quarterly journal *Self Health* is one of the main means of communication with members. Through the journal, a number of campaigns for change have been initiated, including calls for action by Health Authorities to improve the nutritional quality of food served in hospitals; an end to the advertising and promotion of tobacco products and a ban on smoking in public places; greater control on the manner in which some health products are advertised and on the use of unexplained initials after the names of some alternative therapists; a reduction in speed limits to save children and young adults from what is now the greatest risk of serious injury and death for those age groups; and checks on the competence of general practitioners who go on practising after the normal retirement age for other professions (Rigge, 1985). A number of consumer guides have been published, including a *Guide to Alternative Medicine*, a *Guide to Homes for Elderly People*, a *Guide to Second Opinions*, and a *Guide to Hospital Waiting Lists*.

Healthline

In July 1984 the College of Health launched a new telephone information service for the public, called Healthline. The idea was first developed by Gloucester Health Education Service, following the example of the successful TelMed scheme in the United States, and was set up in the UK as a collaborative project between Gloucester, the College of Health and Exeter Health Authority. Over 100 tapes, each between 2–6 minutes long and approved by a panel of medical experts, have been recorded, which provide information on a wide range of health subjects. There are tapes on aspects of keeping healthy and self care, on looking after children and the elderly, on subjects such as sexually transmitted diseases about which people may be embarrassed or reluctant to consult their doctors, and on illnesses such as cancer and heart and circulation disease. The service is free, except for the cost of the telephone call, and is confidential and anonymous. More than 5,000 people used Healthline in London during the first few months of operation. Some fifty new tapes are currently in preparation in response to public demand, and it is hoped that some of these may become available in Bengali and other ethnic minority languages. If the experiment proves successful in the pilot areas of Exeter, Gloucester and London, it is hoped that the Healthline service may expand to other cities with appropriate modifications to all the scripts so that callers are given the addresses of local sources of help wherever possible (Rigge, 1985).

In his launching article in the first issue of *Self Health*, Michael Young placed the College of Health within the context of a wide consumer movement. His concept of an information cooperative is a valuable model for the future:

> I started the Consumers' Association and its magazine *Which*? in order to educate and inform consumers so that they would be on more level terms with producers of goods and services. The Advisory Centre for Education and its magazine *Where*? was later set up to do the same for parents in relation to professional teachers. They were, and are, both 'information cooperatives' – cooperatives whereby members supply the resources for an exchange of information with other members. The time is ripe for a similar effort with an information cooperative for health and one with an eye for action which can lead to practical improvements. Better representation of the consumer interest in the health service could itself be one of these improvements. If the new College does its job it will heighten awareness or our common interest in health.

REFERENCES

'Advice across the chemists' counter' (1985) *Which*?, August, pp. 351-4.
Advice and Legal Representation Project at Springfield Hospital: The

First Year's Work (1983) Springfield Hospital, 61 Glenburnie Road, London, SW17.

The Albany Health Project: The First Five Years (1983) Albany Health Project, The Albany, Douglas Way, London, SE8.

Anderson, R. and Watson, A. (1985), 'The slimline tonic', *Guardian*, 14 November, p. 13.

Andrew, G. and Horsnell, V. (1980) 'The information source libraries cannot ignore', *Library Association Record*, vol. 82(9), pp. 424–5.

Ashton, J. and Seymour, H. (1985) 'An approach to health promotion in one region', *Community Medicine*, vol. 7(2), pp. 78–86.

Ballantyne, D.T. (1974) 'CCTV for patients', *American Journal of Nursing*, vol. 74, pp. 263–4.

Baskerville, P.A., Heddle, R.M. and Jarrett, P.E. (1985) 'Preparation for surgery: information tapes for the patient', *Practitioner*, vol. 229, pp. 677–8.

Beal, C. (1979) 'Studying the public's information needs', *Journal of Librarianship*, vol. 11(2), pp. 130–51.

Beazley, S. (1978), 'Disabled advice services', *British Journal of Occupational Therapy*, vol. 41(2), pp. 55–6.

Bedford, R. (1979) 'Medicine and the media: the need to strengthen the bridge', *Journal of the Royal College of Physicians* (London), vol. 13, pp. 7–14.

Bell, L. (1983) '*An Evaluation of Help for Health*, internal document, Wessex Regional Library and Information Service, Southampton.

Black, Sir D. (1982) '*Inequalities in Health: the Black Report*, ed. Townsend, P. and Davidson, N., Penguin, Harmondsworth.

Blackford, N. (1981) 'Citizens Advice Bureau: call me a CAB!' *Nursing Mirror*, vol. 152(5), pp. 34–5.

Bonfield, A. (1983) 'Television for patient education', *Journal of Audiovisual Media in Medicine*, vol. 6, pp. 140–2.

British Broadcasting Corporation General Advisory Council (1976) *The BBC's Medical Programmes and Their Effect on Lay Audiences*, BBC Publications, London.

Brown, R.L. and Watson, D. (1984) 'Health and patient education: the role we can play', *Journal of Audiovisual Media in Medicine*, vol. 7, pp. 63–6.

Bunch, A. (1979) 'The library at the hub of community information', *Municipal and Public Services Journal*, vol. 87(9), pp. 217–8.

Bunch, A. (1982), *Community Information Services: Their Origin,*

Scope and Development, Bingley, London.

Bunch, A. (1984) *The Basics of Information Work*, Bingley, London.

Burgess, P. (1985) 'Keeping the lines open', *Community Care*, 8 August pp. 16–18.

Burkeman, S. (1980) 'Community health councils – building a constituency', *Royal Society of Health Journal*, vol. 100, pp. 157–60.

'CancerLink: bridging the gap', (1985) *Cancer Care*, vol. 2, pp. 12–14.

Cartwright, A. (1983) *Health Surveys in Practice and in Potential: a critical review of their scope and methods*, London, King's Fund.

Cawkell, A.E. (1980) 'Will information flow to the citizens be improved with videotex systems?', *Aslib Proceedings*, vol. 32(6), pp. 264–9.

Clarke, W.D., Engel, C.E., Jolly, B.C. and Meyrick, R.L. (1976) 'Health education in the doctor's waiting room', *Health Education Journal*, vol. 35, pp. 135–41.

Clarke, W.D., Devine, M., Jolly, B.C. and Meyrick, R.L. (1977) 'Health education with a display machine in the surgery', *Health Education Journal*, vol. 36, pp. 100–13.

Clarke, W.D. (1980) 'Advertising or education: alternative models for patient education', *Journal of Audiovisual Media in Medicine*, vol. 3, pp. 21–2.

Clayden, G. (1985) 'Microcomputers and medical education', *Medical Education*, vol. 19, pp. 76–82.

Clement-Jones, V. (1985) 'Cancer and beyond: the formation of BACUP', *British Medical Journal*, vol. 291, pp. 1021–3.

Cohen, Lord (Chairman) (1964) *Health Education: Report of a Joint Committee of the Central and Scottish Health Services Councils*, HMSO, London.

Community Information Project (1982) *The First Five Years*, Community Information Project, 136 City Road, London, EC1.

Community Information Project (1985) *At the Touch of a Button*, CIP, London.

Creber, J. (1985) 'Public Information in Rural Areas Technology Experiment (PIRATE)', *Program*, vol. 19, pp. 77–9.

CVS in Action (1981) *Information and Resource Centres*, Standing Conference of CVS, NCVO, London.

Darnbrough, A. and Kinrade, D. (1984) *Directory for Disabled People*, 4th edn., Woodhead Faulkner, London.

'Database' (1986) *New Society*, 10 January.

Davies, P. (1985) 'Campaign for hearts and minds in Wales', *Health and Social Service Journal*, vol. 95, p. 322.

Delvin, D. (1981) *'A Patient's Guide to Operations'*, Penguin, Harmondsworth.

Department of Health and Social Security (1981) *Care in Action: A Handbook of Policies and Priorities for the Health and Personal Social Services in England*, HMSO, London.

Directory of Social Action Programmes (1985) Media Project, Volunteer Centre, Berkhamsted.

Dolman, B. (1981) 'General practitioner in the media', *British Medical Journal*, vol. 282(6270), pp. 1123–4.

Drake, R.F. (1980) 'Information for mental health', *Library Association Record*, vol. 82(12), p. 587.

Drennan, V. (1984) *Working in a Different Way: A Research Project Examining Community Work Methods and Health Visiting*, Paddington and North Kensington Health Authority, 16 South Wharf Road, London, W2 1PF.

Drummond, P. (1980) 'Flaws in the indexing tree', *Health and Social Service Journal*, vol. 90, pp. 1470–1.

Eardley, A. and Brown, T. (1985) 'Cancer line', *Nursing Mirror*, vol. 160(4), pp. 16–17.

Eastwood, M. and Smith, I.D. (1973) *Medicine and the mass media*, Royal College of Physicians, (Edinburgh).

Economic Intelligence Unit (1982), *The Home Video Revolution in Western Europe*, Economic Intelligence Unit Special Report No. 144.

Education Act 1981, Ch. 60 Section 10(2), 'Duty of health authorities to notify parents'.

Elliott, D.K. (1984) 'Information and advice services in rural areas', *Library and Information Research News*, vol. 7(25), pp. 21–2.

Ellis, L.B.M., Raines, J.R. and Hakanson, N. (1982) 'Health education using microcomputers', *Preventive Medicine*, vol. 11, pp. 212–24.

Epstein, J. (1983) 'Communicating with the elderly', *Journal of the Market Research Society*, vol. 25(3), pp. 239–62.

'Expanding role for pharmacists', editorial, *British Medical Journal* vol. 2, pp. 911–2.

Farrell, C. and Adams, J. (1981) 'CHCs at work', *CHC News*, no. 65, April.

Fears, D. (1980) *A Citizens' Advice Bureau at Central Middlesex Hospital: An Experiment*, CAB Occasional Paper No. 9, National Association of Citizens' Advice Bureaux, London.

Fisher, B.H. and Cochrane, M. (1982), 'Peckham Health Project: raising health consciousness', *British Medical Journal*, vol. 284, pp. 1, 843–5.

Fletcher, C.M. (1973), *Communication in Medicine,* Nuffield Provincial Hospitals Trust, London.

Fowler, G. (1985) 'Health education in general practice', *Health Education Journal*, vol. 44(1), pp. 44–5.

Fry, J. and Meyrick, R. (1984) 'Patient education' in Fabb, W. and Fry, J., *Principles of Practice management in Primary Care*, MTP Press, Lancaster.

Gann, R. (1981) *Help for Health: The needs of Health Care Practitioners for Information about Organisations in Support of Health Care*, BLR&D Report No. 5613, Wessex Regional Library and Information Service, Southampton.

Gann, R. (1982) *Getting Started: Collecting and Organising Patient Information*, Wessex Regional Library and Information Service, Southampton.

Gann, R. (1983) 'It's your line to the health computer (Joint Care Award)', *Health and Social Service Journal*, vol. 94(4853), pp. 782–3.

Gann, R. (1984) *Information for Care: The First Five Years of the Help for Health Information Service*, Wessex Regional Library and Information Service, Southampton.

Gann, R. (1985) 'Information on self help for health promotion', *Twelfth World Conference on Health Education*, Dublin, Ireland, September.

Gann, R. (1985) 'Information for self care in health and illness', *Fifth International Congress on Medical Librarianship*, Tokyo, Japan, October.

Gann, R. (1986) 'Information for lay care: the Help for Health project in Southampton, UK', in *Information for Primary Health Care*, World Health Organization Regional Office for Europe, Copenhagen (in press).

Gann, R. (1986), 'Patient information', in Picken, F.M. and Kahn, A., *Medical Librarianship in the Eighties and Beyond: A World Perspective*. Mansell, London.

Gillespie, V. and Orton, A. (1985) 'Watching while you wait', *Nursing Times*, vol. 81, pp. 40–1.

Going, M.E. (1981) *Hospital Libraries and Work with the Disabled in the Community*, 3rd edn., Library Association, London.

Graham, J.L. (1980) 'Message and medium: video health education programmes', *Health and Social Service Journal*, vol. 90, pp. 911–2.

Graham, J.L. (1980) 'Focusing on the video show', *Health and Social Service Journal*, vol. 90, pp. 948–9.

Gratton, P. (1985) 'Information as a social need', *Library Association Record*, vol. 87(10), p. 393.

Greater London Citizens' Advice Bureaux Service (1985) *Citizens Advice*, GLCABS, 31 Wellington Road, London, WC2.

Greengross, W. (1981) 'Medicine and the media', *British Medical Journal*, vol. 282, p. 391.

Gregory, J. (1978) *Patients' Attitudes to the Hospital Services*, Royal Commission on the NHS Research Paper No. 5, HMSO, London.

Griffith, H.W. (1982) *Instructions for Patients*, 3rd edn. Saunders, Philadelphia.

Griffiths, R. (1982) 'The Community Health Councils of the future', *Royal Society of Health Journal*, vol. 102(1), pp. 3–6.

Griffiths, R. (1983), *NHS Management Enquiry*, Department of Health and Social Security, London.

Grimshaw, C. (1985) *Inside Advice: The Work of the Citizens' Advice Bureau at Tooting Bec Hospital*, Citizens' Advice Bureau, Tooting Bec Hospital, London, SW17 8BL.

Halpern, S. (1985) 'What the public thinks of the NHS', *Health and Social Service Journal*, vol. 95, pp. 702–4.

Ham, C. (1985) 'Consumerism in the NHS: state of the art', *Health and Social Service Journal*, vol. 94(4950), 'Centre Eight' pp. i–iv.

Harris, J. (1982) 'An investigation of the determinants of the advisory and information service and potential for health education in retail pharmacy', *Health Education Journal,* vol. 41(2), pp. 42–6.

Harris, J.W. (1984) 'Is the pharmacist a credible source of health information?', *Pharmaceutical Journal*, vol. 4, pp. 143–4.

Health Promotion: The Challenge for CHCs (1983) Report of a conference held at King's Fund Centre, King's Fund Centre, London.

Heaton, C. (1985) 'Libraries superfile helping the community', *Local*

Government Chronicle, 27 September, pp. 1096–7.

Horvath, W. (1983) 'Plugging health promotion into the cable TV boom', *Promoting Health*, vol. 4(5), pp. 1–3.

Hurley, G. (1983) *Lucky Break?* Milestone Publications, Project Icarus, Southsea, Hants.

Hutton, A. and Robins, S. (1985) 'What the patient wants from patient participation', *Journal of the Royal College of General Practitioners*, vol. 35, pp. 133–5.

Integrating the Disabled: Report of the Snowdon Working Party (1976) National Fund for Research into Crippling Diseases, Horsham.

Jacobson, B., and Amos, A. (1985) *When Smoke Gets in Your Eyes: Cigarette Advertising Policy and Coverage of Smoking and Health in Women's Magazines, May 1985*, British Medical Association Professional Division and Health Education Council, London.

Jarman, B. (1985) 'Giving advice about welfare benefits in general practice,' *British Medical Journal*, vol. 290, pp. 522–4.

Kania, H. (1985) *Prestel for People*, Council for Educational Technology, London.

Kempson, E. (1984), 'Consumer health information services', *Health Libraries Review*, vol. 1(3), pp. 127–44.

Kitzinger, S. (1979) *The Good Birth Guide*, Fontana, London.

Klein, R. (1984) 'On the spot advice', *Health and Social Services Journal*, vol. 94, pp. 75–6.

Klein, R. (1984) '10,000 projects blossom', *Health and Social Services Journal*, vol. 94, p. 442.

Knight, S. (1980) *Help! I Need Somebody*, 3rd edn., Kimpton, London.

Langridge, C. (1977) 'Community Health Councils: watchdogs or lapdogs?, *Nursing Mirror*, vol. 145(15), pp. 42–3.

Lawes, C. (1984) *Health Education and Spinal Cord Injury*, Leeds Polytechnic Department of Health Education, Leeds LS1 3HE.

Levitt, R. (1980) *The People's Voice in the NHS: Community Health Councils After 5 Years*, King's Fund Centre, London.

Lewis, M.G. (1985) 'Providing library support for a community based mental handicap project: some experiences from a recent setting up exercise', *Aslib Proceedings,* vol. 37(5), pp. 221–9.

Library Association (1980) *Community Information: What Libraries Can Do*, a consultative document, Library Association, London.

Little, K. (1980) 'Advice services and the health worker: a constructive partnership', *Midwife, Health Visitor and Community Nurse*, vol. 16(9), pp. 365–367.

McCron, R. and Dean, E. (1983) *Wellbeing: An Evaluation*, Channel 4, London.

Mann, R.G. (1985) 'Why patient participation groups stop functioning: a general practitioner's viewpoint', *British Medical Journal*, vol. 290, pp. 209–11.

Marsh, G.N. (1980) 'The practice brochure: a patient's guide to team care', *British Medical Journal*, vol. 281, pp. 730–2.

Maxwell, R. and Weaver, N. (1984) *Public Participation in Health: Towards a Clearer View*, King's Fund Centre, London.

Maynes, E.S. (1982) *Prestel in Use: A Consumer View*, National Consumer Council, London.

Metcalfe, D.H.H. (1980) 'Why not let patients keep their own records?' *Journal of the Royal College of General Practitioners*, vol. 30, p. 420.

Midgley, J.M. and Macrae, A.W. (1971) 'Audiovisual media in medical practice', *Journal of the Royal College of General Practitioners*, vol. 21, pp. 346–51.

Moore, N. (1985) 'Information technology in rural areas', *Library Association Record*, vol.87(6), pp. 223, 225, 227.

Morby, G. (1982) '*Know How to Find Out Your Rights*, 2nd edn., Pluto Press and Library Association, London.

Morgan, M. (1984) 'Health education via the friendly local computer', *Health and Social Service Journal*, vol. 94, pp. 1,300–1.

Morgan, M. (1985) 'Health education: a suitable case for new-tech treatment?', *Times Educational Supplement*, 31 May, p. 9.

Morris, P. (1985) 'Bridging the gap', *Nursing Times*, vol. 81, p. 20.

National Association of Citizens' Advice Bureaux (1980) *Chapeltown C.A.B. Disability Project Report September 1979–August 1980*, CAB Occasional Paper No. 12, National Association of Citizens' Advice Bureaux, London.

National Association of Citizens' Advice Bureaux (1984) *Final Report of the Kirklees Ethnic Minority Project: A Project to Study the Information and Advice Needs of Members of Ethnic Minority Groups*, CAB Occasional Paper No. 16, National Association of Citizens' Advice Bureaux, London.

National Consumer Council (1977) *The Fourth Right of Citizenship*,

National Consumer Council, London.

National Consumer Council (1979) *Post Office: Special Agent*, National Consumer Council, London.

National Consumer Council (1982) *Publicity Please: Guidelines on Local Publicity about Information and Advice Centres*, National Consumer Council, London.

National Consumer Council (1982) *Advice Agencies: What They Are and Who Uses Them*, National Consumer Council, London.

National Consumer Council (1983) *Information and Advice Services in the United Kingdom: Report to the Minister of State for Consumer Affairs*, National Consumer Council, London.

National Consumer Council (1983) *Patients' Rights: A Guide for NHS Patients and Doctors*, HMSO, London.

National Council for Social Service (1978) *The Right to Know: a Review of Advice Services in Rural Areas*, Bedford Square Press, London.

Office of Health Economics (1964) *The Pharmacist in Society*, Office of Health Economics, London.

Orriss, H.D. (1974) 'Community Health Councils: watchdogs or lapdogs?', *Nursing Times*, vol. 70(24), pp. 928–9.

Osler, W. (1932) *Aequanimitas, with Other Addresses*, McGraw, New York.

Ottley, P. and Kempson, E. (1982) *Computer Benefits: Guidelines for Local Information and Advice Centres*, National Consumer Council, London.

Paine, T. (1982) 'Patient participation: a survey of patient participation groups in the UK', *British Medical Journal*, vol. 286, pp. 768–72, 847–9.

Parish, P. (1984) *Medicines: A Guide for Everybody*, 5th edn., Penguin, Harmondsworth.

Parish, R. (1983) 'Health education: pointing the way', *Health and Social Service Journal*, vol. 93, pp. 241–2.

Paton, J.S., Shaw, A., Smith, D.C. and McIntyre, E. (1980) 'A multiple choice quiz board for health education', *Journal of Audiovisual Media in Medicine*, vol. 3, pp. 107–8.

Pearse, I.H. (1979) *The Quality of Life: The Peckham Approach to Human Ethology*, Scottish Academic Press, Edinburgh.

The Pharmacists Charter: Extending the role of the pharmacist in the provision of health care to the community (1984) Pharmaceutical

Services Negotiating Committee, Aylesbury, Bucks.

Phillips, M. (1976) 'Advice on the inside', *New Society*, vol. 37(730), pp. 709–10.

Pilkington, E.M. (1979) 'The role of the general practice pharmacist in health education and health maintenance', *Health Education Journal*, vol. 37(3), pp. 187–92.

Pringle, M., Robins, S. and Brown, E. (1985) 'Computer assisted screening: effect on the patient and his consultation', *British Medical Journal*, vol. 290, pp. 1,709–12.

Pritchard, P. (1981) *Patient Participation in General Practice*, Royal College of General Practitioners Occasional Paper No. 17, Royal College of General Practitioners, London.

Pritchard, P. (1983) 'Patient participation in general practice: a practical guide to starting a group', *Medical Annual*, John Wright, Bristol.

Providing a District Library Service: proposals arising from a series of workshops held in 1983 about the contribution library services can make to the provision and use of information in the NHS (1985) King's Fund, London.

'Purposive private library' (1984) *Library Association Record*, vol. 86(1), p. 5.

Rayner, C. (1979) 'Reality and expectation of the British National Health Service consumer', *Journal of Advanced Nursing*, vol. 4, pp. 69–77.

The Recruitment, Training and Development of Health Education Officers (1981) National Staff Committee for Administrative and Clerical Staff, London.

Redfearn, J. (1983) *Libraries Bring Prestel to the Public: A Summary of British Library Supported Research 1979–81*, Library and Information Research Reports 13, British Library Lending Division, Boston Spa.

Research Institute for Consumer Affairs (1984) *Aids for People with Disabilities: A Review of Information Services*, RICA, London.

Richardson, A. (1984) *Working with Self Help Groups: A Guide for Local Professionals*, Bedford Square Press, National Council for Voluntary Organisations, London.

Richardson, A.S. (1969) 'Evaluation of a newspaper column and radio broadcasts for dental education of the public', *Journal of the Canadian Dental Association*, vol. 35, pp. 324–8.

Ricketts, S. (1980) 'Can your Citizens Advice Bureau help you?', *Health Visitor*, vol. 53(9), p. 386.

Rigge, M. (1985), 'A new information cooperative: the College of Health', *Assignation: Aslib Social Sciences Information Group Newsletter*, vol. 2(2), pp. 8–9.

Roberts, E. (1978) 'Consumer satisfaction in the health service: the role of the Community Health Council', *Royal Society of Health Journal*, vol. 98(4), pp. 173–6.

Robinson, S.E. and Roberts, M.M. (1985) 'A women's health shop: a unique experiment', *British Medical Journal*, vol. 291, pp. 255–6.

Rogers, A. (1980) 'Doctor on the air', *Journal of the Royal College of General Practitioners*, vol. 30(219), pp. 629–31.

Rosen, J.L. (1979) 'Aims and achievements of Community Health Councils', *Royal Society of Health Journal*, vol. 99(4), pp. 166–8.

Rosenthal, H. (1983) 'Neighbourhood health projects: some new approaches to health and community work in parts of the United Kingdom', *Community Development Journal*, vol. 18(2), pp. 121–31.

Rowe, M.J. (1984) 'Information for health now, with a happy retirement in view', *Health Libraries Review*, vol. 1(1), pp. 11–15.

Rowland, Y. (1973) 'Citizens' Advice Bureaux: a personal view', *Community Health (Bristol)*, vol. 4(4), pp. 173–8.

Rubin, R.J. (1978) *Bibliotherapy Sourcebook*, Mansell, London.

Saunders, P. (1980) 'Danger for the disabled', *CHC News*, December p. 5.

Saunders, P. (1983) 'Dial A for advice', *Handicapped Living*, vol. 2(4), pp. 17–18.

Sharp, D.K. (1985) 'The Health Education Council Library', *Assignation: Aslib Social Sciences Information Group Newsletter* vol. 2(2), pp. 17–19.

Simpson, R. (1979) *Access to Primary Care*, Royal Commission on NHS Research Paper No. 6, HMSO, London.

Smail, S.A. (1983) 'Health education officer', *British Medical Journal*, vol. 286, pp. 1,941–2.

Smith, C. (1982) *Community Based Health Initiatives: A Handbook for Voluntary Groups*, National Council for Voluntary Organisations, London.

Smith, R. (1983) 'Part-time agony aunt in trousers', *British Medical Journal*, vol. 287, p. 1,029.

Solstad, K. (1985) 'Health education through weekly magazines',

Twelfth World Conference on Health Education, Dublin, Ireland, September.

Somerville, G. (1985) *Community Development in Health: Addressing the Confusions*, King's Fund Centre, London.

South East Thames Regional Health Promotion Group (1984) *Health Promotion: Reality or Illusion*, South East Thames Regional Health Authority, Thrift House, Collington Avenue, Bexhill, East Sussex, TN39 3NQ.

Stanway, A. (1981) *A Dictionary of Operations*, Granada, London.

Strehlow, M.S. (1983) *Education for Health*, Harper and Row, London.

Strickland-Hodge, B. (1985) 'Aslib private viewdata group seminar', *Health Libraries Review*, vol. 2(3), pp. 139–40.

Stroud, J. (1985) 'New vistas via new technology', *Health and Social Services Journal*, vol. 95, pp. 186–8.

Sutherland, I. (1979) *Health Education: Perspectives and Choices*, Allen and Unwin, London.

Tabor, R.B. (1983) *Reflections: A Subject Guide to Works of Fiction, Biography and Autobiography on Medical and Related Topics*, 2nd edn. Wessex Regional Library and Information Service, Southampton.

Tabor, R.B. and Gann, R.E. (1984) 'Information for patients and public' in Morton, L. and Godbolt, S., *Information Sources in the Medical Sciences*, Butterworths, London, pp. 338–49.

Tattershall, R.B. and Marinker, M. (1983) 'Video medicine', *British Medical Journal*, vol. 286, p. 1,428.

Taylor, M. (1983) *Resource Centres for Community Groups*, Community Projects Foundation, 60 Highbury Grove, London, N5 2AG.

Turner, B. and Larcombe, R. (1983) 'Health information and education for inpatients and outpatients via CCTV', *Journal of Audiovisual Media in Medicine*, vol. 6(1), pp. 13–14.

Tyser, P.A. (1975) 'Health education in general practice', *Community Health*, vol. 4, pp. 179–84.

Varnavides, C.K. Zermansky, A.G. and Pace, C. (1984) 'Health library for patients in general practice', *British Medical Journal*, vol. 288, pp. 533–6.

Vickery, D.M. and Fries, J.F. (1980) *Take Care of Yourself*, Unwin Paperbacks, London.

Webb, P. (1981) 'Off air advice: papering the health service cracks', *Media Project News*, October, pp. 37–41.

Webb, P. (1982) 'I just wanted to talk to someone', *Nursing Mirror*, vol. 155(24), pp. 18–22.

'What makes the GP tick?' (1979) *British Medicine*, July 7, pp. 3–7.

Whitehouse, A. (1982) 'Information for living', *Community Care*, 4 March, pp. 14–16.

The Whiteway Health Project: The First Year (1985) Whiteway Health Project, 36 St Michael's Way, Whiteway, Bath.

Whitfield, M. (1968) 'The pharmacist's contribution to medical care', *Practitioner*, vol. 200, pp. 434–8.

Williamson, J.D. and Danaher, K. (1978) *Self Care in Health*, Croom Helm, London.

Wilson, J. (1982) 'Stepping stones to normal life. (Nottingham Self Help Groups Project)', *Health and Social Service Journal*, vol. 92, p. 1,253.

Wilson, J. (1985) 'Self help: does the answer lie in the soil?' *Involve*, no. 22, p. 3.

Wilson, J. (1983) *Self Help Group Starterpack*, Nottingham Self Help Groups Project, 114 Mansfield Road, Nottingham, NG1 3HL.

WIRE (1985), *Wiltshire Information Resource Exchange Project Report 1982 to 1985*, WIRE Project, Community Council for Wiltshire, Wyndhams, St Joseph's Place, Devizes, Wiltshire.

Yeates, R. (1982) *A Librarian's Guide to Private Viewdata Systems*, London and South Eastern Library Region (LASER).

Yeates, R. (1984) 'Viewdata: lessons from Prestel and new opportunities for libraries', *VINE*, vol. 57, pp. 21–6.

Young, M. (1983) 'The four purposes and six methods', *Self Health*, vol. 1(1), pp. 3–4.

4

Health information in other countries

The provision of information on health and illness to patients and the public is by no means confined to the United Kingdom. A number of other countries have equally, if not better, developed services with a similar diversity of agencies involved. To do these justice would require a separate book. In fact several books have already been written on the American scene. The chapter will do no more than give a flavour of health information provision in other countries, concentrating in particular on North America and Northern Europe whose practices are most relevant to the UK. Examples are given of a number of projects and services, with an emphasis on services provided by medical and public libraries.

UNITED STATES

In the United States, as in the United Kingdom, the development of information and advice services for the community can be traced back to the Second World War (Bunch, 1982). Here, a network of Veterans' Information Centers was set up to meet the needs of returning servicemen in 1945. The Centers were modelled on the British Citizens' Advice Bureaux and provided full, up-to-date information on government and community services for veterans. By 1946 there were over 3,000 Veterans' Information Centers (Kahn, 1966), but their role was limited in the range of information covered and the clientele served. By 1949 most Centers had disbanded and did not develop a wider function as the Citizens' Advice Bureaux had in Britain.

In the years that followed, a patchwork provision of community information or 'Information and Referral' (I&R) services developed to provide guidance through the network of services, programmes and agencies available to the post-war American citizen (Childers, 1975). These I&R services tended to be focused on particular groups with special needs, such as the elderly, the sick and the poor. By the early 1950s, well in advance of the United Kingdom, the information needs of hospital patients were beginning to be addressed. The 'activated medical consumer' has been a feature of American society ever since.

In an illuminating article Harris (1978) has traced the chronology of information services for patients in the United States. The first projects of any substance were started by a few health educators on the staff of the National Tuberculosis Association, now known as the Lung Association. These patient education projects of the late 1940s and early 1950s were based on the concept of the informed patient as part of the total health care plan (Jordan *et al.*, 1950). In 1955 the Veterans' Administration studied the problems of non-compliance with drug regimes in its tuberculosis hospitals, and of patients leaving hospitals before medically advised to do so. Effective patient education was singled out as a remedy for both these situations (Beauchamp, 1953).

In the early 1960s voluntary agencies and the Public Health Service funded several successful patient and family education projects concerning heart disease, stroke, cancer and renal dialysis (Fiori, 1974). By the 1970s, health information for the public was a major issue in the United States and, in 1976, the National Health Promotion and Disease Prevention Act became law. The Act provided for the authorisation of grants and contracts for health education projects, training programmes, publications and community health initiatives.

Legal basis of patient information in the USA

The patient's right to know and right to the information on his medical record has been a considerable force in the development of health information services in the USA. The *Report of the Secretary's Commission on Medical Malpractice* (1973) found that there must be more effective communication between doctor and patient with

128

emphasis on a full discussion of diagnosis, prognosis, course of treatment, complications and possible adverse effects. While the notion of informed consent is intended to protect the doctor against litigation, it also recognises the patient's right to information about his condition and relevant self-care procedures (Annas, 1975).

The Patient's Bill of Rights is a culmination of trends in informed consent, medical malpractice and consumer's rights in American society. It was adopted by the American Hospital Association in 1972 and, in at least one instance, has become more than a mere statement of intent. Chapter 688 of Minnesota Laws of 1973 states 'It is declared to be public policy of this state that the interests of patients are protected by the Patient's Bill of Rights' (Curran, 1974). The Health Planning and Resources Development Act of 1975 has as one of its ten national health priorities the development of effective methods for educating the public in personal and preventive health care. The President's Commission for the Study of Ethical Problems in Medicine and Research recommended that 'health care professionals and institutions not only provide information but also assist patients, who request additional information, to obtain it from relevant sources, including hospital and public libraries'.

Health status and cost benefits

The American Hospital Association followed up its Patient's Bill of Rights with a report on *Implementing Patient Education in the Hospital* (1979) reinforced by its *Policy and Statement on the Hospital's Responsibility for Patient Education Services* (1982). In this, the AHA states:

> The hospital has the responsibility to provide patient education services as an integral part of high quality, cost effective care. Patient education services should enable patients, and their families and friends where appropriate, to make informed decisions about health; to manage their illnesses, and to implement follow-up care at home.

Although the American Hospital Association statements are based on a conviction that the patient should be treated humanely and with respect, they are also rooted in pragmatism. As described in Chapter 2, a large number of studies have shown that patient education decreases

129

the length of hospital stay; increases compliance with drug treatment; promotes appropriate use of health services; makes for less fearful and more cooperative patients; and eases the load on health staff. It can be demonstrated that the monetary savings far outweigh the costs of information and education provision for patients. In one study, haemophiliac outpatients and their families received instruction on the management of bleeding problems. After one year the total inpatient days per year for the group declined from 423 to 42, a reduction in hospitalisation costs of 89 per cent (Levin and Britton, 1973). In Los Angeles, the University of Southern California Medical Center introduced a telephone information service for diabetics. The results were a two-thirds reduction in the incidence of diabetic coma over a two-year period, and a total saving in emergency admissions of $1,797,750. The cost of initiating the information service and running it for the two-year period was $20,350 (Miller and Goldstein, 1972).

Because of the considerable cost savings which are possible, patient education has been accepted as a reimbursable service by the major American health care providers including the Health Insurance Council, Blue Cross/Blue Shield, the American Hospital Association and American Medical Association. Health insurance companies have come to realise that educating patients can help reduce hospital stays and re-admissions, and increase patient compliance, thus reducing rising insurance costs (Roth, 1978). In the United States, insurance companies have been major producers and sponsors of health information materials. In view of the interest they necessarily have in the health and longevity of policy holders, it is surprising that British life assurance companies have been so slow to emulate their American counterparts.

Sources of consumer health information

In the United States, the term 'consumer health information' is the one generally used to describe information on health, illness and disability for the public. Eakin, Jackson and Hannigan (1980) have divided consumer health information into the following categories:

1. Personal/patient information including requests for disease information, medical procedures, drugs, pregnancy, child care and related topics.
2. Directory information including requests for names, addresses,

biographical data about physicians, and information about hospitals, health agencies, and medical care services.

3. Publications information including questions about specific books, use of indexes, use of the collection, and library holdings.

4. Factual information including requests for correct spellings, definitions, and facts related to statistics, costs, health manpower and health resources.

The sources of this information for the American individual are, as in the UK, very diverse:

The present picture of consumer health information delivery is characterised by fragmentation rather than cooperation. Consider the array of government and other agencies now involved in health education on the national level: the Bureau of Health Education; the National Center for Health Education; the Office of Health Information and Health Promotion; and the information clearinghouses of various categorical disease programs. Relevant legislation includes the National Health Planning and Resources Act, which defined health information as one of ten national health priorities; the National Health Information and Promotion Act; and the National Consumer Health Information Act.

Health information is not really lacking; in fact it abounds. There are voluntary health organizations for every significant disease, each existing for the purpose of giving information and assistance to those afflicted by the disease and their families. Publications stream out of government agencies. Newspapers, magazines, and television feature articles and programs on medical topics. Health education programs are found in schools, clinics, and hospitals. These are some of the sources available to the public. But where is the public most likely to seek health information? From physicians? From television? From magazine articles or newspaper columns? From pharmacists or nurses or dietitians? From teachers or social workers? From libraries? (Eakin, Jackson and Hannigan, 1980).

The library is potentially an important source of health information. The library at Overlook Hospital in Summit, New Jersey, carried out a community survey in 1980 which examined both the topics on which people would like information and the sources from which they would

131

obtain it. In the previous year, 72 per cent of respondents had a need for information on health and disease. As might be expected, the doctor was the first choice for information for 55 per cent of respondents; the public library with 18 per cent was the next most popular source (Moeller and Deeney, 1982).

Sources of consumer health information in the United States have been described in great detail in Alan Rees and Jodith Janes' invaluable *The Consumer Health Information Sourcebook* (1984). This lists health information clearinghouses, publishers, voluntary organisations, books, pamphlets, periodicals and bibliographies relevant to the lay person. A companion volume *Developing Consumer Health Information Services* (Rees, 1982) concentrates on library-based activities, describing seven major projects in the USA and giving practical advice on designing and implementing similar services. Another useful survey is Myra Madnick's *Consumer Health Education: A Guide to Hospital Based Programs.* (1980). Rather than duplicate these publications in this chapter, instead some trends will be identified and some examples of projects described.

The role of the library

A number of American writers have recognised the contribution which the librarian or information specialist can make to the provision of health information for consumers (Charney, 1978; Harris, 1978; Lunin, 1978; Roth, 1978; Alloway and Salisbury, 1983; Rubin, 1983; Berk, 1985). Indeed, public libraries have addressed themselves to enquiries relating to the health of local users. Unfortunately, until recently, the problem has been the inadequacy of public library collections in health subjects and the lack of specialised knowledge on the part of public library staff (Vaillancourt and Bobka, 1982; Yellott and Barrier, 1983). In response to this need a number of cooperative ventures have been formed, linking the expertise and resources of the medical library with the accessibility and familiarity of the public library. These schemes are usually termed consumer health information networks (or a variant of the term). Early pioneers were the CHIPS and CHIN projects described in more detail later in this chapter.

In Onondaga County Public Library, Syracuse, New York, reference librarians noted an increasing number of health questions which they felt ill-equipped to answer. A solution was the establishment of a Consumer Health Information Consortium (CHIC) of public and health librarians and other agencies involved in the provision of health information for the public, with the objective of cooperative developments of collections, referrals, and shared training. One of the most useful outcomes was the design of a telephone enquiry worksheet aimed at helping librarians to improve their skills in telephone information work (Yellott and Barrier, 1982).

In Tulsa, the city library developed a Health Information Service as a cooperative venture with the Tulsa Medical College and local voluntary and community agencies. The medical library provided free MEDLINE searches and interlibrary loans to the City Library. The Health Information Service participated in a number of community events including health fairs, and provided rooms at the library for free health screening. The library is also a member of the CPR coalition, which is a coalition of health agencies that trains citizens in cardiopulmonary resuscitation (Jennings, 1982). Health promotion consortia are now a major feature of the US health care scene. At the 12th World Conference on Health Education in 1985, a number of speakers described coalitions of local voluntary, commercial and statutory organisations working together to bring health messages to the public. Such schemes span the social and geographical spectrum from the Health Promotion Consortium of Monterey County, California (Simmons, 1985) to Jackson Councy, Illinois (Child, 1985).

An associated development in Illinois has been the establishment of the Community Health Information Resource Project (CHIRP) in Oak Park. This is a cooperative project using the resources of the Oak Park Public Library, the Health Information Center at West Suburban Hospital Medical Center, and the Media Department of the Oak Park High School. There are collections of material at each of the participating institutions and a recommended core bibliography has been prepared for libraries interested in developing similar schemes. It includes all the material bought by CHIRP (Eistenstein, 1984).

The relationship between public and health care libraries and the potential for cooperative ventures has been examined by an Ad Hoc Committee of the Medical Library Association (MLA). The Committee's report (1983) recommended closer ties between public and health care libraries, ranging from the limited involvement of back-up services and interlibrary loans to extensive involvement whereby health care librarians assist in training public librarians in medical resources, trends and terminology, and participate in community outreach programmes.

The potential for cooperation is not confined to increased public library use of medical library resources. As in the UK, the community information collections of many American public libraries include essential information on local resources to help people to cope with the social aspects of illness and, particularly, long-term disability. The Pike's Peak Library District in Colorado has developed an extensive computerised community information system called Maggie's Place. The databases available include a file of all social service agencies in the community, details of day centres, a file of voluntary organisations, an on-line car pool, and a calendar of events. The main library and its branches are equipped with public access computer terminals for users to search the databases directly. In addition, there are over 600 home users of Maggie's Place through dial-up access. Maggie's Place is a very sophisticated example of using information technology to increase community access to local resources (Dowlin, 1983).

Within the hospital, some writers have been at pains to distinguish the role of the librarian from that of patient educator. Patient education should be a detailed process which involves an assessment of the learning needs of the individual patient, and the preparation of a specific programme of education using a variety of appropriate learning methods. Many American hospitals now have patient education or consumer health education departments. The Consumer Health Education Department at Perth Amboy General Hospital, New Jersey, has developed from a one-person operation in 1970 to an impressive department which produces a wide range of materials, and undertakes detailed patient education programmes. These are described in a leaflet *Hard Shell Facts*. The department received the American Hospital Association's National Merit Award for patient education in 1980. An Office of Consumer Health Education forms part of the New Jersey Medical School, Newark (Lazes, 1977; Bryant, 1978). There have been patient education coordinators in Greenville, South Carolina hospitals since the early 1970s (Moran, 1976) while, in North Carolina, the Chapel Hill University Hospital has a central office for patient education responsible for designing, producing, distributing and evaluating materials for patients. Stanford University Hospital in California provides an extensive teaching programme for

134

patients awaiting surgery through its Department of Nursing Service.

The role of the librarian in America is seen as supporting these initiatives by providing information in the form of literature searches and reviews for planners of patient education programmes, to assess the availability of patient education resources both inside and outside the hospital, and to assemble and organise materials for use by professionals and patients (Harris, 1978; Roth, 1978). As an example, the Overlook Hospital in Summit, New Jersey recently built a new hospital library which, from its inception, had a consumer health information centre as part of its design (Moeller and Deeney, 1982). Similar services have been part of the library operation at Central Du Page Hospital, Illinois since 1976 (Rowe, 1980). Hospital librarians in Maryland are becoming involved in consumer health information with an important collection at Springfield Hospital Center, and a Consumer Health Information Network based on the Eastern Shore Regional Library in Salisbury (Harman, 1983). In the health sciences library of a hospital in Nashville, Tennessee, the librarian provides an extensive back-up service to the health education department. The health educators interpret into lay language materials obtained for them by the librarian. In the children's hospital in Detroit the LATCH (Literature Attached to Charts) programme has been extended to information for patients. With the cooperation and recommendation of the physician, articles are attached to the patient's chart which will be helpful to the patient and his family in coping with his illness (McHugh, 1979).

The Strong Memorial Hospital, Rochester, New York has established a paediatric family-patient health education library. The library was founded in 1977 by parents, staff and friends of sick children as a memorial to Sara K. Davidson who died in the hospital at the age of four (Sahler *et al.* 1981). In addition to material for a lay readership the library provides selected professional literature, which can be used in the library or brought to the patient's bedside. A manual on the day-to-day operation of the library has also been published (Weber, 1981). The use of a library trolley to bring health information materials into the wards and clinics has also been tried at the Patient Reference library of the Paoli Memorial Hospital, Pennsylvania (Rickards, 1978) and the Southern California Medical Center (Topper, 1978).

While most of the consumer health information services described have dealt with a whole range of health and illness issues, the particular needs of special client groups have not been forgotten. A whole issue of the *Drexel Library Quarterly* has been devoted to the information needs of disabled people (Senkevitch, 1980), while Ruth Velleman's *Serving Physically Disabled People* (1980) gives practical advice on establishing collections and services. Consumer mental health information has been discussed recently in articles by Angier (1984), Rubinton (1982) and Russell (1982). The contribution of the librarian to bibliotherapy or reading therapy has also been extensively debated (Rubin, 1978; Elser, 1982).

The research and continuing education needs of librarians working in the field of consumer health information have not been overlooked. A number of research and development activities have been undertaken by the School of Information and Library Science at Case Western Reserve University in Cleveland, Ohio, with the cooperation of local health care and library professionals. During 1979 and 1980 the InfoHealth Project based at the library school ran a number of courses designed to improve the knowledge of local public libraries of health issues. The first programme on the topic of cancer consisted of a description of the condition by a medical specialist, followed by an outline of community resources, and basic information materials. This format was used successfully for a number of other health issues (heart disease, child health, women's problems, etc). In connection with these courses, extensive annotated bibliographies of materials were produced. In 1980 the first course on Consumer Health Information Services at any accredited library school was taught at Case Western (Rees, 1982).

The director of InfoHealth was Alan Rees, and his books *The Consumer Health Information Sourcebook* and *Developing Consumer Health Information Services* were further outcomes of the project. Rees has also recognised that a major problem in consumer health information is not only the identification of material for patients, but also its acquisition. In an attempt to overcome this, he has edited a microfiche publishing venture called Consumer Health Information Service (CHIS). For an annual subscription, librarians can receive an indexed microfiche file which reproduces several thousand leaflets from small organisations and publishers in the health field. CHIS is available from Microfilming Corporation of America, 1620 Hawkins Avenue, Sanford, North Carolina. 27330, USA.

Consumer health information in practice

The following case studies illustrate some of the ways in which libraries and other agencies have provided health information to the public in the United States.

Kaiser Permanente Health Library

When the Health Library at Kaiser Permanente Medical Center in Oakland, California opened its doors in 1969, it was the first hospital library to provide a service to lay people. The Health Library began primarily as an audiovisual collection but, since then, it has developed a comprehensive collection of materials for patients and the public in a variety of media, and has been the model for a number of services elsewhere. The Kaiser Permanente Medical Care Program is the world's largest non-governmental health care system.

The library itself occupies a 2,000 square foot site within the hospital and is used by hospital patients, members of the public, outpatients and visitors, and by Oakland health care staff and local organisations. Users can view audiovisual programmes, take free literature, borrow books and tapes (if they are in the Kaiser Permanente Medical Program), buy books and leaflets, and use reference services. There are over 10,000 visitors to the library each year, 60 per cent of whom are self-referred (Collen and Soghikian, 1974; Quay, 1982).

In response to the many enquiries received by the library, a package of information materials has been produced. This includes lists of equipment, sources, books and pamphlets; leaflets describing library services, posters and bookmarks; and examples of leaflets for patients on topics such as diverticulitis, menopause, haemorrhoids, hiatus hernia and warts.

Address: Health Library, Kaiser Permanente Medical Center, 280 West MacArthur Boulevard, Oakland, CA94611, USA.

Veterans' Administration hospitals

In the United States three quarters of hospital admissions are to non-governmental hospitals, under some form of private insurance scheme. The state-funded sector is predominantly made up of longstay and mental hospitals. A notable exception is the Veterans' Administration network of state-funded hospital and outpatient centres found throughout the United States. As we have seen, the Veterans' Administration was a pioneer in patient education as long ago as 1953. This tradition has continued with consumer health information centres and libraries to be found in many VA hospitals.

The VA Medical Center in Miami, Florida, opened a patient library in 1977 (Roth, 1979). The library offers reference facilities, a lending collection, subscriptions to a range of journals, giveaway leaflets from organisations such as the American Heart Association and the United Ostomy Association. There is an audiovisual area with video players, tape-slide machines and telephone connections to TelMed.

Address: Veterans' Administration Medical Center, 1201 NW 16th Street, Miami, FL 33125, USA.

In San Francisco, the VA Hospital has a Patient Education Resource Center (PERC) which is used by patients and staff. Patients and their families are served on a self-referral basis as well as through 'consult sheets' or prescriptions for information completed by hospital staff. Books, pamphlets, periodicals, audiovisual materials and models may be used in the PERC library or on the wards. For topics which are not adequately covered by existing commercial media, the Center will assist in producing material in-house.

Address: Patient Education Resource Center, Veterans' Administration Hospital, 4150 Clement Street, San Francisco, CA 94121, USA.

A Patient Education Center/Library (PECL), which opened at the Minneapolis VA Medical Center in 1979, has now become one of the leading services of its kind in the USA. Its collection includes 2,000 patient or family health information books and over 400 audiovisual aids. In addition, there is a collection of 3,000 recreational books. Like the Kaiser Permanente library, the PECL occupies an area of some 2,000 square feet. Besides providing standard reference and lending services, the Minneapolis library is also the focus of a range of other consumer health information activities. PECL is part of the Twin Cities Biomedical Consortium, a group of 31 health sciences libraries in Minneapolis and St Paul. The consortium publishes a regular newsletter, *Consumer Health Info* designed to inform librarians, health educators, and other health professionals of health information resources available. PECL is particularly interesting because here the

138

librarian is also responsible for coordinating the production of in-house patient information sheets, including writing, coordination with artists and photographers, and the clinician review process. An extensive range of leaflets has been produced. This is particularly strong in the areas of tests and procedures (with leaflets on arthrogram, blood tests, bronchoscopy, colonoscopy, ERCP, endoscopy, IVP, cardiac catheterisation etc.) and cancer therapy (radiotherapy and chemotherapy). The librarian, Lionelle Elsesser, has also produced a useful guide to identifying, selecting and assessing material for a consumer health library (Elsesser and Epstein, 1983).

Address: Patient Education Center/Library, Veterans' Administration Medical Center, 54th St. and 48th Ave. South, Minneapolis, MN 55417, USA.

Community Health Information Network (CHIN)

The Community Health Information Network (CHIN) began in the mid-1970s as a cooperative health information service composed of a hospital library (Mount Auburn Hospital, Cambridge, Massachusetts) and the public library systems of the six towns which form the hospital's catchment area within Greater Boston. CHIN was one of the earliest projects that attempted to bring together the skills and resources of public and health sciences libraries, with the aim of making up-to-date and reliable health information more widely available (Gartenfeld, 1978; Gartenfeld, 1982).

The services developed by CHIN included access to hospital library stock by the public (usually through interlibrary loan rather than direct access); hospital library back-up for the public library enquiry service; provision of reading lists, subject bibliographies and a union list of CHIN books; in-service training programmes to introduce public librarians to health information; and the development of locally-based collections of leaflets, newsletters, indexes of support groups etc. Like PECL in Minneapolis, CHIN has also produced its own guidelines for evaluating health information for consumers (Dalton and Gartenfield, 1981).

For most of its history, CHIN has been supported primarily through grant funding or 'soft money'. Staff were hired for limited periods of time to carry out specific projects. At best, the project included a network coordinator, a librarian, a health educator, and research and development staff but, at other times, there have been the frustrating financial problems familiar to all who have worked on short-term funding. Despite this, CHIN remains the model for cooperative health information projects.

Address: CHIN, Mount Auburn Hospital, 330 Mount Auburn St. Cambridge, Mass. 02238, USA.

Consumer Health Information Program and Services (CHIPS)

Alongside CHIN, the other pioneer of hospital/public library cooperation is the Consumer Health Information Program and Services/Salud y Bienestar (CHIPS). CHIPS is a bilingual consumer health information service operated by a hospital library and a public library in the neighbouring towns of Torrance and Carson in Los Angeles County, California. The two libraries, located one mile apart, serve more than two million people of multi-ethnic background (Goodchild, 1982).

As in the CHIN project, major elements of CHIPS have been reciprocal interlibrary lending and joint in-service training. The public library staff have received training on health matters, while the hospital library staff have been trained to deal with the public. A newsletter has been produced, a series of bibliographies and a number of journal articles published to share the CHIPS experience with other librarians (Goodchild, 1978: Sorrentino et al., 1979; Fierberg et al., 1983).

There has been a strong emphasis on promotion and publicity of CHIPS. The library at the Los Angeles County Harbor – UCLA Medical Center has been promoted as the natural focus of patient education activities and resources. The hospital's Patient Education Committee on which the library is represented, sponsors an annual Patient Education Poster Fair and has produced a *Patient Education Directory*. A Patient Education on Wheels cart service has been introduced, whereby a library trolley, stocked with Spanish and English language pamphlets for patients and families and staffed by bilingual college students and volunteers, is taken to hospital clinics.

Address: CHIPS, 150 East 216th St., Carson, CA90745 USA.

Tel-Med

Tel-Med is a cassette tape library of health care information which the public can contact over the telephone. Like the Health Line service in the UK, users dial a switchboard and either request a specific tape number from the Tel-Med catalogue or ask the operator whether a tape exists on a topic which interests them. The tapes have an average length of three to seven minutes.

Tel-Med was conceived and developed by the San Bernardino County Medical Society in California in 1972. Since then, its use has grown dramatically with Tel-Med centres in most major cities and many smaller communities in the United States (Okel and Holderfield, 1974; Sager, 1978). The original library of 50 tapes has expanded to cover several hundred topics. One of the most important aspects of the service is its confidentiality. This may account for the high number of calls on delicate subjects such as sexuality and masturbation, VD, AIDS, pregnancy, and drug abuse.

Evaluation of the knowledge and use of Tel-Med by the public and by doctors (Diseker *et al.*, 1980 and 1981) indicates that its value is recognised by both groups. However, there is still some concern amongst doctors about its potential for unsound self-diagnosis. Another concern is that Tel-Med's existence seems less well known amongst those of lower educational and income levels, who might benefit most from its use.

Address: Tel-Med, 22700 Cooley Drive, Colton, CA 92324, U.S.A.

Local health information centres and clearinghouses

A different type of service is the health information centre which is not affiliated to a library, although it may have a library of its own. There are now many centres of this kind in the USA. The Consumer Health Information Center (CHIC) in Salt Lake City is a good example. CHIC provides a free library of books and pamphlets relating to health. It also acts as a clearinghouse for local organisations and services, and issues a calendar of community health events and offers a programme of lectures and health screenings. The Center is staffed by a health educator and a coordinator but most of the public contact work is done with trained volunteers (Berk, 1985).

The Center for Medical Consumers and Health Care Information was founded in New York in 1976 with the aim of encouraging lay people to take a greater responsibility for their own health. The Center contained one of the earliest health libraries designed for non-professionals, consisting of a collection of consumer health books, medical textbooks and directories, medical and scientific journals, and a cuttings file of health information. In addition, a Telephone Health Library was developed using tapes in part supplied by Tel-Med and in part written by Center staff (Levin, 1978).

Also in New York, the Lenox Hill Hospital's Health Education Center offers a walk-in health education 'shop'. The Center supplies leaflets, shows videotapes, holds lectures and provides a free Tel-Med service to over 100,000 people a year. A Sleepline is available 24 hours a day, seven days a week which gives an automatic message designed to send callers to sleep, without the use of drugs. An additional service which has recently been introduced is the Relaxation Booth – 'a new experience to help stressed New Yorkers to lower their tension levels' (Alexander, 1985). This is a soundproofed private booth where callers to the Center can listen to a tape on relaxation techniques while watching a video tape of tranquil nature scenes.

Address: Lenox Hill Hospital Health Education Center, 1080 Lexington Avenue, New York, NY10021, USA.

Some information centres have concentrated on acting as clearing-houses for the provision of information about self-help groups. As in the UK and Europe, these clearinghouses typically provide common services and training for groups as well as information about the groups themselves. There are several models for establishing a clearinghouse. The Westchester Self Help Clearinghouse in New York is jointly funded by mental health agencies and a univeristy. The New York City Self Help Clearinghouse is also university-linked while the Chicago Self Help Center is independently operated and funded (Borck and Aronowitz, 1982).

Since 1981, the New Jersey Self Help Clearinghouse has been providing 'a high tech approach to maximising high touch support resources' (Madara, 1985). In a service with some similarities to Help for Health in the UK, a database of over 3,000 self-help groups in New Jersey has been set up on an IBM System 34 computer. This provides instant retrieval of information for personal callers and those using the clearinghouse's toll-free telephone lines, as well as camera-ready copy for directories of organisations. Most interestingly, the clearinghouse database contains the names of people interested in starting new self-help groups. This has led to the establishment of over 180 new groups over the last three years.

Address: New Jersey Self Help Clearinghouse, Saint Clare's Hospital, Community Mental Health Center, Denville, New Jersey, U.S.A.

Planetree Center

San Francisco's Planetree Center is an example of a very ambitious and well-funded health information centre and is worth looking at in more detail. The Planetree project began four years ago as a resource centre on health and illness for the public. A library of over 2,000 books has been set up, including not only popular publications but also the major medical texts. There are subscriptions to the major medical journals such as *Lancet* and *New England Journal of Medicine*, and *Index Medicus* is held from 1981 to the present. An index to local resources lists health agencies, clinics, practitioners and self-help groups. In addition to its own resources, the Planetree Center also has access to the main medical libraries in the San Francisco Bay area.

The Planetree Health Resource Center operates on an annual budget of $125,000; has memberships ranging from $35 a year for individuals up to $5,000 for corporations; has library cards at $10 each for borrowing books and tapes for a 14-day period; averages 600–700 patrons per month; receives about 100 mail requests for information each month; and has over 1,200 members and library card holders. The annual membership fee entitles members one in-depth research pack on a topic of the member's choice. The pack includes material from the medical and popular literature, lists of organisations and services, and a computer search where relevant.

In association with the People's Medical Society, the Planetree Health Resource Center has produced a guide to setting up a library of this kind entitled *How to Start a People's Medical Library* (Phelan and Schmalz, 1984). The guide gives advice on checking what already exists in local public libraries and voluntary organisations; siting the library; fundraising; publicity; basic stocks; American booksellers. As well as the library, the Center runs a bookshop selling a selection of the best health care books for the lay person, audiocassettes, and health products ranging from blood pressure kits to babyfood grinders. There is also a health food restaurant. It is a non-profit making organisation funded by grants, membership fees, fundraising events and individual contributions.

In 1985 the Center went one stage further by securing funding totalling $416,000 to open a model unit at the Pacific Medical Center (Perlman, 1985). At the new unit, patients are encouraged to study their own medical charts and to write their own reports of progress and setbacks. They are given written material explaining every aspect of their illness, and the staff are always ready to explain more. Nutritionists help families and patients to prepare their own meals in the unit's own kitchen. The Kaiser Foundation has provided additional funding for an independent two-year evaluation by the University of Washington.

Address: Planetree Health Resource Center, 2040 Webster St., San Francisco CA 94115, USA.

People's Medical Society

The People's Medical Society was launched in 1983 as a consumer organisation dedicated to helping people reform the medical system and create better health for themselves. Like the British College of Health the Society aims to make active health consumers out of passive medical patients. The Society is an independent non-profit making organisation with funding from membership subscriptions, trusts, and Rodale Press, a publishing company with a long history of involvement in health issues. In addition to Robert Rodale, the directors of the Society include Lowell Levin, Professor of Public Health at Yale, and Patricia Phelan of the Planetree Center.

The declared aims of the People's Medical Society are to promote self care, wellness, and a greater personal responsibility for health. However, the real driving force behind the Society is the commercial basis of health care in the United States. As in the UK, concern about health care costs is a social and political issue. The American public is becoming increasingly concerned about spiralling medical costs. In the United States these are a matter of personal finance, with the result that the American health care consumer is concerned with quality and value for money in health in the same way as he would be with any other product or service.

In response to this, the People's Medical Society has produced a series of Health Action Kits which give consumers guidelines and detailed checklists to help them in evaluating their nursing home, or their physician. In order to help consumers choose the highest quality care at the lowest prices the Society also makes known the costs and quality of local medical services and insurance plans, and in an attempt to prevent unnecessary surgery it has identified wide variations in rates of surgery for particular conditions in different parts of the country. Publications include a newsletter and the guide to starting a people's medical library described above.

 Address: People's Medical Society, 14E Minor St., Emmaus, PA
     18049, USA.

National centres and federal clearinghouses

During the past 10-15 years the US Department of Health and Human Services has been responsible for the development and operation of numerous health information centres or clearinghouses. An extremely useful guide *Health Information Resources in the Federal Government* has been produced by the DHHS (1984). The directory lists federal agencies, bureaux, clearinghouses and institutes that can provide information on health-related topics, and is available from the National Health Information Clearinghouse. Federal health information clearinghouses are also the subject of a chapter in *Developing Consumer Health Information Services* (Freeman, 1982) and of a useful summary article entitled 'Where to find what in the federal government: a ready reference' (Behrens, 1984). DHHS clearinghouses and information centres are also listed, along with the material they produce in the DHHS bibliography *Staying Healthy* (1984).

 The most useful first point of contact for tracing health information resources is the National Health Information Clearinghouse. The NHIC is part of the Office of Disease Prevention and Health Promotion of the US DHHS and serves professionals and consumers alike. A computer database contains details of over 2,000 government agencies, professional societies and volunteer groups who produce health information materials. Directories, resource lists and bibliographies are produced. *Health Finders* is a series of bulletins listing materials and organisations which provide information on a number of subjects.

 Address: National Health Information Clearinghouse, PO Box
     113, Washington, D.C. 20133–1133 USA.

In addition to the general first-stop clearinghouse function provided by NHIC there are also clearinghouses for specific topics. These can provide information, materials or services aimed at helping individuals to stay healthy and to understand and cope with health problems:

Arthritis Information Clearinghouse, PO Box 9782, Arlington VA 22209

Cancer Information Service, National Cancer Institute Bldg. 31, Room 10 A18, Bethesda, MD 20205

Center for Health Promotion and Education, 1600 Clifton Rd. Bldg. 14, Atlanta, GA 30333

Clearinghouse for Occupational Safety and Health Information, 4676 Columbia Parkway, Cincinatti, OH 45226

Clearinghouse on Child Abuse and Neglect Information, PO Box 1182, Washington, DC 20013

Clearinghouse on the Handicapped, Switzer Building, Room 3132, 330 C St. S.W., Washington, DC 20202

Food and Drugs Administration Office of Consumer Affairs, Public Inquiries, 5600 Fishers Lane, Rockville, MD 20857

High Blood Pressure Information Center, 120/80, National Institute of Health, Bethesda, MD 20205

National Clearinghouse for Alcohol Information, PO Box 2345, Rockville, MD 20852

National Clearinghouse for Drug Abuse Information, PO Box 416, Kensington, MD 20795

National Clearinghouse for Family Planning Information, PO Box 2225, Rockville, MD 20852

National Diabetes Information Clearinghouse, Box NDIC Bethesda, MD 20205

National Digestive Diseases Education and Information Clearing-house, 1555 Wilson Blvd, Suite 600, Rosslyn, VA 22209

National Information Center for Handicapped Children and Youth, 1555 Wilson Blvd, Suite 600, Rosslyn, VA 22209

National Institute of Mental Health, Public Inquiries Section, Park-Lawn Bldg., Room 15C–17, 5600 Fishers Lane, Rockville, MD 20857

Office on Smoking and Health, Technical Information Center, Park Bldg., Room 1–10, 5600 Fishers Lane, Rockville, MD

Sudden Infant Death Syndrome Clearinghouse, 3520 Prospect St. NW, Suite 1 Washington, DC 20057

The services provided through the federal government are com-plemented by the work of centres in professional organisations, the voluntary sector and academic departments.

The National Self Help Clearinghouse is a non-profit making organisation which acts as a nationwide referral source to local self-help groups and/or national self-help organisations. It has close links with a network of 27 regional self-help clearinghouses. It has published a number of booklets including one on starting a self-help group and a newsletter *Self Help Reporter* which appears five times a year.
Address: National Self Help Clearinghouse, 33 West 42nd St., Room 1222, New York NY 10036, USA.

In 1978 the American Hospital Association established the Center for Health Promotion to assist hospitals in implementing effective health and patient education activities. It has developed information packets to respond to requests on a wide range of topics and publishes *Promoting Health*, a bi-monthly journal for patient, community and employee health promotion professionals.
Address: Center for Health Promotion, American Hospital Association, 840 N. Lake Shore Dr., Chicago, IL 60611, USA.

The Division of Health Education at the University of Alabama has become a focus for research and reporting on patient education activities. For several years now, an interesting *Patient Education Newsletter* has been published which contains articles and listings of events and materials. The *Newsletter* was edited by Edward Bartlett, Professor of Public Health, and from 1986 onward will be appearing as part of the Elsevier journal *Patient Education and Counseling* also edited by Bartlett.

Address: Division of Health Education, School of Public Health, University of Alabama at Birmingham, AL 35294, USA.

In the US, as in the UK, voluntary organisations such as the American Heart Association, the American Cancer Society and the American Diabetes Association are major providers of health information materials. *The Consumer Health Information Sourcebook* (Rees and Janes, 1984) provides an excellent listing of these.

Databases

Several authors have indicated the problems of identifying information materials and organisations in the field of consumer health information where bibliographic control is notoriously poor (Kolner, 1984; Lipsett and Schultz, 1984). Two American online databases are now making this task a little easier.

DIRLINE is an online database compiled by the National Reference Center of the Library of Congress and the National Health Information Clearinghouse, and made available as part of the National Library of Medicine's MEDLARS system. The database contains records for several thousand organisations which either provide health information themselves or can make referrals to appropriate experts. The organisations listed in the directory include libraries and information centres, federal, state or local government offices, university departments and research centres, and voluntary organisations. There are approximately 1,000 non-US information sources listed.

CHID (*Combined Health Information Database*) is a joint venture from five clearinghouses which aims to fill a gap in biomedical databases. The database comprises five individual sub-files – Arthritis; Diabetes; Digestive Diseases; High Blood Pressure; Health Education.

These sub-files are produced respectively by the Arthritis Information Clearinghouse, Arlington, Virginia; the National Diabetes Information Clearinghouse, Bethesda; the Digestive Diseases Clearinghouse, Bethesda; the High Blood Pressure Information Center, Bethesda; the Center for Health Promotion and Education, Atlanta, Georgia. The entire database or individual sub-files can be searched.

The database currently contains over 17,000 references to journal articles, monographs, proceedings and reports relevant to professionals, patients and the public (Lunin, 1984). Particularly useful is the inclusion of ongoing programmes of research and grey literature. Pamphlet material from voluntary organisations comprises a major element of the grey literature and can be impossible to trace by other means. The compilers are sensitive to the demands which may be made on a small voluntary organisation following the inclusion of their material in an international database so, when a document is entered on the database, a letter is sent to the organisation warning it to expect increased orders. There is currently interest in establishing a national deposit collection of this material, possibly on microfiche.

CHID has been available on the host BRS since January 1985. By sharing the costs of mounting the database, the five agencies involved have been able to keep their costs to a minimum. A *CHID Search Reference Guide* is available from Combined Health Information Database, Box NDIC/CHID, Bethesda, MD 20892, USA.

CANADA

In Canada, as in Europe and the United States, there is increasing attention being given to lay involvement in health care and the associated access to health information (Kelner, 1985). Lay participation has occasionally led to conflict. In one community health centre is Saskatchewan a wide measure of patient control was introduced. However, the doctors soon felt under threat and, in 1974, all ten clinic physicians resigned following allegations of unchecked interference by those lacking medical knowledge (Young, 1975).

Despite these local differences of opinion, the Social Development Directorate of Health and Welfare Canada has, for the last few years, been actively engaged in supporting lay participation and self-help initiatives. One form of support has been the production of

149

information materials including a manual *Helping You Helps Me* which is designed to help self-help groups get started and maintain themselves. Over 15,000 copies of the manual have been distributed since November 1983. In addition, two films have been produced about the experiences of people in self-help groups: one in English called *We've Been There* and one in French *Les Coulisses de l'Entraide*. An extensive bibliography on self help has also been compiled (Todres, 1984).

Health and Welfare Canada is also funding the production of a Canadian *Self Help Newsletter* which is distributed by the Canadian Council on Social Development, to approximately 10,000 individuals and groups who have an interest in self help.

> Address: Health and Welfare Canada, 654 Brooke Claxton Building, Turney's Pasture, Ottawa, KIA 1B5, Canada.

An issue discussed at the national consultation on self-help groups sponsored by Health and Welfare Canada has been the establishment of national clearinghouses on self-help groups. This notion has now been dropped in favour of the development of regional clearinghouses. In Montreal, a Mutual Aid Centre has been established to enable self-help groups to collaborate with each other and pool their resources. Information is available for groups and the general public, and the Centre also promotes research and holds symposia. A Self Help Clearinghouse has also been set up in Toronto with funding from Health and Welfare. Services planned include a centralised telephone information service on the groups that exist within the city, the publication of newsletters and other information materials, the establishment of a self-help library and training for group leaders.

> Address: Metro Toronto Self Help Clearinghouse, 246 Bloor Street West, 5th Floor, Toronto, Ontario M55 1A1, Canada.

The Network Centre for Self Care in Victoria is a project designed to support the growing network of people (both professionals and lay people) in Western Canada who are actively promoting self care. A microcomputer database has been set up listing organisations, research projects, key individuals and publications. A quality quarterly journal called *Wellspring* is produced. *Wellspring* includes articles, letters, reviews and a calendar of local events. It is a readable and attractive example of what a clearinghouse can achieve. Like the other clearinghouses described, the Network Centre for Self Care has been funded by seed money from Health and Welfare Canada.

Address: Network Centre for Self Care, 435 Simcoe St., Victoria, British Columbia, V8V 4T4, Canada.

Libraries

In 1974–75 Henry Goodman of the University of Calgary visited the eastern half of Canada as part of a project involving the examination of community information services. The study tour also took in the United States, Western Europe and the Middle East. He found evidence almost everywhere of the rapid development of 'one-stop citizens' information services' – in other words, ready-access information centers designed to help people to cope with the problems of everyday life, including health problems (Bunch, 1982). One of the earliest library initiatives was the 'Link' Information and Referral System established by North York Public Library in 1971. The system arose out of a request made to the library in 1970 by the North York Mental Health Council for the formation of an agency to supply information to the local community. 'Link' now provides a central point of reference to residents of North York seeking information about local organisations and services (Goldman, 1976). In 1973, Pyper analysed the proliferation of neighbourhood information centres in Canada and expressed some concern about the development of poorly stocked and staffed independent schemes, running in parallel to the community information activities of local public libraries. Some guidelines for more constructive and cooperative ventures are offered (Pyper, 1973).

The growth of community information services in the public library sector in the 1970s was mirrored by an increased interest in patient education schemes in Canadian hospitals. There was a growing realisation that the informed patient is a partner in health care (Robinson, 1974). Patient education became part of the curriculum in nurse education (Jenny, 1978; Redman, 1975). Experimental projects were set up involving patient teaching clinics (McCone, 1973), audiovisual materials (Briant, 1974) and self-care manuals (Buck *et al.*, 1976; Landry, 1978). Library services developed to support these activities. At the University of Alberta Health Sciences Centre a patient education resource file was established. Patients can visit the collection which is housed in the Audiovisual Library of the Medical Sciences Building, or materials can be taken out to patients in clinics, wards or other hospitals (Bidwell, 1979). The role of the librarian and the ethical implications of the provision of information to patients and the public have since been discussed by a number of Canadian librarians (Eagleton, 1983; Farber, 1983; Groen, 1983; Prince, 1983).

Clinical librarianship and the patient

Canada is the home of one of the most innovative projects in patient information, the clinical librarianship project at McMaster University Medical Centre, Ontario. The clinical librarianship project was initiated at McMaster in 1975. At that time a number of similar schemes were being set up in the United States. Librarians in these programmes accompanied professionals on their ward rounds and in their clinics, and provided information in response to problems that occurred (Cimpl, 1985; Claman, 1978; Colianni, 1978; Schnall and Wilson, 1976).

The McMaster clinical librarianship project differed from the others in that it provided an information service for patients and families as well as for health professionals. In addition, non-physician members of the medical team were encouraged to use the service. If a need for patient information emerged on a ward round, the librarian returned to the library and assembled a package of material from a file of pamphlets, simply written journal articles and information about local self-help groups, which was then delivered to the patient before discharge from the hospital (Marshall and Hamilton, 1978; Marshall, 1982). The McMaster project has been closely evaluated and the results and subsequent discussion on the implications for library services (Marshall and Haynes, 1983) are of enormous value.

Address: Health Sciences Library, McMaster University, Hamilton, Ontario L85 4J9, Canada.

AUSTRALIA

In 1973 the Australian National Hospitals and Health Services Commission produced a report on *A Community Health Programme for Australia*. Its objectives included involving people in decision making about their own health and health services, and 'leading people to understand that even scientific medicine has its limitations so that many disorders have no cure, while others are self-limiting and need no treatment'. Information was crucial to decision-making and to self management of health problems.

One outcome of the *Community Health Programme* was the Consumer Health Involvement Project (CHIP) in New South Wales. Here the Western Metropolitan Health Region got together with the University of New South Wales to appoint a coordinator whose aim was to encourage local people to become intelligent and informed health consumers (Bates, 1976). Interviews and surveys in the shopping centre and meetings with community groups were used to find out what local people really wanted from their health services, rather than what professionals thought they wanted. At one health centre, a committee of consumers was set up called the Fairfield Health Resources Committee. The committee acted rather like a patient participation group in the UK, providing a consumer input to the management of the centre and arranging public meetings on health topics of interest to local people.

Another project, this time in Brisbane, aimed at increasing self responsibility in health through support for self-help groups (Brownlea, 1980). The project claims to have led to 'new working relationships between providers and clients based upon the concept of participatory care and co-caring'. The growth of a self-help movement in Australia has been recognised in the recent establishment of an Australian Self Helping Health Care Association. The Association published its first newsletter in 1985 which includes an article by Professor Arthur Brownlea of the Brisbane project.

Address: Australian Self Helping Health Care Association, c/o Health Research Team, School of Environmental Studies, Griffith University, Nathan, Qld 4111, Australia.

Increasingly, Australian hospitals and health centres are providing information materials for patients. The 'How to succeed in practice by really trying' section of *Australian Family Physician* in June 1982 was devoted to some examples of patient information literature issued by the Blackburn Clinic, Victoria, the Croydon Practice, New South Wales and also by the Queenstown Medical Centre in New Zealand (Carson and Murtagh, 1982). In addition to publishing their own literature, some hospitals are also setting up information points where a wide range of materials can be made available to patients, relatives and visitors. At Flinders Medical Centre, Bedford Park, South Australia there is an information desk staffed by a nurse dealing with over 600 enquiries a month.

Health Information Centre, Westmead Hospital

One of the most impressive health information projects in Australia is based at the Westmead Hospital in the suburbs of Sydney. The service began in 1980 with the formation of a Paediatric Health Education Unit, part of the University of Sydney but based at the hospital. The philosophy of the Unit is to provide understandable, factual information to patients and parents about common health issues; to assist patients and parents to manage their own health and diseases better at home and to know when to obtain medical assistance; and to encourage patients and parents to become less dependent. Staff included a health education officer, several paediatricians involved part-time, a secretary and two part-time research nurses. Using an in-house printing press, wordprocessor and audiovisual unit, an excellent series of patient education leaflets has been produced, covering common childhood problems such as asthma, gastroenteritis, and febrile convulsions, as well as tests and procedures.

In 1984 the service was extended by the appointment of a librarian to develop a health information centre. A collection of over 250 books and 1,000 pamphlets has been established, all of which have been reviewed and approved by relevant specialists. In due course, audiovisual materials will be added to the collection, which is available for use by staff and students of Westmead Hospitals, community health staff, patients and the public. The centre, now called Health Link, was opened by the Minister of Health in September 1985. The most recent venture is the publication of a guide to books and pamphlets, entitled *A Guide to Consumer Health Information*.

Address: Health Link Health Information Centre, Westmead Hospital, Westmead, New South Wales 2145, Australia.

EUROPE

Since the late 1960s there has been an upsurge of interest in the greater

154

participation of people in the running of their own lives, and health care is no exception. One manifestation of this has been the mushrooming of self-help activities. This seems to be a phenomenon more concentrated in Northern Europe, perhaps because in Southern Europe there are more traditional networks for support in the family and church.

Word Health Organization

The World Health Organization has taken a particular interest in these developments. The Declaration of Alma Ata (1978) holds that primary care is central to the provision of preventive, promotive, curative and rehabilitative services, and that self help is an important component of primary health care in all countries. In 1975 the World Health Organization held the first major conference on self help and health, the International Symposium on the Role of the Individual in Primary Care, in Copenhagen. The outcome of the conference was the publication of *Self Care: Lay Initiatives in Health* (Levin, 1979). This report, and the one prepared by David Robinson (1981) following a further consultation on the WHO Self Help and Health Symposium at Leuven, Belgium, were particularly concerned with establishing a glossary of terminology to be used in describing self-care and self-help activities. Briefly the accepted definitions were that the whole system of non-professional health care could be described as 'lay health care'. People acting for themselves or their intimates are said to engage in 'self care'. People joining together to cope with a particular problem through mutual support, information and social activities, are said to form a 'self-help group'. Larger organisations that provide assistance to groups or individuals in self care are referred to as 'self-help organisations' (or in the UK generally, 'voluntary organisations'). When people engage in helping others on a voluntary basis this is labelled 'volunteer care'.

A further outcome of these discussions was the establishment of the International Information Centre on Self Help and Health, a World Health Organization collaborating centre based originally in Hamburg and now at the Catholic University of Leuven in Belgium. The brief for the Centre has been to undertake a review of the state of the art in self help in Europe, including the production of bibliographies and glossaries; to act as a clearinghouse for information exchange between institutions and individuals involved in relevant research; and to organise meetings of these researchers and practitioners. Two meetings have been organised at Hohr-Grenzhausen in Germany. The first, in 1982, looked at the need for support systems for self-help groups (such as the Nottingham Self Help project). The second, in 1983, concentrated on relationships between professional health care and self help. The centre produces a very informative newsletter which reviews self-help developments in Europe.

Address: International Information Centre on Self Help and Health, E. van Evenstraat 2C, B-3000 Leuven, Belgium.

The agency responsible for the World Health Organization's support for self care in Europe has been the Health Education Unit of the World Health Organization Regional Office for Europe. In recent years, health education has come increasingly to the foreground in the work of the WHO Regional Office and the current emphasis is very much on lay and community participation in health care. One of the main problems in the European Region has been seen as a lack of knowledge of lay resources amongst health professionals, the public and politicians. The Health Education Unit is now collecting information on lay health initiatives, and in particular is involved in networking between 'consumer oriented health documentation centres' throughout Europe.

The Regional Officer for Health Education, Ilona Kickbusch, has, with Stephen Hatch of the Policy Studies Institute in London, been responsible for an indispensable overview *Self Help and Health in Europe*. This examines the self-help phenomenon, how it is viewed from the perspectives of medical practitioners, researchers and psycho-analysts, and goes on to examine examples of self help in practice from hypertension clubs in Croatia, through the All Russian Society for the Deaf – a self-help (*samoobsluzhivanie*) group dating from pre-revolutionary days – to self-care activities in Lapland (Hatch and Kickbusch, 1983). The World Health Organization, through its organisation of meetings, encouragement of research and its recommendations to member states, has lent the weight of its moral authority to the legitimisation of self help in Europe.

WHO recommendations regarding self help were taken into account by the Committee of Ministers of the Council of Europe who, in 1980, formulated a recommendation to the member states regarding 'the patient as an active participant in his own treatment'. In this recommendation the Council emphasised the need for a change in the doctor-patient relationship, indicating that the patient has a right to more self reliance, increased participation and more information on illness and treatment.

Address: World Health Organization Regional Office for Europe, Scherfigsvej 8, DK-2100 Copenhagen Ø, Denmark.

FRANCE

In France many of the 'alternative' and consumer movements can be dated back to the events of 1968. In order to give help and advice to those accused of political activities in 1968, a network of law centres or Boutiques de Droit was established. Modelled on these, the first health shop (Boutique de Santé) was opened in 1977 in Tours. The Tours centre was followed by several in the *arrondissements* of Paris; the first being in the 10th, and shortly afterwards in the 13th and 9th. Frequently organised by committed radicals, they mainly offered information to the public on health issues and arranged meetings. Attempts to involve local people were not always successful and several Boutiques de Santé closed down. An exception is the Group Santé du 9e, Paris, which is made up largely of non-professionals who organise well attended weekly debates. Several independent self-help groups have been established (for cancer patients and asthma sufferers, for example). The Centre de Santé à Charonne in the 11th *arrondissement* has published its own journal *S. comme Santé* since 1979.

During the 1970s in France, the developing consumer movement turned its attention to drugs and the pharmaceutical industry. The publication in 1974 of Dr Pradal's *Guide des médicaments les plus courants* criticising the influence of the pharmaceutical industry caused a furore. Pradal was taken to court by the industry, and the case received extensive media coverage. In 1977 Pradal and others launched *L'Impatient*, a journal for 'the defence and information of health care consumers'. *L'Impatient* has some similarities to the British health care consumers' journal *Self health* published by the College of Health. Each provides information on health rights, gives practical advice on self help and self care, regularly features alternative

157

therapies and attempts to expose malpractices and unequal distribution of resources. *L'Impatient* now has over 20,000 subscribers.

Address: *L'Impatient*, 9 Rue Saulnier, 75009, Paris, France.

In the only really accessible review of lay health initiatives in France Alf Trojan (1983) wonders whether there is a great deal of self-help activity in France. Mutual aid is little reported in France and the usual explanation is 'French people are too individualistic for things like that'. However Trojan reports the appearance of a directory of self-help groups in 1978 (*Resources spéciales*, 1978). A recent bibliography (Bruneau and Rioux, 1981) suggests that there are at present between 3–5,000 voluntary organisations in France, comprising what is called 'la vie associative'. In 1981 an umbrella organisation FONDAtion pour la Vie Associative was established. Its membership includes self-help groups for disabled people and for parents of handicapped children. A linked development has been the founding, also in 1981, of the Fédération Nationale d'Usagers de la Santé (FeNGUS), a national federation of health shops, patient participation groups and health consumer groups.

Addresses:FONDA (Foundation pour La Vie Associative), 18 rue de Varenne, 75007 Paris, France.

Fédération National d'Usagers de la Santé, 5 bis, rue des Haudriettes, 75003, Paris, France.

GERMANY

The health movement in Germany can also be linked to the radical and alternative movements of the 1960s and 1970s. Its forms of organisation and aims are similar to the women's movement and the ecological movement. Many of those active in lay health initiatives in Germany are also involved with the Green Party (Die Grunen) and campaigns for a new public health policy have been described as an 'ecology of health' (Huber, 1983).

A major step in the development of this movement in Germany was the *Gesundheitstag* which took place in Berlin in 1980. This alternative health fair was held at the same time as the 83rd German Medical Congress known as the 'Doctors' Parliament' and attracted a good deal of attention. Over 10,000 participants took part in discussions, seminars and working groups. A health publications company (Verlag Gesundheit) was founded to publish reports arising from the conference. In Berlin, the first health shop (Gesundheitsladen EV) was set up to provide a source of information on self-help groups and alternative health care. This became the model for new health shops in more than 30 towns throughout the Federal Republic of Germany. These act as contact points and information centres for their regions. In autumn 1981, the Hamburg health shop organised the second *Gesundheitstag*. This time 20,000 people attended, double the numbers of the first.

In Germany, as in other European countries, there is little evidence of widespread library involvement in health information for the public. Here the characteristic organisation is the health shop or clearinghouse. Information-giving is an important activity, but so is the provision of practical support to local groups through meeting facilities, training and common services such as typing and printing. In the July 1985 issue of *Voluntary Action*, Judy Wilson describes a visit to several German self-help clearinghouses. Judy heads the Nottingham Self Help Team which is similar in its approach to the European clearinghouses. In Hamburg a clearinghouse called KISS (Kontakt und Informationsstelle für Selbsthilfegruppen) has been established. The centre has a very efficient information service which deals with 300 enquiries a month from individuals and professionals seeking self-help groups. The databank of 750 local self-help groups is deliberately stored in a manual form, since the Germans are very touchy about civil liberties and the possibilities for abuse of automated systems (Wilson, 1985).

There is now a national clearinghouse, Deutsche Arbeitsgemein- schaft Selbsthilfegruppen based in Berlin. This is first and foremost an information centre, with a staff of three. They deal with a high level of enquiries, and a recent television appearance brought 700 requests for information. The centre also acts as the secretariat for meetings of the 50 local clearinghouses which now exist in Germany. A magazine called *Selbsthilfegruppen Nachricten* (*Self Help News*) is published.

Address: Deutsche Arbeitsgemeinschaft Selbsthilfegruppen e.V., Albrecht-Achilles Str. 65, D-1000, Berlin, 31 West Germany.

THE NETHERLANDS

The European country which bears the greatest similarity to the United Kingdom in its approach to health information for the public is the Netherlands. In particular, there is a growing interest in patient education in Dutch hospitals, a movement supported by the Dutch government which, in its Patient Policy Memoranda (*Nota patientbeleid*) of 1981 and 1983 allocated an important role to health education in a wide range of Dutch health-care fields. There is increasing awareness that providing information to hospital patients is an integral part of public health education and several hospitals have introduced studies and activities to develop patient education programmes (Jonkers, 1984).

Patient education

In a valuable review article Visser (1984) has described 82 reports of patient education activities in the Netherlands. As has been found elsewhere, one of the most frequent complaints of Dutch hospital patients concerns lack of information. The Dutch Consumers Union found that 45 per cent of former patients interviewed complained of having received no information before admission and 25 per cent considered the information regarding treatment inadequate (Consumers Union, 1976).

Many Dutch hospitals are now attempting to redress the situation. Booklets are available in nearly all Dutch hospitals giving general information on hospital facilities, admission procedures etc. The Werkgroep 2000 Adviescentrum voor Patienten Initiatieven in Amersfoort has produced a survey of information folders given to patients in Dutch hospitals (*Distorting Mirrors*, 1976). The Academic Hospital in Leiden has over 100 leaflets available for patient use of which leaflets issued by Excerpta Medica on medical conditions, tests and procedures are widely used (Dekkers and Heezius, 1981); to date only a few hospitals are using videotapes but those that have are generally positive in their opinion of their effectiveness (Meuwissen and van der Beek, 1981). A telephone information service has recently been introduced for cancer patients and their families (Van Dam *et al.* 1983).

In 1985 the Dutch Ministry of Welfare, Health and Culture asked

160

the Department of Health Education at the University of Limburg to carry out a national survey of patient education activities in Dutch hospitals (Liederkerken, 1985). A questionnaire was sent to all directors of Dutch hospitals (229 hospitals) of which 129 responded. This showed that 60 per cent of the respondents were spending money on producing patient education materials; 29 per cent had a patient education committee; 19 per cent had a patient education coordinator (usually a nurse); and 19 per cent had a written policy on patient education within the hospital. An interesting additional finding was that 37 per cent of the hospital directors felt that patient education activities had considerable importance in hospital public relations.

In the province of Zuid Holland the Provincial Cross Organisation, in association with the Dutch Heart Foundation, has set up a programme of discussion meetings for cardiac patients and their partners (Gercama, 1985). The patients and their partners meet seven times in groups of 8 to 12, for two hours weekly. The groups give patients the opportunity to share experiences of heart attack, hospitalisation, heart surgery and rehabilitation. In addition, experts speak to the groups on topics such as relaxation, exercise, taking drugs and welfare benefits. The Dutch Heart Foundation has now agreed to fund a national project based on the Zuid Holland experience.

Since 1982, the Dutch National Hospital Institute (National Ziekenhuisinstituut) has been undertaking research in the field of patient education. A particular study has been made of diabetic patient education at the Bethesda Hospital in Hoogeven, which has been a highly successful programme.

Address: National Ziekenhuisinstituut, Oudlaan, 4, PO Box 9697, Utrecht, GR 3506, Netherlands.

The Netherlands Institute of General Practitioners (Nederlands Huisartsen Instituut) started a research project into patient education in general practice in 1981. Like his British counterpart, the Dutch general practitioner is the key figure in health care delivery and is, as a rule, the first point of contact for the patient, who only has access to specialist hospital care through him. Most GPs in the Netherlands are in one-doctor practices with an average of about 2,500 patients.

The Netherlands Institute of General Practitioners research project involved interviews with GPs about their experiences and attitudes to patient education. The results (Spronk and Warmenhoven, 1984) do not make optimistic reading. While most GPs recognised the problems of communicating medical information to patients, the majority were also ambivalent or openly hostile to information sources outside their immediate control. Indeed, 60 per cent expressed negative feelings about self-help groups and, when questioned further, most gave as their reason the quality of information supplied by the groups. Although the use of leaflets in the consultation appears to be a more accepted method of patient education, only 37 per cent were positive about using them, and only 17 per cent favoured the idea of a health information centre open to patients.

Address: Nederlands Huisartsen Instituut, PO Box 2570, 3500 GN, Utrecht, Netherlands.

Self-help groups

Despite the views of Dutch GPs, there is a large number of voluntary health organisations in the Netherlands. Some take the form of self-help groups centred around specific illnesses and disabilities while others are more generally concerned with patients' rights, and are rather like patient participation groups in the United Kingdom.

The Werkgroep 2000 Adviescentrum voor Patienten Initiatieven has as its goal 'the emancipation of patients'. It is an independent organisation but receives an annual grant from the Dutch Ministry of Health. The W2000 Project, as it is known, runs an information service on the activities of patient participation groups or 'patients' unions', as well as specific self-help groups. It produces a magazine and leaflets, some of which translate. health care legislation into everyday language.

Address: Werkgroep 2000, Koningin Wilhelminalaan, 17, 3818 HN, Amersfoort, Netherlands.

In Tilburg, a self-help support project has produced a five-volume guide 'Self help groups in the Netherlands'. This gives a comprehensive account of the structure and activities of 67 national associations of self-help groups, subdivided into those dealing with health and social problems.

Address: Projektgroep Zelfhulp Tilburg, Katholieke Hogeschool, Hogesschoollaan 225, PO Box 90153, 5000 Le Tilburg, Netherlands.

Self help forms part of the curriculum in the Faculty of Medicine in the State University of Limburg in Maastricht, founded in 1974. The justification for the establishment of an eighth medical school in Holland lies among other things in its concentration on teaching and research in primary care, and in the possibility of experimentation in the form and content of medical education (Bremer-Shulte, 1983). Part of the research activity at the Faculty has been the Patient Counselling and Patient Organisation (PACO) project. A leaflet describing the project (in English) entitled *Towards a Self-Care Supportive Health System* is available from the faculty. Support groups for psoriasis patients have been studied as an example of self help in practice (Bremer-Shulte, *et al.*, 1985). A clearinghouse on self help and health has been established to provide a source of information, research and training for professionals and groups alike. Evaluation of the clearinghouse has shown that, although it is well known and used by local groups, general practitioners rarely use its services or refer patients to it. 80 per cent of contacts come from within its immediate geographical surroundings.

Address: PACO Project, Rijksuniversiteit Limburg, Medical Faculty, PO Box 616, 6200 MD, Maastricht, Netherlands.

Libraries

The published literature does not indicate an extensive involvement of Dutch public or medical libraries in lay health information, although a British Library report does describe public library outreach services in general (Brown, 1981).

The one library service worth describing in some detail, however, is the Dutch Health Education Centre in Utrecht. The Dutch Health Education Centre (Centrum Dienstverlening) opened in 1981 and soon built up an extensive library of materials relevant to health education, health promotion and self care. Thirty per cent of its stock is in languages other than Dutch, mainly English. The library is currently undergoing an extensive automation exercise. After evaluating a number of computer systems during 1985, the ADLIB package, which runs on a Prime minicomputer, was selected. The database will include a register of ongoing research as well as the library file of over 15,000 records, which is expected to increase by 1,500 new items each year. The system, which will be used for information retrieval, generation of additions lists etc., is to be installed in January 1986. Allowing for a year of data input, it should be available to users by March 1987.

As well as in-house use by the Health Education Centre the database will be used online by 40 institutions involved in health education throughout the Netherlands. Because of the large amount of foreign literature included, it is anticipated that there will be interest from bodies such as the Health Education Council in the UK. (The software package is able to convert English subject headings into Dutch.) Future plans include the use of video disks to store pamphlet material and journal articles (DeVries, 1985).

Address: Centrum Dienstverlening, Da Costakade 45, PO Box 5104, 3502 JC, Utrecht, Netherlands.

DENMARK

The right of patients to receive information on their own health has been a point of discussion in the Scandinavian countries for some years (Andersen, 1975; Salling, 1974). In Denmark the presence of the World Health Organization Regional Office for Europe in Copenhagen has been influential. Patients attending the Rheumatology and Physical Medicine Department of the Hvodovre Hospital in Copenhagen have participated in a project whereby they write their own notes in the form of a diary (O'Donnell, 1984; Turner, 1984). When patients first visit the hospital they write a story of their illness in a file. These files are then kept by the patient's bed and each day patients, nurses or doctors add accounts of how the patients feel and what they and the doctors have agreed to do. If the doctor recommends a particular drug or treatment, written information about its action, why it is needed and possible side effects goes into the diary. If patients have questions about their illness which they find difficult to express verbally they can also be entered. After some initial reservations, doctors and nurses as well as patients have accepted the scheme with enthusiasm.

SWEDEN

In Sweden, consumer demands for better information on health and illness have resulted in a new health law, *Hälso och Sjukvardsnämn-den*. The new Act came into force in 1983 and states that:

... a good health and medical care service shall be of a high quality and that the patients need for security, as far as care and treatment are concerned, shall be met based on respect for the patient's own decisions and integrity, and that it should promote good contacts between the patient and nursing staff. The care and treatment shall, as far as possible, be formulated and carried out in consultation with the patient. The patient shall be given information on his health status and about the treatment methods that can be offered. (Engstrom, 1984)

The law places a responsibility on local health authorities to make information available to patients and the general public, and to assist self-help groups to publish their leaflets and other information (Kempson, 1984). For example, the Gothenburg health authority has an information department which produces its own consumer health information literature and helps local voluntary groups to do the same. These leaflets are mainly distributed to the public through health professionals, though some are sent to public libraries and local authority information centres. A catalogue of health information material available in Sweden (*Patient information katalog*) is published by Spri – the Swedish Institute for Health and Social Welfare Planning. This covers leaflets, films, tape–slides and books produced by a wide range of organisations, from self-help groups through health authorities to pharmaceutical companies.
Address: Spri, Box 27310, 10254, Stockholm, Sweden.

In addition to the health authority information services there are also well established telephone information services (Sjukvård-supplysningen) for the public in Gothenburg and Stockholm. These are available 24 hours a day, are staffed by nurses employed by the health authority, and will give information and advice on a wide range of topics including illnesses, and the possible side effects of medicines patients have been prescribed by their doctor.
None of these services, however, are provided by libraries or librarians. Hospital library services in Sweden are provided by the public library and are predominantly recreational. This reflects the

situation in public libraries where any form of information service is very much the exception (Kempson, 1984).

DEVELOPING COUNTRIES

In the West, despite the differences in health care systems, there is a general expectation that medical care from doctors is available and fairly easily accessible to all who require it. This is by no means the case in many developing countries where doctors are few and where access to health workers may be difficult (McEwen *et al.*, 1983). From the need to meet this enormous gap in service provision has resulted some of the more imaginative innovations and changes in policy backed by the World Health Organization. Integral to the WHO target of 'Health for All by the Year 2000' has been the development of the 'barefoot' health worker or health auxiliary in primary care.

The role of the auxiliary worker has been described by Katherine Elliott (1979):

> Auxiliary workers can carry most of the primary health care burden because experience has shown that primary health care services work most satisfactorily when they make use of local people, who remain part of the community they serve but who have been given the right kind of technical and social training to enable them to respond effectively to local needs. They then become an invaluable resource for the new style of health services which are required to meet the target set by the World Health Organization of health for all by the year 2000.

In several developing countries experimental schemes have been established which involve the provision of basic medical training to village health workers who then act as a link with health care professionals in medical centres. Tanzania was one of the first countries to build a health care system on this basis (Gish, 1973). Health auxiliary schemes in Sudan, Pakistan and Iran, as well as the role of the traditional birth attendant are reviewed in McEwen, Martini and Wilkins' *Participation in Health* (1983).

The recruitment, training and supervision of village health workers and traditional birth attendants, and the creation of village health

166

posts in the People's Republic of Benin has been described by Bichmann (1985). A variety of manuals, handbooks and flow charts have been designed for use by these 'barefoot' health workers (*Barefoot Doctor's Manual*, 1974; *The Primary Health Care Worker*, 1977; Revolutionary Health Committee of Hunan Province, 1978). The Teaching Aids at Low Cost (TALC) service – a teaching activity of the Institute of Child Health at the University of London – distributes low-cost, appropriate health education materials (books, slide sets, posters, flannelgraphs) for use in developing countries.

Address: TALC, PO Box 49, St. Albans, Herts., United Kingdom.

A recent issue of *Health Education Journal* carries an interesting account of a doctor's elective period spent at a Village Health Worker project in Andhra Pradesh, India (Mariasy, 1984). Here, health education is seen as an integral part of village health care, and the village health worker acts as a public relations officer and an interpreter between village people and the hospital workers. She uses basic visual aids such as flash cards, posters, and, where facilities permit, slides and film strips, to put over basic health information. The Central Health Education Board in India has produced a 'mother and child health package' as the core of its health education drive. This covers the whole course of motherhood from pregnancy to feeding and immunisation of children, and includes advice on antenatal care, delivery, lactation, the postnatal period, and family planning. 'Small families are healthy families' is the message.

What role, if any, is there for librarians in providing health information for the community in the developing countries? The World Health Organization sees the supply of appropriate information to the right people at the right time as a key factor in its 'health for all by 2000' campaign (Ruff, 1985). Since libraries play an important role in this overall strategy, WHO has developed the concept of the national focal point library which is based on the simple idea whereby WHO would have one nominated library in each country where its own publications could be deposited and through whom it could channel help and advice (Carmel, 1984). In many parts of the world, notably in South East Asia, Eastern Africa, the Western Pacific and the Middle East, national focal point libraries have been involved in development of policies and priorities for library services, establishment of an infrastructure for health library cooperation, and maintenance of links with national and international information systems. These are important developments, but are removed from the immediate information needs of the health care consumer.

In the limited literature from the developing countries on library involvement in health information for the lay public, we are fortunate to have a recent article on the library's role in patient education in diabetes from the Bangladeshi Institute of Research and Rehabilitation in Diabetes, Endocrine and Metabolic Disorders (BIRDEM) in Dacca (Miah, 1985). Here the BIRDEM library is providing information materials (in particular, audiovisual aids) for medical teachers, physicians, dietitians, paramedical personnel and patients who are taking part in the diabetes patient education programme. BIRDEM is the only well equipped diabetic clinic in the country where free treatment is given. As a result, access to treatment and information services for this illness is severely limited. In an attempt to overcome some of these problems the Diabetic Association of Bangladesh is training village social workers and paramedical staff who work at village level to detect diabetes, give information and supervise treatment.

In a thoughtful and perceptive article William Martin (1984) has questioned whether western models of library service are appropriate for export to developing countries. Some Third World observers have seen Western-style community information services as the solution to the problems of obtaining information on the essentials of everyday life (Adimorah, 1983). There is no doubt about the need for information, but what is more questionable is its nature, format and relevance. Martin quotes the radical voice of Adolphe Amadi who argues for a recognition of the difference between oral and literate cultures. In both environments the need for information is the same: it is the milieux that differ (Amadi, 1981). Clearly, universal literacy remains a long-term goal for many emerging nations and any system which emphasises print-based information in a largely non-literate society is asking for trouble.

Majid Rahnema (1982) has emphasised the potential value of oral resources using cassette recorders for conveying information to rural communities. A tape can record and reproduce messages in any language or dialect, enabling people themselves to participate in the acquisition, production and dissemination of information. It is hard to overlook the part played by the tape cassette in the Iranian revolution 'when all the might of the Shah's military and political machine proved useless against the words of an 80-year old purveyed to the millions in oral form' (Martin, 1984). A further appropriate use of the oral tradition to put over information on health issues may be found in Papua New Guinea, where the Ruan Ruan Travelling Theatre performs a repertoire of Coffee, Water, Nutrition and Family Planning plays. Similar theatre projects exist in Botswana and Zambia, where a medium has been discovered which reaches people in need of information far more directly and effectively than print.

The experience of developing countries reminds us of the power of information and of its limitations. Information in itself solves nothing. Knowledge is power only when it can be used effectively; when the social, political and cultural environment allows us to use information to change our lives for the better. Healthy choices must become the easy choices. The path to real improvement in health status is a steep and sometimes rocky one, progressing from knowledge through understanding and changes in belief to action. Information may only be the first step but, without it, we cannot even begin the climb.

REFERENCES

Adimorah, E.N.O. (1983) 'An analysis of progress made by public libraries as social institutions in Nigeria', *Unesco Journal of Information Science, Librarianship and Archives Administration*, vol. 5 (3).

Alexander, R. (1985) 'Lenox Hill Hospital adds a wave of calm', *New York Times*, 12 May.

Alloway, C.S. and Salisbury, C. (1983) 'Issues in consumer health information services', *RQ*, vol. 23 (2), pp. 143-9.

Amadi, A. (1981) 'The emergence of a library tradition in pre- and post-colonial Africa', *International Library Review*, vol. 13, p. 65.

American Hospital Association, (1972) *A Patient's Bill of Rights*, AHA, Chicago.

American Hospital Association (1979) *Implementing Patient Education in the Hospital*, AHA, Chicago.

American Hospital Association (1982) *Policy and Statement on the Hospital's Responsibility for Patient Education Services*, AHA, Chicago.

Andersen, K.L. (1975) 'Patients' needs for information on their own health', (translation) *Sygeplejersken*, vol. 75 (44), pp. 15, 20 (in Danish).

Angier, J.J. (1984) 'Issues in consumer mental health information', *Bulletin of the Medical Library Association*, vol. 72 (3), pp. 262–5.

Annas, G.J. (1975) *The Rights of Hospital Patients*, Avon Books, New York.

Barefoot Doctor's Manual, (1974) US Department of Health, Education and Welfare, Washington.

Bates, E.M. (1976) 'Consumer participation in the health services', *International Journal of Health Education*, vol. 19, pp. 45–50.

Beauchamp, G.E. (1953) 'Patient education and the hospital program', *US Veterans' Administration Bulletin*, vol. 10 (88), p. 3.

Behrens, R.A. (1984) 'Where to find what in the federal government: a ready reference', *Promoting Health*, vol. 5 (6), pp. 6–8.

Berk, R. (1985) 'Access to consumer health information', *The Reference Librarian*, vol. 12, pp. 195–206.

Bichmann, W. (1985) 'Primary health care: a new strategy? Lessons to learn from community participation' in Laaser, U., Senault, R. and Viefhaus, H., *Primary Health Care in the Making*, Springer, Berlin.

Bidwell, C.M. (1979) 'Patient education resource file', *Medical Teacher*, vol. 1 (3), pp. 153–4.

Borck, L.E. and Aronwitz, E. (1982) 'The role of the self help clearinghouse', *Prevention in Human Services*, vol. 1 (3), pp. 121–9.

Bremer-Shulte, M. (1983) 'Self help and medical education' in Hatch, S. and Kickbusch, I., *Self Help and Health in Europe*.

Bremer-Shulte, M., Cormane, R.H., van Dijk, E. and Wuite, J. (1985) 'Group therapy of psoriasis', *Journal of the American Academy of Dermatology*, vol. 12 (1), pp. 61–7.

Briant, N. (1974), 'When you make your own tape ...', *Canadian Nurse*, vol. 70 (12), pp. 38–9.

Brown, R. (1981) *Outreach in the Netherlands: An Experiment in the Public Library Service to Disadvantaged Groups with Particular Reference to the Role of the Nederlands Bibliotheek en Lektuur Centrum (NBLC)*, BLR & D Report No. 5689.

Brownlea, A. (1980) 'Participatory health care', *Social Science and Medicine*, vol. 14D (2), pp. 139–46.

Bruneau, C. and Rioux, J.P. (1981) *Les associations en France 1930–1980*, Institut d'Histoire du Temps Présent, Paris.

Bryant, N.H. (1978) 'Consumer health education in New Jersey community hospitals', *Journal of Community Health*, vol. 3 (3), pp. 259–70.

Buck, C., Simpson, H., and Stewart, M. (1976) 'The potential value of a patients' manual for self care', *Canadian Family Physician*, vol. 22, pp. 385–91.

Bunch, A. (1982) *Community Information Services: Their origin, Scope and Development*, Clive Bingley, London.

Carmel, M. (1984) 'The World Health Organization and national focal point libraries', *Focus on International and Comparative Librarianship*, vol. 15 (3), pp. 27–8.

Carson, N.E. and Murtagh, J.E. (1982) 'Patient information', *Australian Family Physician*, vol. 11 (6), pp. 470–1.

Charney, N. (1978) 'Ethical and legal questions in providing health information', *California Librarian*, vol. 39, pp. 25–33.

Child, R.C. (1985) 'Health promotion objectives in Southern Illinois', *12th World Conference on Health Education, Dublin, 1985.*

Childers, T. (1975) *The Information Poor in America,* Scarecrow Press, New Jersey.

Cimpl, K. (1985) 'Clinical medical librarianship: a review of the literature', *Bulletin of the Medical Library Association*, vol. 73 (1), pp. 21–8.

Claman, G.G. (1978) 'Clinical medical librarians: what they do and why', *Bulletin of the Medical Library Association*, vol. 66 (4), pp. 454–8.

Colianni, L.A. (1978) 'Clinical medical librarians in a private teaching hospital setting', *Bulletin of the Medical Library Association*, vol. 66 (4), pp. 420–5.

Collen, F.B. and Soghikian, K. (1974) 'A health education library for patients', *Health Service Reports,* vol. 89, pp. 236–43.

Commonwealth Health Department (1981) *Promoting Health: Prospects for Better Health Throughout Australia*, Australian Government Publishing Service, Canberra.

Consumers Union (1976) 'Hospital experiences of ex-patients' (translation), *Consumenten Reisgids*, vol. 24, pp. 486–91 (in Dutch).

Council of Europe: Committee of Ministers (1980) *The Patient as an Active Participant in his own Treatment,* Recommendation No. R (80) 4.

Curran, W.J. (1974) 'The patient's bill of rights becomes law,' *New England Journal of Medicine*, vol. 290, pp. 32–3.

Dalton, L. and Gartenfeld, E. (1981) 'Evaluating printed health information for consumers', *Bulletin of the Medical Library Association*, vol. 69 (3), pp. 322–4.

DeVries, J. (1985) 'The library of the Dutch Health Education Centre', *12th World Conference on Health Education, Dublin, 1985.*

Dekkers, F. and Heezius, T. (1981) 'Information for patients in the second line' (translation), *Med. Contact*, vol. 36, pp. 1,125–8 (in Dutch).

Diseker, R.A., Michielutte, R. and Morrison, V. (1980) 'Use and reported effectiveness of Tel-Med: a telephone health information system', *American Journal of Public Health*, vol. 70 (3), pp. 229–34.

Diseker, R.A., Michielutte, R. and Morrison, V. (1981) 'An assessment of Tel-Med utilization by physicians and dentists', *American Journal of Public Health*, vol. 71 (10), pp. 1,168–70.

Distorting Mirrors: A Study of Information Folders Given to Patients in Hospitals (translation) (1976) Werkgroep 2000, Amersfoort, Netherlands (in Dutch).

Dowlin, K.E. (1983) 'Public access to information' in Keren, C. and Perlmutter, L., *The Application of Mini and Microcomputers in Information Documentation and Libraries*, North Holland, Oxford.

Eagleton, K. (1983) 'The role of the hospital library in providing health information', *Bibliotheca Medica Canadiana*, vol. 5 (2), pp. 53–7.

Eakin, D., Jackson, S.J., and Hannigan, G.G. (1980), 'Consumer health information: libraries as partners', *Bulletin of the Medical Library Association*, vol. 68 (2), pp. 220–9.

Eistenstein, E. (1984) *Selected List of Health Information Titles for Public Libraries: A Recommended Core Bibliography*, CHIRP, Oak Park, Illinois.

Elliott, K. (1979) *Auxiliaries in Primary Health Care: An Annotated Bibliography*, Intermediate Technology Publications, London.

Elser, H. (1982) "Bibliotherapy in practice', *Library Trends*, vol. 30 (4), pp. 647–59.

Elsesser, L. and Epstein, H. (1983) 'Beyond the core bibliography: a guide to developing a consumer health library', *Promoting Health* vol. 4 (3), pp. 4–6.

Engstrom, B. (1984) 'The patient's need for information during hospital stay', *International Journal of Nursing Studies*, vol. 21 (2), pp. 113–30.

Farber, J.M. (1983) 'The role of social work in providing health care information', *Bibliotheca Medica Canadiana*, vol. 5 (2), pp. 44–6.

Fierberg, J., Berliner, M.A., Goodchild, E. and Gil-Gomez, M. (1983) 'The hospital library as a focus of patient education activities and resources', *Bulletin of the Medical Library Association*, vol. 71 (2), pp. 224–6.

Fiori, F. (1974) 'Health education in a hospital setting', *Health Education Monographs*, vol. 2, pp. 11–29.

Fraser, M.D.E. (1979) 'Your health – my health – everyone's health', *Bibliotheca Medica Canadiana*, vol. 1 (3), pp. 86–9.

Freeman, T.S. (1982) 'Federal health information clearinghouses, in Rees, A.M., *Developing Consumer Health Information Services*.

Gartenfeld, E. (1978) 'The Community Health Information Network: a model for hospital and public library cooperation', *Library Journal*, vol. 103 (7), pp. 1,911–14.

Gartenfeld, E.. (1982) 'Community Health Information Network (CHIN) Boston' in Rees, A.M., *Developing Consumer Health Information Services*.

Gercama, J. (1985) 'Discussion meetings for cardiac patients and their partners', *12th World Conference on Health Education, Dublin 1985*.

Gish, O. (1973) 'Doctor auxiliaries in Tanzania', *Lancet*, vol. 2, pp. 1,251–4.

Goldman, P. (1976) 'LINK information and referral service', *Ontario Library Review*, vol. 60 (3), pp. 166–71.

Goodchild, E.Y. (1978) 'The CHIPS project: a health information network to serve the consumer', *Bulletin of the Medical Library Association*, vol. 66 (4), pp. 432–6.

Goodchild, E. (1982) 'Consumer Health Information Program and Services/Salud y Bienestar (CHIPS), Los Angeles' in Rees, A.M. *Developing Consumer Health Information Services*.

Groen, F. (1983) 'Provision of health information has legal and ethical aspects', *Canadian Library Journal*, vol. 40 (6), p. 359.

Harman, S.E. (1983) 'Patient health information services: new frontier for hospital librarians in Maryland', *Maryland State Medical Journal*, vol. 32 (9), pp. 676–7.

Harris, C.L. (1978) 'Hospital based patient education programs and the role of the hospital librarian', *Bulletin of the Medical Library Association*, vol. 66 (2), pp. 210–17.

Hatch, S. and Kickbusch, I. (1983) *Self Help and Health in Europe: New Approaches to Health Care*, World Health Organization Regional Office for Europe, Copenhagen.

Health Information Resources in the Federal Government (1984) US Department of Health and Human Services, Washington, DC., DHHS (PHS) Publication no. 84–50146.

Huber, E. (1983) 'Health enters green pastures: the health movement in the Federal Republic' in Hatch, S. and Kickbusch, I., *Self Help and Health in Europe*.

Jennings, K. (1982) 'Health Information Service, Tulsa' in Rees, A.M. *Developing Consumer Health Information Services*.

Jenny, J. (1978) 'Patient teaching as a curriculum thread', *Canadian Nurse*, vol. 74 (2), pp. 28–9.

Jonkers, R. (1984) *Current Health Education Research*, Central Services Health Education and Social Scientific Information and Documentation Centre, Bunnik, Netherlands.

Jordan, E.F., Mailander, W. and Schmidt, S.J. (1950) *Patient Education at Rutland Heights Hospital*, National Tuberculosis Association, New York.

Juell, C.A. (1977) 'Brief survey of public information services at privately supported medical school libraries: comparison with publicly supported medical school libraries', *Bulletin of the Medical Library Association*, vol. 65, pp. 292–5.

Kahn, A. (1966) *Neighbourhood Information Centers: A Study and Some Proposals*, Columbia University School of Social Work, New York.

Kelner, M. (1985) 'Fostering local networks for a healthy public', *Radical Community Medicine*, summer 1985, pp. 38–41.

Kempson, E. (1984) 'Consumer health information services', *Health Libraries Review*, vol. 1 (3), pp. 127–44.

Kolner, S.J. (1984) 'A regional union list as an online catalogue for consumer health information', *Bulletin of the Medical Library Association*, vol. 72 (1), pp. 29–30.

Landry, M.G. (1978) 'Questions and answers: avoiding the obvious with a patient information booklet', *Canadian Medical Association Journal*, vol. 118 (9), pp. 1,130–1,131.

Lazes, P.M. (1977) 'Health education project guides outpatients to active care', *Hospitals*, vol. 51 (4), pp. 81, 82, 84, 86.

Levin, A.A. (1978) 'Medical consumerism and health information', *Bulletin of the American Society for Information Science*, vol. 4 (4), p. 19.

Levin, L.S., Katz, A.H. and Holst, E. (1979) *Self Care: Lay Initiatives in Health*, Prodist, New York.

Levin, P.H. and Britton, A.F.H. (1973) 'Supervised patient management of haemophilia', *Annals of Internal Medicine*, vol. 78, pp. 195–201.

Liederkerken, P. (1985) 'Policy development of patient education in Dutch hospitals', *12th World Conference on Health Education, Dublin, 1985*.

Lipsett, L.F. and Schultz, C. (1984) 'The role of annotated bibliographies in information dissemination', *Bulletin of the Medical Library Association*, vol. 72 (2), pp. 180–6.

Lunin, L.F. (1978) 'Information for health is an issue', *Bulletin of the American Society of Information Science*, vol. 4 (4), p. 11.

Lunin, L.F. (1984) 'Combining databases: challenges, achievements, expectations (Combined Health Information Database)' in Flood, B., *Challenges to an Information Society*, Knowledge Industry Publications for ASIS, White Plains.

McCone, C. (1973) 'Preadmission patient teaching clinic', *Canadian Nurse*, vol. 69, p. 39.

McEwen, J., Martini, C.J.M. and Wilkins, N. (1983) *Participation in Health*, Croom Helm, London.

McHugh, P. (1979) *Consumer Health Information*, Ealing College of Higher Education, BLR & D Report No. 5520.

Madara, E.J. (1985) 'The self help clearinghouse operation: tapping the resource development potential of I & R services', *Information and Referral: the Journal of the Alliance of Information & Referral Systems*, vol. 7 (1), pp. 42–58.

Madnick, M.E. (1980) *Consumer Health Education: A Guide to Hospital Based Programs*, Nursing Resources, Wakefield, Mass.

Mariasy, Y. (1984) 'A village health worker's project in the Chuddapah district of Andhra Pradesh', *Health Education Journal*, vol. 43 (4), pp. 107–11.

Marshall, J.G. and Hamilton, J.D. (1978) 'The clinical librarian and the patient: report of a project at McMaster University Medical

Centre', *Bulletin of the Medical Library Association*, vol. 66 (4), pp. 420–25.

Marshall, J.G. (1982) 'McMaster University Health Sciences Library and Hamilton Public Library, Hamilton, Ontario' in Rees, A.M., *Developing Consumer Health Information Services*.

Marshall, J.G. and Haynes, R.B. (1983) 'Patient education and health outcomes: implications for library service', *Bulletin of the Medical Library Association*, vol. 71 (3), pp. 259–62.

Martin, W.J. (1984) 'The potential for community information services in a developing country', *IFLA Journal*, vol. 10 (4), pp. 385–92.

Meuwissen, J.H.J.M. and van der Beek, L.J.M. (1981) 'Audiovisual help in patient guidance' (translation), *Med Contact*, vol. 36, pp. 403–6 (In Dutch).

Miah, M. Farid Hossain (1985) 'A patients' education programme in diabetes mellitus: the library's role', *Health Libraries Review* vol. 2 (3), pp. 108–11.

Miller, L.V. and Goldstein, J. (1972) 'More efficient care of diabetic patients in a county hospital setting', *New England Journal of Medicine*, vol. 286, pp. 1,388–91.

Moeller, K.A. and Deeney, K.E. (1982) 'Documenting the need for consumer health information', *Bulletin of the Medical Library Association*, vol. 70 (2), pp. 236–9.

Moran, M.K. (1976) 'Patient education coordinators in Greenville, S.C. hospitals', *Public Health Reports*, vol. 91 (3), pp. 274–5.

National Hospitals and Health Services Commission (1973) *'A Community Health Programme for Australia*.

Nota patientbeleid [Patient policy memorandum] (1981) Ministry of Health and Environmental Hygiene, The Hague, Netherlands.

Nota patientbeleid [Sequel to patient policy memorandum] (1983) Ministry of Health and Environmental Hygiene, The Hague, Netherlands.

O'Donnell, M. (1984) 'Secrecy: the most dangerous disease of them all', *Guardian*, 4 April.

Okel, B.B. and Holderfield, H. (1974) 'Tel-Med: an experiment in patient health education', *Journal of the Medical Association of Georgia*, vol. 63, pp. 369–70.

Perlman, D. (1985) 'Medicine that emphasizes the role of the patient,' *San Francisco Chronicle*, 12 September pp. 19, 21.

Phelan, P. and Schmalz, R. (1984) *How to Start a People's Medical Library*, People's Medical Society, Emmaus, Pennsylvania.

The Primary Health Care Worker (1977) World Health Organization, Geneva.

Pradal, H. (1974) *Guide des Médicaments les plus courants*, Seuil, Paris.

Prince, B. (1983) 'Health information from the public library', *APLA Bulletin*, vol. 47 (1), p. 3.

Pyper, T. (1973) 'What is the role of the neighbourhood information centre?', *Canadian Welfare*, September–October, pp. 13–14, 24.

Quay, C.K. (1982) 'Health library of the Kaiser Permanente Medical Care Program' in Rees, A.M., *Developing Consumer Health Information Services.*

Rahnema, M. (1982) 'The sound library: a tool for development', *Unesco Journal of Information Science, Librarianship and Archives Administration*, vol. 4 (3), pp. 152–3.

Redman, B.K. (1975) 'Guidelines for quality of care in patient education', *Canadian Nurse*, vol. 71 (2), pp. 19–21.

Rees, A.M. (1982) *Developing Consumer Health Information Services*, Bowker, New York.

Rees, A.M. and Janes, J. (1984) *The Consumer Health Information Sourcebook*, 2nd edn. Bowker, New York.

Report of the Secretary's Commission on Medical Malpractice (1973) Department of Health Education and Welfare, Washington DC.

Report to the Medical Library Association Board of Directors from the Ad Hoc Committee on Consumer Health Information (1983) Medical Library Association, Chicago.

Résources Spéciales (1978) *Alternatives* (Paris), no. 6–7.

Revolutionary Health Committee of Hunan Province (1978), *A Barefoot Doctor's Manual*, Routledge & Kegan Paul, London.

Rickards, D.J. (1978) 'Providing health care information to patients in a small hospital', *Bulletin of the Medical Library Association*, vol. 66 (3), pp. 342–5.

Robinson, D. (1981) *WHO, Self Help and Health*. Institute for Health Studies, University of Hull.

Robinson, L.A. (1974) 'Patient's information base: a key to care', *Canadian Nurse*, vol. 70 (12), pp. 34–6.

Roth, B.G. (1978) 'Health information for patients: the hospital library's role', *Bulletin of the Medical Library Association*, vol. 66

(1), pp. 14–17.

Roth, B.G. (1979) 'Patient health education: one library's experience', *South Eastern Regional Medical Library Program Notes*, no. 32, p. 1.

Rowe, D.B. (1980) 'Open medical library provides valuable community service', *Hospitals*, vol. 54, pp. 115–17.

Rubin, R.J. (1978) *Bibliotherapy Sourcebook*, Oryx Press, London.

Rubin, R.J. (1983) 'Public access to health information: the librarians response', *RQ*, vol. 22 (4), pp. 409–10.

Rubinton, P. (1982) 'Mental health: information, libraries and services to the patient', *Library Trends*, vol. 30 (4), pp. 513–659.

Ruff, B. (1985) 'An overview of the World Health Organization's policies concerning health and documentation centres', *Health Libraries Review*, vol. 2, pp. 99–104.

Russell, L.H. (1982) 'Patient education for the mentally ill', *Library Trends*, vol. 30 (4), pp. 631–45.

Sager, D.J. (1978) 'Answering the call for health information (Tel-Med dial access system)', *American Libraries*, September, pp. 480–82.

Sahler, O.J.Z., Satterwhite, B.B. and Reynolds, J.D. (1981) 'The pediatric family – patient health education library: the issue of access to information', *Pediatrics*, vol. 68 (3), pp. 374–8.

Salling, A.L. (1974) 'Let us hear about attempts at patient information' (translation), *Sygeplejersken*, vol. 74 (45), p. 11 (in Danish).

Schnall, J.E. and Wilson, J.W. (1976) 'Evaluation of a clinical medical librarianship program at a university health sciences library', *Bulletin of the Medical Library Association*, vol. 64, pp. 278–83.

Senkevitch, J.J. (1980) 'Information services to disabled individuals', *Drexel Library Quarterly*, vol. 16 (2), April.

Simmons, R. (1985) 'Health promotion consortia in California', *12th World Conference on Health Education, Dublin, 1985.*

Sorrentino, S., Goodchild, E.Y. and Fierberg, J. (1979) 'Cataloging procedures and catalog organization for patient education materials', *Bulletin of the Medical Library Association*, vol. 67 (2), pp. 257–60.

Spronk, V.R.A. and Warmenhoven, M. (1984) 'Patient education in general practice: opinions of general practitioners', *Patient Education and Counselling*, vol. 5 (2), pp. 68–75.

Staying Healthy: A Bibliography of Health Promotion Materials

(1984) US Department of Health and Human Services, Washington DC.

Todres, R. (1984) *Self Help Groups: An Annotated Bibliography 1970–1982*, National Self Help Clearinghouse, New York.

Topper, J.M. (1978) 'Hospitals as centres for consumer health information', *Bulletin of the American Society of Information Science*, vol. 4 (4), pp. 13–14.

Trojan, A. (1983) 'Groupes de santé: the users' movement in France' in Hatch S. and Kickbusch, I. *Self Help and Health in Europe*.

Turner, J. (1984) 'Patient jottings', *Sunday Times*, 26 February.

Vaillancourt, P.M. and Bobka, M. (1982) 'The public library's role in providing consumer health information', *Public Library Quarterly*, vol. 3 (3), pp. 41–9.

Van Dam, F., Klein Poelhuis, E., Heshusins, M. and Van Koppen, C. (1984) 'The Information Center of the Queen Wilhelmina Foundation: a study of users and their questions', *WEGO Symposium, Rotterdam, December 16 1983*.

Velleman, R. (1980) '*Serving Physically Disabled People: An Information Handbook for all Librarians*, Bowker, New York.

Visser, A.P. (1984) 'Patient education in Dutch hospitals', *Patient Education and Counselling*, vol. 6 (4), pp. 178–89.

Weber, S. (1981) *Manual for the Development and Day to Day Operation of an in-Hospital Health Education Library*, Sarah K. Davidson Family Patient Library, University of Rochester, New York.

Wilson, J. (1985) 'Can you kill with kindness?', *Voluntary Action*, vol. 3 (6), p. 10.

Yellott, L. (1982) 'Onondaga County Public Library and the Consumer Health Information Consortium (CHIC), Syracuse' in Rees, A.M., *Developing Consumer Health Information Services*.

Yellott, L. and Barrier, R. (1983) 'Evaluation of a public library's health information service', *Medical Reference Services Quarterly*, vol. 2 (2), pp. 31–51.

Young, K.T. (1975) 'Lay-professional conflict in a Canadian community health centre', *Medical Care*, vol. 13 (11), pp. 897–904.

5

Getting started: collecting and organising health information

In 1982 the Wessex Regional Library and Information Service produced an information pack based on the experiences of the Help for Health Information Service. This chapter is an updated and amended version of those sections of the pack which have been found most useful. It aims to help those setting up health information services to make the right contacts, establish basic collections of health-related publications and to organise this material for use.

WHERE TO FIND OUT

This is a guide to the major sources of information on services, organisations and publications of relevance to health. Included are the major umbrella groups and national organisations dealing with various aspects of health, illness and disability. Those listed have well developed information and publication services. Local health information services should become members or ask to be placed on mailing lists in order to receive information on a regular basis. Only those organisations dealing with health and disability in a general way, or covering a number of issues are listed. There are literally thousands of specialist organisations which it would be impossible to list individually. For information on these consult one of the directories listed later in this chapter.

NATIONAL ORGANISATIONS

Health Information

BLAT CENTRE FOR HEALTH AND MEDICAL EDUCATION, BMA House, Tavistock Square, London, WC1H 9JP Tel: 01 388 7976 World Health Organization collaborating centre, providing information on health education activities. Particularly concentrates on educational technology. BLAT has an information library, a film library and production departments. Publishes a current awareness bulletin, *BLAT Information*.

COLLEGE OF HEALTH, 18 Victoria Park Square, London, E2 9PF Tel: 01 980 6263
Organisation for health care consumers, run along similar lines to the Consumers Association. Publishes a quarterly magazine *Self Health* and a series of guides to health care services. The College of Health has also set up Healthline, the phone-in tape library on health topics.

HEALTH EDUCATION COUNCIL, 78 New Oxford Street, London, WC1A 1AH Tel: 01 631 0930
The Health Education Council is a national body funded largely by the DHSS and serving England, Wales and Northern Ireland. The HEC produces a wide range of free leaflets for the public on various aspects of keeping healthy. The HEC Resource Centre produces 22 invaluable Source Lists on topics such as Cancer education and Mental Health, a monthly list of recent additions (books and audiovisual materials) and a monthly 'Journal articles of interest'. For Scotland, contact: SCOTTISH HEALTH EDUCATION GROUP, Woodburn House, Canaan Lane, Edinburgh, EH10 4SG Tel: 031 447 8044

HELP FOR HEALTH, Wessex Regional Library Unit, South Academic Block, Southampton General Hospital, Southampton, SO9 4XY Tel: 0703 777222 ext 3753/779091
Primarily a local service for the Wessex Region on self-help organisations and self-help publications. Help for Health will also give general information to enquirers from elsewhere in the country.

PATIENTS ASSOCIATION, Room 33, 18 Charing Cross Road, London, WC2H OHR Tel: 01 240 0671
Represents and furthers the interests of patients through an individual advice service on patients' rights, and by spreading information on patients' interests. Publishes a newsletter, *Patient Voice*.

Self help and voluntary action

NATIONAL COUNCIL FOR VOLUNTARY ORGANISATIONS, 26 Bedford Square, London, WC1B 3HU Tel: 01 636 4066
National agency for the maintenance and promotion of voluntary social action. Information and resource centre providing training, legal, publishing, information and advisory services for voluntary organisations, nationally and locally. Publications list available (Bedford Square Press). NCVO provides the secretariat for the National Association of Councils of Voluntary Service. Also based at NCVO is the Community Health Initiatives Resource Unit (CHIRU) and the National Self Help Support Centre.

VOLUNTEER CENTRE, 29 Lower King's Road, Berkhamsted, Herts. HP4 2AB Tel: 04427 73311
National agency concerned with volunteers in health, social and penal services. Information centre on recruitment, work and training of volunteers. Encourages and publishes research on voluntary action. Publications list available.

Alternative and complementary medicine

COUNCIL OF COMPLEMENTARY AND ALTERNATIVE MEDI-CINE, 10 Belgrave Square, London, SW1 Tel: 01 235 9512
Determines standards of education, training, ethics and discipline for alternative practitioners.
INSTITUTE FOR COMPLEMENTARY MEDICINE, 21 Portland Place, London, W1N 3AF Tel: 01 631 4571
Provides information on alternative therapies and can put enquirers in touch with local practitioners.

Blind

IN TOUCH, BBC Broadcasting House, London, W1A 1AA

Produces quarterly bulletins summarising information from the radio programme *In Touch*. The bulletins are also available in Braille, Moon or on cassette tape.

ROYAL NATIONAL INSTITUTE FOR THE BLIND, 224/228 Great Portland Street, London, W1N 6AA Tel: 01 388 1266
Provides an information and advisory service on accommodation, aids, education etc. RNIB has a library service, publishes material in inkprint and Braille, and administers the British Talking Book Service for the Blind.

Broadcasting

BROADCASTING SUPPORT SERVICES, Room 17, 252 Western Avenue, London, W3 6XJ Tel: 01 992 5522
Provides follow-up services for programmes on BBC, Channel 4 and ITV. It publishes viewers' guides, runs telephone helplines, and letter-answering services. A standing order subscription service to all viewers' guides is now available.

MEDIA PROJECT, Volunteer Centre, 29 Lower King's Road, Berkhamsted, Herts. HP4 2AB Tel: 04427 73311
The project is looking at the role of television and radio, nationally and locally, in the broad field of social action. Information is available on programmes on health and disability as well as areas such as literacy, ethnic minorities, and community work. A *Directory of Social Action Programmes* is published which lists television and radio programmes by subject and gives addresses of stations, and there is a periodical, *Media Project News*.

Cancer

BACUP (BRITISH ASSOCIATION OF CANCER UNITED PATIENTS) 121/3 Charterhouse Street, London, EC1M 6AA Tel: 01 608 1661
National information service staffed by experienced cancer nurses. Provides information on treatment, research, support groups and practical help, and publishes leaflets.

CANCERLINK, 46a Pentonville Road, London, N1 9HF Tel: 01 833 2451
Cancer information service linked to a network of patient support groups in London and elsewhere.

Children

CONTACT A FAMILY, 16 Strutton Ground, London, SW1P 2HP Tel: 01 222 2695
Links families with a handicapped child to other families in a similar situation and area. A useful source of contacts for less common syndromes.

NATIONAL ASSOCIATION FOR THE WELFARE OF CHILDREN IN HOSPITAL (NAWCH) Argyle House, 29/31 Euston Road, London, NW1 2SD Tel: 01 833 2041
Information and advisory service for parents whose children are about to enter hospital. Initiates research and holds study days and conferences. Conducts surveys of hospital facilities. Publications list available. Publishes a newsletter *Update*.

NATIONAL CHILDREN'S BUREAU, 8 Wakley Street, London, EC1V 7QE Tel 01 278 9441
Multi-disciplinary centre concerned with children's needs in the family and society. Initiates a wide range of research. Provides an information and library service. Publications list available. Publishes a journal *Concern* and produces an excellent series of reading lists and summaries of research (*Highlights*).

NATIONAL LIBRARY FOR THE HANDICAPPED CHILD, Blyton Handi-Read Centre, Lynton House, Tavistock Square, London, WC1H 9LT Tel: 01 387 7016
Reference library and advisory service on all aspects of reading and the handicapped child. Includes books for and about children with reading handicaps, periodicals, audiovisual equipment, computer equipment and software.

Deaf

ROYAL NATIONAL INSTITUTE FOR THE DEAF, 105 Gower

Street, London, WC1E 6AH Tel: 01 387 8033
Has a library and information service and a technical advisory service on hearing aids and other equipment. Publishes a journal *Soundbarrier*.

Disability

DISABILITY ALLIANCE, 25 Denmark Street, London, WC2 8NJ Tel: 01 240 0806
A federation of over 50 organisations of and for disabled people, campaigning for a comprehensive income scheme for disabled people as a right. Provides welfare rights information and advice, and sponsors local rights services. Publishes *Disability Rights Handbook*.

DISABLED LIVING FOUNDATION, 380/384 Harrow Road, London, W9 2HU Tel: 01 289 6111
An information service on all aspects of disability. Specialist advisory services on Incontinence, Music, Clothing, Visual Handicap, and an Aids Centre. Aimed primarily at professionals but also helps disabled people and their relatives. Publications list available. Produces excellent information sheets as part of its information service.

DISABLEMENT INCOME GROUP, Toynbee Hall, 28 Commercial Street, London, EC1 Tel: 01 247 2128
Both a pressure group for a national disability income and a charitable trust concerned with education, research and publication. Provides an advisory service on welfare rights and services for disabled people. Publications list available. Publishes a magazine entitled *Progress*.

NATIONAL INFORMATION FORUM, c/o Disabled Living Foundation, 380/384 Harrow Road, London, W9 2HU Tel: 01 289 2791
Successor to the International Year of Disabled People Information Committee. Now an umbrella group with representatives from many disability and information organisations. Concerned with research into information needs and provision, production of training materials, and conferences and seminars on good practice in dissemination of information in the disability field.

ROYAL ASSOCIATION FOR DISABILITY AND REHABILITA-
TION (RADAR), 25 Mortimer Street, London, W1N 8AB Tel: 01 637
5400
Coordinating body with nearly 400 member organisations. Specialist
information available on access, education, holidays, housing and
mobility. Publications list available. Publishes a glossy magazine
Contact, and a very informative *Bulletin*.

Elderly

AGE CONCERN ENGLAND, 60 Pitcairn Road, Mitcham, Surrey
CR4 3LL Tel: 01 640 5431
A centre of policy, research, publication and information on all
subjects regarding the welfare of old people. Acts as the headquarters
for over 1,000 Age Concern organisations throughout the country.
Publications list available. Publishes the informative *Age Concern
Information Circular*.

CENTRE FOR POLICY ON AGEING, 25–31 Ironmonger Row,
London, EC1V 3QP Tel: 01 253 1787
Undertakes policy studies on a variety of subjects relevant to the
elderly. Has a library and information service which produces
bibliographies and current awareness literature.

Ethnic groups

CENTRE FOR ETHNIC MINORITY HEALTH STUDIES, Field
House Teaching Centre, Duckworth Lane, Bradford, BD9 6RJ Tel:
0274 490324
Aims to bring together in one place information about the health of
ethnic minorities in Britain. Has a resource centre and information
service and organises seminars and conferences.

COMMISSION FOR RACIAL EQUALITY, Elliott House, 10/12
Allington Street, London, SW1E 5EH Tel: 01 828 7022
Set up under the Race Relations Act 1976 to help promote equality
and good relations between people of different racial groups.
Publishes material in the area of race and health, and can provide
details of local Community Relations Councils.

COMMUNITY HEALTH GROUP FOR ETHNIC MINORITIES, 2nd Floor, 13 Macclesfield Street, London, W1V 7HL Tel: 01 439 8765 A resource centre and information service on health and ethnic groups. 'Ethnic Switchboard' gives advice on health, social and legal matters to people in their own language. Interpreting and translating service is available for health and social workers.

Mental handicap

ROYAL SOCIETY FOR MENTALLY HANDICAPPED CHILDREN AND ADULTS (MENCAP) 117/123 Golden Lane, London, EC1V ORT Tel: 01 253 9433 Specialist advisory and information services for the public and for professionals on all aspects of mental handicap. Finances research and holds conferences and meetings. Regional offices provide liaison for 450 local groups. Publications list available. Publishes a magazine *Parents' Voice* and a regular information pack *Communications*.

Mental health/addictions

ALCOHOL CONCERN, 305 Gray's Inn Road, London, WC1X 8QF Tel: 01 833 3471 The national agency on alcohol misuse. Supports local services and training initiatives, has a library and information service, and publishes a journal *Alcohol Concern*.

GOOD PRACTICES IN MENTAL HEALTH, 380/384 Harrow Road, London, W9 2HU Tel: 01 289 2034 Collects and disseminates information on good ideas and practices in mental health services locally. There are GPMH projects in many parts of the country.

INSTITUTE FOR THE STUDY OF DRUG DEPENDENCE, 1/4 Hatton Place, Hatton Garden, London, EC1N 8ND Tel: 01 430 1991/2/3 Information unit for professionals and the general public on drug and solvent abuse. Does not cover smoking or alcoholism.

MIND: NATIONAL ASSOCIATION FOR MENTAL HEALTH, 22

Harley Street, London, W1N 2ED Tel: 01 637 0741
Information and advisory service on all aspects of mental health, (both mental illness and mental handicap). Legal and welfare rights service to protect the rights of patients and staff. Arranges conferences and short courses on a wide range of mental health issues. Publications list available. Publishes a journal *OpenMind*.

Women

MIDWIVES INFORMATION AND RESOURCE SERVICE (MIDIRS), National Temperance Hospital, 112 Hampstead Road, London, NW1 2LT Tel: 01 387 3755
Information service for midwives and others interested in all aspects of pregnancy and childbirth. Produces information packs, and offers a source of information on research and practice.

WOMEN'S HEALTH INFORMATION CENTRE (WHIC), 52 Featherstone Street, London, EC1 Tel: 01 251 6580
National information and resource centre for women's health issues. Maintains a library of information materials and coordinates a network of women's health groups. Publishes *WHIC Newsletter* and fact sheets on individual topics.

LOCAL ORGANISATIONS

Library, information and advice services

CITIZENS' ADVICE BUREAUX
Over 900 local bureaux, staffed mainly by trained volunteers but often with a paid organiser, providing generalist information and advice on any topic to the public. Addresses appear in telephone directories under CITIZEN'S ADVICE BUREAU or may be obtained from: NATIONAL ASSOCIATION OF CITIZENS' ADVICE BUREAUX, 115–123 Pentonville Road, London, N1 9LZ Tel: 01 833 2181.
NACAB provides each bureau with a monthly pack of information materials, including sheets on new legislation, new official leaflets and background reading.

DIAL GROUPS (DISABLEMENT INFORMATION AND ADVICE LINES)
Independent local advisory and information services run by disabled people for disabled people. Available to anyone with a question on disability (disabled people, their relatives, professionals etc). Local groups may have a variety of names.

DIAL UK: NATIONAL ASSOCIATION OF DISABLEMENT INFORMATION AND ADVICE LINES, Victoria Buildings, 117 High Street, Clay Cross, Derbyshire, S45 9DZ Tel: 0246 864498
Advises on the establishment and development of local groups.

LOCAL AUTHORITY INFORMATION SERVICES
District Council information centres vary enormously. Some are merely public relations exercises, others offer little more than information on leisure and tourism, but they may produce lists of local organisations which are available on request.

NATIONAL HEALTH SERVICE LIBRARIES
Usually based in District General Hospitals, NHS libraries offer a range of services (including information enquiries) to NHS staff. Some NHS Regions have formal Regional Library Services, others cooperate on an *ad hoc* basis. Increasingly, services are open to all NHS staff in hospital and community, and some libraries are prepared to offer services to local self-help groups and members of the public.

NEIGHBOURHOOD ADVICE CENTRES
Informal community-based advice centres, set up either by voluntary or statutory agencies to provide information on issues such as housing, welfare benefits, law etc. May take the form of: CONSUMER ADVICE CENTRES, HOUSING ADVICE CENTRES, LEGAL ADVICE CENTRES, WELFARE RIGHTS ADVICE CENTRES.

ADVICE SERVICES ALLIANCE, 18 Queen Anne's Gate, London SW1.
FEDERATION OF INDEPENDENT ADVICE CENTRES, 13 Stockwell Road, London, SW9.

PUBLIC LIBRARIES
Many public libraries have begun to develop community information

services by adding to their stock in areas which had once been the province of advice bureaux, and by developing indexes of local information. Addresses appear in telephone directories under LIBRARIES.

COMMUNITY INFORMATION PROJECT, 136 City Road, London, EC1 Tel: 01 251 8616
The Community Information Project encourages the development of local community information services based in public libraries and elsewhere. Information is maintained on local projects and publications. The Project now has a particular specialism in the use of information technology for community information and publishes a newsletter *Computanews*.

Coordinating bodies for voluntary activity

COMMUNITY COUNCILS
Independent rural bodies made up of voluntary and statutory member organisations usually on a county basis. Provide a general information and advice service on local matters, and often produce directories of local services.

NATIONAL COUNCIL FOR VOLUNTARY ORGANISATIONS, 26 Bedford Square, London, WC1B 3HU Tel: 01 636 4066
Provides information on the network of community councils.

COUNCILS FOR VOLUNTARY SERVICE
Councils for Voluntary Service act as umbrella groups for local voluntary organisations, offering services such as secretarial assistance and printing, and promoting new groups where a need emerges. Usually serving urban areas with a smaller catchment area than a Community Council. They often produce directories of local organisations. May also be called COUNCILS OF COMMUNITY SERVICE, HELPING SERVICES COUNCILS.

NATIONAL COUNCIL FOR VOLUNTARY ORGANISATIONS, 26 Bedford Square, London, WC1B 3HU Tel: 01 636 4066
Provides information on local CVS activity.

National Health Service

COMMUNITY HEALTH COUNCILS
The consumer's voice in the National Health Service, consisting of members of the public representing various voluntary and statutory bodies. They advise and help patients with rights, complaints etc., and provide information on local health services. Often publish guides to local statutory and voluntary help. Addresses appear in telephone directories under COMMUNITY HEALTH COUNCILS or from: ASSOCIATION OF COMMUNITY HEALTH COUNCILS FOR ENGLAND AND WALES, Mark Lemon Suite, Barclays Bank Chambers, 254 Seven Sisters Road, London, N4 2HZ Tel: 01 272 5459

HEALTH EDUCATION SERVICES
Health Education Services at District Health Authority level aim to promote healthy living and to provide information on health topics. Collections of audiovisual aids, posters, leaflets etc. are available, some produced locally, others by the Health Education Council. Some are now taking the name Health Promotion Service to reflect a broader outlook. Addresses appear in telephone directories under NATIONAL HEALTH SERVICE, or the name of the District Health Authority, or from: HEALTH EDUCATION COUNCIL, 78 New Oxford Street, London, WC1A 1AH Tel: 01 631 0930

Other statutory services

DEPARTMENT OF HEALTH AND SOCIAL SECURITY
Provides information on the range of National Insurance and supplementary benefits, including those for the ill and disabled. Leaflets about the different benefits are available free of charge. Addresses appear in telephone directories under HEALTH AND SOCIAL SECURITY, DEPARTMENT OF.

EDUCATION DEPARTMENT
Provides information on educational facilities, including careers, adult education and specialist advice for disabled people. Addresses appear in telephone directories under the name of the local authority (County Council) followed by EDUCATION DEPARTMENT.

SOCIAL SERVICES DEPARTMENT

Provides information on services such as meals on wheels, home helps, old people's homes, child care etc. Can also advise on problems with housing, finance, education, disablement and rehabilitation etc. Addresses appear in telephone directories under name of local authority (County Council) followed by SOCIAL SERVICES DEPARTMENT.

A SHELF OF REFERENCE BOOKS

This is a guide to a shelf of basic reference books giving information on statutory and voluntary health care services. The content is based on a working reference collection used by the Help for Health Information Service and the comments arise from observations of usefulness by the Help for Health staff. Local directories form a vital part of any information collection and while it is not, of course, possible to list these here they should be collected to supplement national information. The total cost of the reference books is approximately £300.

Dictionaries

Butterworths Medical Dictionary (1980) Butterworths, London, 2nd edn. £19.50 ISBN: 0 407 00193 X
All health information services need a medical dictionary. This may seem an expensive one but a comprehensive authoritative British dictionary is an essential buy.

Magalini, S.I., and Scrasia, E. (1981) *Dictionary of Medical Syndromes* Lippincott, Philadelphia, 2nd edn. £57.25 ISBN: 0 397 50503 5
A health information service is likely to receive a number of enquiries on rare syndromes. This dictionary is an invaluable source for synonyms, signs, symptoms, etiology, diagnosis and prognosis. It is very expensive but is worth trying to afford.

Directories – health and social services

Family Welfare Association (1985), *Guide to the Social Services*, 73rd ed.

192

Family Welfare Association, London, £7.65, ISBN 0 900954 25 6
Annual guide to the administration of the British welfare state.
Includes personal social services, the structure of the NHS, welfare
benefits, taxation, housing, education, employment and immigration.

Hospitals and Health Services Yearbook (1985) Institute of Health
Services Management, London, £45.00 ISBN: 0 901003 37 9
This may seem expensive but it is the major annual directory of the
National Health Service. Includes a listing by Regional Health
Authority of all hospitals, health centres, NHS administrative offices,
community health councils etc., in the UK. In addition there are
details of government departments, professional bodies and other
organisations, summaries of reports and a directory of suppliers of
equipment.

Social Services Yearbook (1985/6) Longman, Harlow, Essex £27.00
ISBN: 0 582 90407 2
Important guide to social welfare provision in the UK. Main part is a
directory of social services arranged by county and including social
services offices, children's homes, special schools, day centres etc. Also
includes education authorities, health authorities, hospitals, government departments, and voluntary agencies.

National Consumer Council (1983) *Patients' Rights*: *A Guide for NHS
Patients and Doctors* HMSO, London, £1.50 ISBN: 0 11 701044 8
Explains the rights and duties of patients and their doctors and
outlines GP and hospital services available, how to make use of them
and how complaints procedures work when things go wrong.

Directories – voluntary organisations and self-help groups

Charities Aid Foundation (1985), *Directory of Grant-making Trusts*
CAF Publications, Tonbridge, Kent £45.00 ISBN: 0 904757 24 2
A comprehensive reference book which offers access to 2400 grant-
making bodies with a total income of over £482 million. Expensive
and not easy to use but it could pay for itself if funding is obtained!

Charities Digest (1985) Family Welfare Association, London, £7.65
ISBN: 0 900954 21 3

Not a complete guide to registered charities but a selective list of over 1,200 charities with details of their objectives and work (supplied by the charities themselves). Particularly useful for benevolent funds which are not easy to trace elsewhere.

Mental Health Foundation (1985) *Someone to Talk To Directory*, Routledge & Kegan Paul, London, £21.00 ISBN: 0 901944 08 4
Directory of over 10,000 self-help groups, the most comprehensive yet published. A brave attempt though the mix of national and local groups, the absence of a name index, and the sheer size make it difficult to use.

National Council for Voluntary Organisations (1985), *Voluntary Organisations: An NCVO Directory 1985/6* NCVO, London, £5.95 ISBN: 0 7199 1137 0
Published annually since 1928 this is the most useful directory of voluntary organisations and self-help groups available. It lists alphabetically over 800 leading voluntary organisations with a subject index. There is a good health content.

Patients Association (1984), *Self Help and the Patient* 9th edn. Patients Association, London, £2.50
A reasonably priced directory of the main national self-help groups (250 in all) arranged by subject.

Health and illness

Booth, J. (1983) *Handbook of Investigations* Harper & Row, London, £4.50 ISBN 0 06 318235 1
Many people have to undergo tests and investigations which may be routine to staff but which can be a cause of great anxiety to patients. Information on tests can be hard to find and this guide to 50 procedures fills a gap in the popular literature.

Griffith, H.W. (1982) *Instructions for Patients* 3rd edn. Saunders, Philadelphia, £29.00 ISBN: 0 7216 42861
Unique, looseleaf compendium of information sheets for patients, which are designed to be removed and photocopied. Covers a very wide range of illnesses and symptoms, from abdominal pain to

varicose veins, as well as special diets, tests, anatomical diagrams etc. An unbeatable fall-back when no information can be found elsewhere.

Parish, P. (1984) *Medicines: A Guide for Everybody* 5th edn. Penguin, Harmondsworth, £4.95 ISBN 0 14 051122 9
The most useful and accessible popular pharmacopoeia. Contains a comprehensive list of medicines which can be obtained on prescription or over the counter with uses, precautions, adverse effects and dosages.

Stanway, A. (1981) *A Dictionary of Operations*, Paladin, London, £2.50 ISBN: 0 586 08368 5
A clear guide to having an operation which includes going into hospital, an A–Z guide to common and less common operations, and a summary of procedures and investigations.

Vickery, D.M., Fries, J.F., Muir Gray, J.A., and Smail, S.A. (1980) *Take Care of Yourself*, Unwin, London, £3.95 ISBN: 0 04 616018 3
Well designed guide which uses self diagnosis flowcharts to give home treatment advice for over seventy common medical problems.

Disability

Bransbury, L., Rock, P., and Levy, B.A. (1984) *Compass: The Direction Finder for Disabled People*, Disablement Income Group, London, £2.25
Designed to point disabled people in the right direction for helpful organisations, services, benefits and aids. A guide to where to go rather than a comprehensive manual, and a useful buy.

Darnbrough, A. and Kinrade, D. (1985) *Directory for Disabled People*, 4th edn. Woodhead-Faulkner, Cambridge, £11.50 ISBN: 0 85941 255 5
Utterly invaluable guide to opportunities and services for disabled people (sensory and mental as well as physical handicaps). Covers benefits, aids, housing, education, employment, mobility, holidays, leisure. Includes addresses of many useful organisations and a publications list.

Disability Rights Handbook (1986) Disability Alliance, London, £2.40
Indispensable cheap annual guide to rights, benefits and services.

Concentrates on cash benefits with detailed information on eligibility, claiming, appealing etc., but also covers mobility, housing, retirement, complaints. There is an alphabetical list of several hundred disability organisations at the end of the book.

Royal Association for Disability and Rehabilitation (1986) *Holidays for Disabled People*, RADAR, London, £2.00
Help for Health receives more enquiries on holidays for people with special needs than on any other topic. This directory of hotels, guest houses, self catering and group holidays is indispensable, and a bargain. Information is given on access, level of care, special diets etc.

Wilshere, E.R., *Equipment for the Disabled*. Mary Marlborough Lodge, Oxford
A comprehensive series of illustrated booklets on aids and equipment, covering most areas of daily living for disabled people. Gives illustrations of equipment with price, manufacturer, and description. Constantly updated. Available singly or as a set. The following titles are available: Clothes and dressing; Communication; Disabled child; Disabled mother; Hoists and walking aids; Home management; Housing and furniture; Incontinence and stoma care; Leisure and gardening; Outdoor transport; Personal care; Wheelchairs.

KEEPING UP-TO-DATE

Keeping up-to-date is a major problem for any information service. This is a list of the most important journals, newsletters, information bulletins, current awareness services, and abstracting and indexing services. As with reference materials these should be supplemented by local publications. The national daily and Sunday papers (especially the *Guardian*, *The Times*, *Observer* and *Sunday Times*) and general and women's magazines (especially *Which* and *Good Housekeeping*) are also useful sources. The approximate annual cost of these subscriptions is £400 a year.

Journals, newsletters and bulletins

Age Concern Information Circular. Monthly. £8.00 a year. Age Concern England, 60 Pitcairn Road, Mitcham, Surrey.

News on legislation, social security, pensions, voluntary organisations, press releases. Each issue contains a list of recent periodical articles in the field of ageing, reviews of new publications, and details of courses and conferences.

The Bulletin. Monthly. £4.50 a year. Royal Association for Disability and Rehabilitation (RADAR), 25 Mortimer Street, London, W1N 8AB
Extremely useful guide to new legislation, employment, mobility, conferences, exhibitions. Good publications section.

Communications. 3 times a year. £7.00 a year. MENCAP, 123 Golden Lane, London EC1
Information pack containing news and views; briefing on recent reports and articles; copies of new Government, Health Education Council, and voluntary organisation leaflets. Especially valuable because it not only alerts to new publications but, in many cases, includes them in the pack.

Community Health News. 10 times a year. Cost on application. Association of Community Health Councils for England & Wales, 254 Seven Sisters Road, London, N4 2HZ
Primarily for CHC secretaries and members. Includes news from ACHCEW and individual local CHCs, an "information wanted" section, and useful details of the publications and activities of a range of health related organisations.

Disabled Living Foundation Information Service. Bi-monthly. Cost on application. Disabled Living Foundation, 380–384 Harrow Road, London, W9 2HU
Essential. Consists of newsletter and indexed information sheets on all aspects of daily living. The newsletter is a particularly up-to-date guide to new legislation; benefits and services; publications; meetings. The titles of the information sheets are: Beds; Chairs; Communication; Eating and Drinking Aids; Hoists and Lifting Equipment; Leisure Activities; Sport and Physical Recreation; Personal Care; Personal Toilet; Transport; Walking Aids; Wheelchairs; Household Equipment; Household Fittings; Incontinence; Clothing; Footwear; Children's Aids; School Furniture.

Disability Now. Monthly. Free but donations appreciated. Spastics Society, 12 Park Crescent, London, W1N 4EQ
Newspaper on all aspects of disability (not just cerebral palsy). Includes a diary, parliamentary briefing, reviews, a problem page and features.

Family Planning Today. Quarterly. £3.00 a year. Family Planning Information Service, 27/35 Mortimer Street, London, W1N 7RJ
News sheet giving details of current issues in family planning, fertility, sex education etc. Useful synopses of articles from the press and medical journals.

Handicapped Living. Monthly. £10.00 a year. A.E. Morgan Ltd., Stanley House, 9 West Street, Epsom, Surrey KT18 7RL
Widely available, glossy magazine on living with a disability. Particularly strong on aids and equipment, transport, leisure, holidays. Also includes horoscopes, a problem page, 'Pat's Piece' by disabled journalist Pat Saunders, and classified advertisements.

Health Education News. Bi-monthly. Free. Health Education Council, 78 New Oxford Street, London, WC1A 1AH
News of latest Health Education Council campaigns, new leaflets, posters etc. Most of the HEC material described is available from local health education departments. The newspaper is particularly useful for locally produced material which might otherwise be missed.

Health Visitor. Monthly. £20.00 a year. B. Edsall Ltd., 124 Belgrave Road, London, SW1V 2BL
Official journal of the Health Visitors Association (members receive it free). As well as HVA news and articles it has book and film reviews, details of self-help groups and a particularly useful 'Information wanted' section where health visitors offer or ask for contacts for rare disorders.

Health Libraries Review. Quarterly. £29.00 a year. Blackwell Scientific Publications, Osney Mead, Oxford, OX2 OEL
Official journal of Library Association Medical Health & Welfare Libraries Group (reduced rates for members). Original articles and news of current developments in health and welfare library and

information services. Regular 'Patient Information' column describes projects and services, gives details of self-help groups and reviews publications.

Involve. 8 times a year. £7.50 a year. Volunteer Centre, 29 Lower King's Road, Berkhamsted, Herts. HP4 2AB
News and articles on volunteering in the health and social services field. Useful 'Bulletin' current awareness service gleaned from more than 200 journals, press releases and other material received by the Volunteer Centre.

Maternity Action. Bi-monthly. £5.00 a year. Maternity Alliance, 59–61 Camden High Street, London, NW1 7JL
Focus on maternity issues, benefits and rights, parliamentary news, details of publications from the Maternity Alliance and other groups.

Midwives Information and Resource Service (MIDIRS). 3 packs a year. £20 for libraries and information services (other costs on application). MIDIRS, National Temperance Hospital, 112 Hampstead Road, London, NW1 2LT
Loose-leaf information packs containing selection of articles from journals in the field of midwifery and childbirth, unpublished papers, news from voluntary organisations, foreign material, reports and news.

Multiple Sclerosis Society Bulletin. Monthly. £2.00 a year. Multiple Sclerosis Society, 25 Effie Road, London, SW6 1EE
Good update on all aspects of disabled living. Valuable for details of both organisations and publications and generally very up-to-date. Includes CRACK News (for younger MS sufferers).

Media Project News. Bi-monthly. £12.50 a year. Volunteer Centre Media Project, 29 Lower King's Road, Berkhamsted, Herts. HP4 2AB
Interesting features on community involvement through the media of television and radio, particularly on a local basis. Subscription includes two editions of *Directory of Social Action Programmes* and two case studies.

New Generation. Quarterly. £8.00 a year. National Childbirth Trust, 9

199

Queensborough Terrace, London, W2 3TB
Designed for NCT teachers, breastfeeding counsellors, and postnatal supporters. Includes features on aspects of NCT work but is particularly useful for its book reviews, news of other organisations and excellent summaries of articles from medical and nursing journals.

New Society. Weekly. £42.00 a year. New Society, 14–16 Farringdon Lane, London, EC1R 3AV
New Society has always included articles of relevance to self care and health information but it is even more useful now that it contains NCVO's *Voluntary Action* as a centre pullout. This is an indispensable update on activities and publications of voluntary organisations.

Nursing Times. Weekly. £45.00 a year. Macmillan Journals, Farndon Road, Market Harborough, Leics. LE16 9NR
Now incorporating *Nursing Mirror* this is essential reading for keeping up-to-date with developments not only in nursing but in health care generally. The monthly *Community Outlook* supplement is particularly useful and includes information on patient organisations and publications, and pullout fact sheets.

Open Mind. Bi-monthly. £7.00 a year. MIND, 22 Harley Street, London, W1N 2ED
The most important journal in the field of mental health. Original articles, news, benefits information, letters, book reviews and a very good listings page.

Parents Voice. Quarterly. MENCAP, 123 Golden Lane, London, EC1Y ORT
A readable journal of high standard. Original articles by professionals and parents; letters; details of MENCAP publications and reviews of others; news from regions.

Patient Education and Counseling. Quarterly. $81.00 Elsevier Scientific Publishers, PO Box 85, Limerick, Ireland
An expensive journal which many information services would not wish to hold themselves. However it is worth persuading a local medical library to take out a subscription. It is a multidisciplinary research journal on patient education around the world (with an

American bias). It now contains *Patient Education Newsletter* which was formerly available separately.

Self Health. Quarterly. £10.00 a year (membership). College of Health, 18 Victoria Park Square, London, E2 9PF
Magazine for health care consumers. Includes good original features, 'Action for Health' news pages, alternative medicine round-up, reviews and letters.

Spinal Injuries Association Newsletter. Quarterly. £15.00 a year (membership). Spinal Injuries Association, Yeoman House, 76 St. James' Lane, London, N10 3DF
A particularly good newsletter containing valuable information on all aspects of disability, not merely spinal injuries. Topics include aids, benefits, employment, holidays, housing, mobility, recreation. Reviews of new publications.

Self Help Spotlight. Bi-monthly. Cost on application. Share Community, 140 Battersea Park Road, London, SW11 4NB
Always interesting. Brief articles on self-help activity in community arts, alternative technologies and lifestyles, housing etc., as well as health groups. Also describes interesting American groups, books and events.

WHIC Newsletter. £10.00 a year (membership). Women's Health Information Centre (WHIC), 52 Featherstone Street, London, EC1
Membership of WHIC entitles members to regular newsletters on women's health issues, self-help fact sheets on specific topics, and broadsheets on the social causes of ill health.

Current awareness lists, abstracts and indexes

BIMH Current Awareness Service. Monthly. £12.00 a year. British Institute of Mental Handicap, Wolverhampton Road, Kidderminster, Worcs. DY10 3PP
Current awareness bulletin on books, journal articles, audiovisual material, and conferences in the field of mental handicap. Covers topics such as education, arts, sexuality, specific disorders.

Community Currents. Bi-monthly. £9.50 a year. Community Projects Foundation, 60 Highbury Grove, London, N5 2AG
Digest of new information about key issues in community life and community action (including health and information services). Over 100 journals are scanned and a selection of books and meetings. Covers some of the same ground as *Voluntary Forum Abstracts.*

Health Education Council Resource Centre and Library lists. Monthly. Free. Health Education Council, 78 New Oxford Street, London, WC1A 1AH
Recent additions to the library: Recent additions to the resource centre; Journal articles of interest to health educators.
Invaluable current awareness lists arranged by subjects.

Health Visitors Association Current Awareness Bulletin. Quarterly. £6.00 a year. Health Visitors Association, 36 Eccleston Square, London, SW1V 1PF
At Help for Health more enquiries are received from health visitors than any other group. A health information service will find it useful to keep up-to-date with developments in health visiting and community nursing. This is a subject listing (from abortion to welfare rights and women's health) with brief abstracts.

Popular Medical Index. Quarterly. £20.00 a year. Mede Publications, 77 Norton Road, Letchworth, Herts. SG6 1AD
A unique subject index giving coverage of periodical articles and books on health topics at a lay level. Covers disease, medical treatment, positive health (slimming, diet, exercise) and alternative medicine. Indexes not only the main medical and nursing journals but also a number of women's magazines.

Voluntary Forum Abstracts. Bi-monthly. £12.50 a year. National Council for Voluntary Organisations, 26 Bedford Square, London, WC1B 3HU
Joint NCVO/Volunteer Centre publication. Excellent coverage of voluntary sector, social policy, social welfare (including health and disability), social structure and social environment. Detailed abstracts of journal articles, books and reports with indexes by subject, author, title and organisation.

BUILDING A HEALTH INFORMATION COLLECTION

Having developed a collection of basic reference materials and current awareness publications, health information services will need to expand the collection in response to specific local needs. This section gives some guidance on building up a basic health information collection in specifc subject areas. Where possible two or three books, some free or cheap booklets or leaflets, and relevant periodicals are suggested for each of the main topics on which Help for Health receives enquiries. The list is arranged according to the Help for Health subject headings. Prices are not included as it may be some time before a specific item is required, and the current cost should then be checked. Do remember that many of the booklets are produced by small voluntary organisations operating on a tight budget. Always send a large adequately stamped envelope. When writing, ask for a publications list and details of membership of the organisation. It may well be worth becoming a member to receive new literature on a regular basis. It is tempting to call this section 'The tip of the iceberg'. It represents only a small proportion of the enormous number of popular health publications but it does list some of the more useful material for a core collection. For publications in areas not covered by this list, consult one of the directories of self-help groups for a relevant organisation.

Series

There are several excellent series of health publications for a lay readership. Contact the following for a full list:

British Medical Association, *Family Doctor* series, BMA House, Tavistock Square, London, WC1H 9JP
Chambers *Coping with* series, W & R Chambers, 43/45 Annandale Street, Edinburgh, EH7 4AZ
Churchill Livingstone *Patient Handbooks*, Robert Stevenson House, 1–3 Baxter's Place, Leith Walk, Edinburgh
Human Horizons series, Souvenir Press, 43 Gt. Russell St., London, WC1B 3PA
Martin Dunitz *Positive Health Guides*, 154 Camden High Street, London, NW1

Oxford University Press *The Facts* series, Oxford University Press, 116 High Street, Oxford, OX1 4BR

Scriptographic Publications, 92–104 Carnwath Road, London, SW6 3H8

Sheldon Press *Overcoming common problems* series and *Health care for women* series, SPCK House, Marylebone Road, London, NW1 4DU

Thorsons Publishers Ltd., Denington Estate, Wellingborough, Northants, NN8 2RQ.

The Aged

BOOKS

Coni, N., Davison, W., and Webster, S. (1984) *Ageing: The Facts.* Oxford University Press.

Dartington, T. (1980) *Family Care of Old People*, Souvenir Press, London.

Gray, J.A.M. (1983) *Better health in retirement*, Age Concern, Mitcham, Surrey.

Greengross, W. (1985) *Ageing: An Adventure in Living*, Souvenir Press, London.

BOOKLETS/LEAFLETS

Looking After Yourself in Retirement, Health Education Council, 78 New Oxford Street, London, WC1A 1AH

Your Rights for Pensioners, Age Concern, 60 Pitcairn Road, Mitcham, Surrey.

AIDS (Acquired Immune Deficiency Syndrome)

BOOKLETS/LEAFLETS

AIDS and the Blood, Haemophilia Society, PO Box 9, 16 Trinity Street, London, SE1 1DE

AIDS: More Facts for Gay Men, Terrence Higgins Trust, BM AIDS, London, WC1N 3XX

Some Facts about AIDS, Health Education Council, 78 New Oxford Street, London, WC1A 1AH

Alcoholism

BOOKS
Chick, J. (1984) *Drinking Problems*, Churchill Livingstone Patient Handbooks, Edinburgh.
Goodwin, D.W. (1981) *Alcoholism: The Facts*. Oxford University Press.

BOOKLETS/LEAFLETS
Alcohol: Time to Cut Down? Alcohol Concern, 305 Gray's Inn Road, London, WC1.
That's the Limit: A Guide to Sensible Drinking, Health Education Council, 78 New Oxford Street, London, WC1A 1AH

PERIODICALS
Alcohol Concern, Alcohol Concern.

Allergy

BOOKS
Hanssen, M. (1984) *E for Additives*, Thorsons, Wellingborough.
Steel, M. (1986) *Understanding Allergies*, Consumers' Association, London.

BOOKLETS/LEAFLETS
Look at the label, Ministry of Agriculture, Fisheries and Food, Publications Unit, Lion House, Willowburn Trading Estate, Alnwick, Northumberland, NE66 2PF

Alternative medicine

BOOKS
College of Health (1984) *Guide to Alternative Medicine*, College of Health, London.
Hafen, B. and Frandsen, K. (1984) *An A–Z of Alternative Medicine*, Sheldon Press, London.
Stanway, A. (1982) *Alternative Medicine: A Guide to Natural Therapies*, Penguin, Harmondsworth.

BOOKLETS/LEAFLETS
Series of leaflets on major therapies, British Holistic Medical Association, 179 Gloucester Place, London, NW1 6DX

Anorexia nervosa

BOOKS
Melville, J., *The ABC of Eating: Coping with Anorexia, Bulimia and Compulsive Eating*, Sheldon Press, London.
Palmer, R. (1980) *Anorexia Nervosa: A Guide for Sufferers and Their Families*, Penguin, Harmondsworth.

PERIODICALS
Feedback, National Information Centre for Anorexic Family Aid, Sackville Place, 44/48 Magdalen Street, Norwich, NR3 1JE

Arthritis

BOOKS
Hart, F.D. (1981) *Overcoming Arthritis*, Martin Dunitz, London.
Moll, J.M.H. (1983) *Arthritis and Rheumatism*, Churchill Livingstone Patient Handbooks, Edinburgh.
Scott, J. (1980) *Arthritis and Rheumatism: The Facts*, Oxford University Press.

BOOKLETS/LEAFLETS
Arthritis and You: Answers to Some Common Questions, Arthritis Care, 6 Grosvenor Crescent, London, SW1X 7ER
Series of booklets, Arthritis and Rheumatism Council for Research, 41 Eagle Street, London, WC1

PERIODICALS
Arthritis News, Arthritis Care.
In Contact: Information and News for the Young Arthritic, Arthritis Care.

Asthma

BOOKS
Clarke, T.J.H. (1984) *Adult Asthma*, Churchill Livingstone Patient Handbooks, Edinburgh.

Milner, A.D. (1984) *Asthma in Childhood*, Churchill Livingstone Patient Handbooks, Edinburgh.

BOOKLETS/LEAFLETS
Series of leaflets, Asthma Society, St Thomas's Hospital, Lambeth Palace Road, London, SE1 7EH
Series of leaflets, Chest, Heart and Stroke Association, Tavistock House North, Tavistock Square, London, WC1 9JE

Autism

BOOKS
Wing, L. (1980) *Autistic Children: A Guide for Parents*, Constable, London.

PERIODICALS
Communication, National Autistic Society, 276 Willesden Lane, London, NW2
Newsletter, National Autistic Society.

Back pain

BOOKS
Jayson, M. (1981) *Back Pain: The Facts*. Oxford University Press.
Porter, R.W. (1983) *Understanding Back Pain*, Churchill Livingstone Patient Handbooks, Edinburgh.
Stoddard, A. (1981) *The Back: Relief from Pain*. Martin Dunitz.

BOOKLETS/LEAFLETS
Mind your Back, Health Education Council, 78 New Oxford Street, London, WC1A 1AH
Series of booklets, Back Pain Association, 31–33 Park Road, Teddington, Middx. TW11 OAB

PERIODICALS
Talk Back, Back Pain Association.

Bereavement

Kubler-Ross, E. (1982) *Living with Death and Dying*, Souvenir Press, London.

Lake, T. (1984) *Living with Grief*, Sheldon Press, London.

BOOKLETS/LEAFLETS
What to do After a Death, DHSS Leaflets Unit, PO Box 21, Stanmore, Middx. (or local offices).
Series of leaflets, CRUSE: The National Organisation for the Widowed and their Children, 126 Sheen Road, Richmond, Surrey.
Series of leaflets for bereaved parents, Compassionate Friends, 6 Denmark Street, Bristol, BS1 5DQ

PERIODICALS
Bereavement Care, CRUSE
CRUSE Chronicle, CRUSE

Blindness

Dobree, J.H. and Boulter, E. (1982) *Blindness and Visual Handicap: The Facts*, Oxford University Press.
Royal National Institute for the Blind (1984) *Directory of Agencies for the Blind in the British Isles and Overseas*, RNIB, London.

BOOKLETS/LEAFLETS
Series of leaflets, Royal National Institute for the Blind, 224/8 Great Portland Street, London, W1N 6AA

PERIODICALS
In Touch Bulletin, In Touch, BBC, Broadcasting House, London, W1A 1AA.

Breast Cancer

BOOKS
Baum, M. (1981) *Breast Cancer: The Facts*, Oxford University Press.
Faulder, C. (1982) *Breast Cancer: A Guide to its Early Detection and Treatment*, Virago, London

BOOKLETS/LEAFLETS
Living with the loss of a breast, Health Education Council, 78 New Oxford Street, London, WC1A 1AH

Series of booklets, Mastectomy Association, 26 Harrison Street, London, WC1

Cancer

BOOKS
Directory of Cancer Research and Welfare Organisations (1984) Charities Aid Foundation, Tonbridge.
Scott, R.B. (1979) *Cancer: The Facts*, Oxford University Press.
Williams, C. (1983) *All About Cancer: A Practical Guide to Cancer Care*, Wiley Chichester.

BOOKLETS/LEAFLETS
Can You Avoid Cancer: A Guide to Reducing Your Risks, Health Education Council, 78 New Oxford Street, London, WC1A 1AH
Patient Information Series, Royal Marsden Hospital, Fulham Road, London, SW3

PERIODICALS
Cancer Relief News, National Society for Cancer Relief, 30 Dorset Square, London, NW1 6QL

Cerebral Palsy

BOOKLETS/LEAFLETS
Series of booklets, Spastics Society, 12 Park Street, London, W1N 4EQ

PERIODICALS
Disability Now, Spastics Society.

Child care

BOOKS
Gilbert, P. (1984) *Common Childhood Illnesses*, Sheldon Press, London.
Lask, B. (1985) *Children's Problems: A Parents' Guide to Understanding and Tackling Them*, Martin Dunitz, London.
Leach, P. (1979) *Baby and Child*, Penguin, Harmondsworth.

Child, handicapped

BOOKS
Carr, J. (1980) *Helping Your Handicapped Child*, Penguin, Harmondsworth.
Cunningham, C. and Sloper, P. (1978) *Helping Your Handicapped Baby*, Souvenir Press, London.
McCormack, A.E. (1985) *Coping With Your Handicapped Child*, Chambers, Edinburgh.
Russell, P. (1984) *The Wheelchair Child*, 2nd edn. Souvenir Press, London.

BOOKLETS/LEAFLETS
Help Starts Here: For Parents of Children With Special Needs, Voluntary Council for Handicapped Children, 8 Wakley Street, London, EC1V 7QE.

Child, hospitalised

BOOKLETS/LEAFLETS
Series of booklets, National Association for the Welfare of Children in Hospital, Argyle House, 29/31 Euston Road, London, NW1 2SD.

PERIODICALS
Update, National Association for the Welfare of Children in Hospital.

Cystic fibrosis

BOOKLETS/LEAFLETS
Series of leaflets, Cystic Fibrosis Research Trust, 5 Blyth Road, Bromley, Kent, BR1 3RS.

PERIODICALS
Cystic Fibrosis News, Cystic Fibrosis Research Trust.

Deafness

BOOKS
Directory of Organisations for the Deaf and Hard of Hearing (1984)

Charities Aid Foundation, Tonbridge.
Nolan, M. and Tucker, I.G. (1981) *The Hearing Impaired Child and the Family*, Souvenir Press, London.

BOOKLETS/LEAFLETS
Series of booklets, National Deaf Children's Society, 45 Hereford Road, London, W2 5RH.
Series of booklets, Royal National Institute for the Deaf, 105 Gower Street, London, WC1E 6AH.

PERIODICALS
Soundbarrier, Royal National Institute for the Deaf.

Dementia

BOOKLETS/LEAFLETS
Caring for the Person with Dementia, Alzheimer's Disease Society, Bank Buildings, Fulham Broadway, London, SW6 1EP.
Who Cares?, Health Education Council, 78 New Oxford Street, London, WC1A 1AH.
Who Cares about the Relatives?, MIND, 22 Harley Street, London, W1N 2ED.

Depression

BOOKS
Hauck, P. (1984) *Depression: Why it Happens and How to Overcome It*, Sheldon Press, London.
Rowe, D. (1983) *Depression: The Way Out of Your Prison*, Routledge, London.

Diabetes

BOOKS
Bloom, A. (1982) *Diabetes Explained*, 4th edn. MTP, Lancaster.
Dolger, H. and Seeman, B. (1984) *How to Live with Diabetes*, Penguin, Harmondsworth.
Farquhar, J.W. (1981) *The Diabetic Child*, Churchill Livingstone Patient Handbooks, Edinburgh.

211

Tattersall, R. (1981) *Diabetes: A Practical Guide for Patients on Insulin*, Churchill Livingstone Patient Handbooks, Edinburgh.

BOOKLETS/LEAFLETS
The diabetic's handbook, series of booklets, British Diabetic Association, 10 Queen Anne Street, London, W1.

PERIODICALS
Balance, British Diabetic Association.

Disabled people

BOOKS
Darnbrough, A. and Kinrade, D. (1984), *Motoring and Mobility for Disabled People*, RADAR, London.
Hale, G. (1983) *The New Sourcebook for the Disabled*, Heinemann, London.
Halliburton, P. and Quelch, K. (1981), *Get Help: A Guide for Social Workers to the Management of Illness in the Community*, Tavistock, London.
Jay, P. (1984) *Coping with Disability*, Disabled Living Foundation, London.

BOOKLETS/LEAFLETS
Aids for the Disabled; *Help for handicapped People*; *Which benefit? 60 Ways to Get Cash Help*, DHSS Leaflets Unit, PO Box 21, Stanmore, Middx. HA7 1AY (or local offices).
Door to Door: A Guide to Transport for Disabled People, Department of Transport, 2 Marsham Street, London, SW1P 3EB.

PERIODICALS
CONTACT, Royal Association for Disability and Rehabilitation, 25 Mortimer Street, London, W1N 8AB.
Progress, Disablement Income Group, Attlee House, 28 Commercial Street, London, E1 6LR.

Down's Syndrome

BOOKS
Cunningham, C. (1982) *Down's Syndrome: An Introduction for Parents*, Souvenir Press, London.

212

BOOKLETS/LEAFLETS
Help for Those with Down's Syndrome, and series of other leaflets, Down's Children's Association, 4 Oxford Street, London, W1R 9FL.

PERIODICALS
Down's Children's Association News, Down's Children's Association.

Drug abuse

BOOKS
Directory of Organisations Concerned with Drug Misuse (1985) Charities Aid Foundation, Tonbridge.
Drug Abuse Briefing: A Guide to the Effects of Drugs and to the Social and Legal Facts about their Non-Medical Use in Britain (1984) Institute for the Study of Drug Dependence, London.
Leech, K. (1983) *What Everyone Should Know About Drugs*, Sheldon Press, London.

BOOKLETS/LEAFLETS
Drug Misuse: A Basic Briefing; *What Every Parent Should Know About Drugs*; *What Parents Can Do About Drugs*, Department DM, DHSS Leaflets Unit, PO Box 21, Stanmore, Middx. HA7 1AY.

Drugs and medicines

BOOKS
Medawar, C. (1984) *The Wrong Kind of Medicine*, Consumers' Association, London.
Melville, J. (1984) *The Tranquilliser Trap and How to Get Out of It*, Fontana, London.
Trimmer, E. (1983) *Good Housekeeping's Guide to Medicines*, Ebury Press, London.

BOOKLETS/LEAFLETS
Follow the Medicines Code, Health Education Council, 78 New Oxford Street, London, WC1A 1AH.
Medicines: The Right and Wrong Way of Handling Medicines, Royal Society for the Prevention of Accidents, Cannon House, The Priory, Queensway, Birmingham, B4 6BS.

Tranquillisers: Hard Facts, Hard Choices, MIND, 22 Harley Street, London, W1N 2ED.
Trouble With Tranquillisers, Release, 347a Upper Street, London, N1.

Dyslexia

BOOKS
Hornsby, B. (1984) *Overcoming Dyslexia: A Straightforward Guide for Families and Teachers*, Martin Dunitz, London.
BOOKLETS/LEAFLETS
Dyslexia: The Hidden Handicap, British Dyslexia Association, Church Lane, Peppard, Oxon. RG9 5JN.
Series of leaflets, Helen Arkell Dyslexia Centre, 14 Crondace Road, London, SW6 4BB.

Eczema

BOOKS
Atherton, D.J. (1984) *Your Child With Eczema*, Heinemann, London.
Orton, C. (1981) *Learning to Live With Skin Disorders*, Souvenir Press, London.

BOOKLETS/LEAFLETS
Series of leaflets, National Eczema Society, Tavistock House North, Tavistock Square, London, WC1H 9SR.

PERIODICALS
Exchange, National Eczema Society.

Epilepsy

BOOKS
Hopkins, A. (1981) *Epilepsy: The Facts*, Oxford University Press.
Laidlaw, M. (1983) *Epilepsy Explained*, Churchill Livingstone Patient Handbooks, Edinburgh.

BOOKLETS/LEAFLETS
Series of leaflets, British Epilepsy Association, Crowthorne House, New Wokingham Road, Wokingham, Berks RG11 3AY.

214

Series of leaflets, National Society for Epilepsy, Chalfont Centre, Chalfont St Peter, Gerrards Cross, Bucks. SL9 ORJ.

PERIODICALS
Epilepsy Now, British Epilepsy Association.

Eye care

Youngson, R. (1985) *Everything You Need to Know about your Eyes*, Sheldon Press, London.

BOOKLETS/LEAFLETS
Series of leaflets, Optical Information Council, Temple Chambers, Temple Avenue, London, EC4Y ODT.

Family planning

BOOKS
Bromwich, P. and Parsons, T. (1984) *Contraception: The Facts*, Oxford University Press.
Kane, P. (1983) *Which? Guide to Birth Control*, Consumers' Association, London.

BOOKLETS/LEAFLETS
Series of leaflets, Family Planning Information Service, 27–35 Mortimer Street, London, W1A 4QW.

Haemophilia

BOOKLETS/LEAFLETS
Series of booklets, Haemophilia Society, 16 Trinity Street, London, SE1 1DE.

Heart

BOOKS
Hampton, J.R. (1981) *All About Heart Attacks*, Churchill Livingstone Patient Handbooks, Edinburgh.
Mulcahy, R. (1984) *Beat Heart Disease*, Martin Dunitz, London.

Shillingford, J.P. *Coronary Heart Disease: The Facts*, Oxford University Press.

BOOKLETS/LEAFLETS
Beating Heart Disease, Health Education Council, 78 New Oxford Street, London, WC1A 1AH.
Series of booklets, British Heart Foundation, 102 Gloucester Place, London, W1H 4DH.
Series of booklets, Chest, Heart and Stroke Association, Tavistock House North, Tavistock Square, London, WC1 9JE.
Series of booklets, Coronary Prevention Group, 60 Great Ormond Street, London, WC1N 3HR.

PERIODICALS
Heart to Heart, Coronary Prevention Group.

Hypertension

BOOKS
Lewis, P. *High Blood Pressure*, Churchill Livingstone Patient Handbooks, Edinburgh.
O'Brien, E. and O'Malley, K. (1983) *High Blood Pressure: What It Means for You and How to Control It*, Martin Dunitz, London.

BOOKLETS/LEAFLETS
Is it Blood Pressure? British Heart Foundation, 102 Gloucester Place, London, W1H 4DH.
Facts About High Blood Pressure, Chest, Heart and Stroke Association, Tavistock House North, Tavistock Square, London, WC1 9JE.

Incontinence

BOOKS
Feneley, R.C. (1984) *Incontinence*, Churchill Livingstone Patient Handbooks, Edinburgh.

BOOKLETS/LEAFLETS
Incontinence: A Very Common Problem, Health Education Council,

78 New Oxford Street, London, WC1A 1AH.
Notes on Incontinence, Disabled Living Foundation, 380–384 Harrow Road, London, W9 2HU.

Kidney

BOOKS
Cameron, S. (1981) *Kidney Disease: The Facts*, Oxford University Press.

Leukaemia

BOOKLETS/LEAFLETS
Series of booklets, Leukaemia Research Fund, 43 Great Ormond Street, London, WC1N 3JJ.

Menopause

BOOKS
Coope, J. (1984) *The Menopause: Coping With the Change*, Martin Dunitz, London.
Mackenzie, R. (1985) *Menopause: A Practical Self Help Guide for Women*, Sheldon Press, London.

BOOKLETS/LEAFLETS
The Change of Life, Health Education Council, 78 New Oxford Street, London, WC1A 1AH.

Mental handicap

BOOKS
Whelan, E. and Speake, B. (1979) *Learning to Cope*, Souvenir Press, London.
Worthington, A. (1982) *Coming to Terms with Mental Handicap*, Helena Press, Huddersfield.

BOOKLETS/LEAFLETS
Mental Handicap, Fact sheet 2, MIND, 22 Harley Street, London, W1N 2ED.

Myths, Campaign for People with Mental Handicaps, 12a Maddox Street, London, W1R 9PL.
Series of leaflets, MENCAP, 123 Golden Lane, London, EC1Y ORT.

PERIODICALS
In Touch Newsletter, In Touch Trust, 10 Norman Road, Sale, Cheshire, M33 3DF.

Mental health

BOOKS
Gostin, L. (1983) *A Practical Guide to Mental Health Law*, MIND, 22 Harley Street, London, W1N 2ED.
Melville, J. (1980) *First Aid in Mental Health*, Allen and Unwin, London.
Smith, N. (1983) *Mental Disorder: What You Should Know*, Greenway Press, Croydon.

BOOKLETS/LEAFLETS
Series of leaflets, MIND.

Migraine

BOOKS
Rose, F.C. (1980) *Migraine: The Facts*: Oxford University Press.
Wilkinson, M. (1982) *Migraine and Headaches*, Martin Dunitz, London.

BOOKLETS/LEAFLETS
Series of leaflets, British Migraine Association, 178a High Road, Byfleet, Weybridge, Surrey.

PERIODICALS
British Migraine Association Newsletter, British Migraine Association.

Motor neurone disease

BOOKLETS/LEAFLETS
Series of leaflets, Motor Neurone Disease Association, 61 Derngate, Northampton, NN1 1UE.

218

Multiple sclerosis

BOOKS
Dowie, R. (1981) *Learning to Live with MS*, Multiple Sclerosis Society, London.
Matthews, B. (1985) *Multiple Sclerosis: The Facts*, 2nd edn. Oxford University Press.

BOOKLETS/LEAFLETS
So you Have MS? and series of information sheets, Multiple Sclerosis Society, 25 Effie Road, London, SW6 1EE.

PERIODICALS
MS News, Multiple Sclerosis Society.

Muscular dystrophy

BOOKLETS/LEAFLETS
Muscular Dystrophy Handbook, and series of leaflets, Muscular Dystrophy Group, 35 Macauley Road, London, SW4 OQP.

Parkinson's disease

BOOKS
Godwin-Austen, R. *The Parkinson's Disease Handbook*, Sheldon Press, London.
Stern, G. and Lees, A. (1982) *Parkinson's Disease: The Facts*, Oxford University Press.

BOOKLETS/LEAFLETS
Series of booklets, Parkinson's Disease Society, 36 Portland Place, London, W1 3DG.

PERIODICALS
Parkinson Newsletter, Parkinson's Disease Society.

Patients

BOOKS
A Patient's Guide to the National Health Service, Consumers' Association, London.

Guide to Hospital Waiting Lists and other guides. College of Health, London.

BOOKLETS/LEAFLETS
Series of information sheets, Patients' Association, Room 33, 18 Charing Cross Road, London, WC2H OHR.

PERIODICALS
Patient Voice, Patients' Association.
Patient Participation, National Association for Patient Participation, Mrs Joan Mant, Hazelbank, Peaslake, Surrey, GU5 9RJ.

Phobias

BOOKS
Goodwin, D.W. (1983) *Phobia: The Facts*, Oxford University Press.
Lewis, D. (1984) *Fight Your Phobia and Win*, Sheldon Press, London.
Mitchell, R. (1982) *Phobias: What They Mean, How They Occur, What Can Be Done to Treat Them*, Penguin, Harmondsworth.

BOOKLETS/LEAFLETS
Agoraphobia and Other Phobias, Factsheet 8, MIND, 22 Harley Street, London, W1N 2ED.

Pregnancy and childbirth

BOOKS
Bourne, G. (1979) *Pregnancy*, Pan, London.
Evans, R. (1984) *Maternity Rights Handbook,* Penguin, Harmondsworth.
National Childbirth Trust (1985) *Pregnancy and Parenthood*, 2nd edn., Oxford University Press.
Phillips, A. (1983) *Your Body, Your Baby, Your Life*, Pandora Press, London.

BOOKLETS/LEAFLETS
Series of leaflets, Health Education Council, 78 New Oxford Street, London, WC1A 1AH.

Series of information sheets and booklets, National Childbirth Trust, 9 Queensborough Terrace, London, W2 3TB.

Premenstrual syndrome

BOOKS
Dalton, K. (1983) *Once a Month*, Fontana, London.
Sanders, D. (1985) *Coping with Periods*, Chambers, London.

Psoriasis

BOOKS
Marks, R. (1981) *Psoriasis: A Guide to one of the Commonest Skin Diseascs*, Martin Dunitz, London.

BOOKLETS/LEAFLETS
What is Psoriasis? Psoriasis Association, 7 Milton Street, Northampton, NN2 7JG.

PERIODICALS
Beyond the Ointment, Psoriasis Association.

Schizophrenia

BOOKS
Tsuang, M.T. (1982) *Schizophrenia: The Facts*, Oxford University Press.

BOOKLETS/LEAFLETS
Schizophrenia, Fact sheet 5, MIND, 22 Harley Street, London, W1N 2ED.
Series of booklets, National Schizophrenia Fellowship, 78/9 Victoria Road, Surbiton, Surrey, KT6 4NS.
Series of booklets, Schizophrenia Association of Great Britain, Bryn Hyfryd, The Crescent, Bangor, Gwynedd, LL57 2AG.

PERIODICALS
Newsletter of Schizophrenia Association, Schizophrenia Association.

Sex

BOOKS
Brown, P. and Faulder, C. (1979) *Treat Yourself to Sex*, Penguin, Harmondsworth.
Comfort, A. (1982) *The Joy of Sex*. Quartet, London.

BOOKLETS/LEAFLETS
Series of leaflets, Family Planning Information Service, 27–35 Mortimer Street, London, W1A 4QW.
Series of leaflets on sex and disability, Sexual and Personal Relationships of Disabled People (SPOD), 286 Camden Road, London, N7.

Smoking

BOOKS
STOP: A Guide to Non-Smoking (1981) Penguin, Harmondsworth.

BOOKLETS/LEAFLETS
Series of leaflets, Action on Smoking and Health (ASH), 5–11 Mortimer Street, London, W1N 7RH.
Series of leaflets, Health Education Council, 78 New Oxford Street, London, WC1A 1AH.

Spina bifida

BOOKS
Welch, C. (1985) *Spina Bifida and You*, Association for Spina Bifida and Hydrocephalus, London.

BOOKLETS/LEAFLETS
Series of booklets, Association for Spina Bifida and Hydrocephalus, 22 Upper Woburn Place, London, WC1H OEP.

PERIODICALS
Link, Association for Spina Bifida and Hydrocephalus.

Spinal injuries

BOOKS
Fallon, B. (1978) *Able to Work*, Spinal Injuries Association, London.
Fallon, B. (1978) *So You're Paralysed*, Spinal Injuries Association, London.

PERIODICALS
SIA Newsletter, Spinal Injuries Association, Yeomans House, 76 St James Lane, London, N10.

Stoma care

BOOKS
Mullen, B.D. (1980) *The Ostomy Book: Living Comfortably with Colostomies, Ileostomies and Urostomies*, Ileostomy Association, London.

BOOKLETS/LEAFLETS
Series of leaflets, Colostomy Welfare Group, 38–39 Eccleston Square, London, SW1V 1PE.
Series of leaflets, Ileostomy Association, Amblehurst House, Chobham, Woking, Surrey, GU24 8PZ.

PERIODICALS
IA Journal, Ileostomy Association.
In Touch, Franklin Medical, Freepost, High Wycombe, Bucks, HP12 3BR.

Stress

BOOKS
Madders, J. (1984) *Stress and Relaxation*, 3rd edn. Martin Dunitz, London.
Tyrer, D. (1983) *How to Cope with Stress*, Sheldon Press, London.
Weekes, C. (1984) *Self Help for your Nerves*, Angus & Robertson, London.

Stroke

BOOKS
Jay, P. (1985) *Help Yourselves: A Handbook for Hemiplegics and Their Families*, 4th edn. Ian Henry, London.
Law, D. and Paterson, B. (1980) *Living After a Stroke*, Souvenir Press, London.
Rose, F.C. and Capildeo, R. (1981) *Stroke: The Facts*, Oxford University Press.

BOOKLETS/LEAFLETS
Recovery from a Stroke, British Heart Foundation, 102 Gloucester Place, London, W1H 4DH.
Series of booklets, Chest Heart and Stroke Association, Tavistock House North, Tavistock Square, London, WC1 9JE.

PERIODICALS
Hope; *Look Forward*; *CHSA News*, Chest, Heart and Stroke Association.

Sudden infant death, stillbirth and miscarriage

BOOKS
Borg, S. and Lasker, J. (1982) *When Pregnancy Fails: Coping with Miscarriage, Stillbirth, and Infant Death*, Routledge & Kegan Paul, London.
Knight, B. (1983) *Sudden Death in Infancy*, Faber, London.
Oakley, A., McPherson, A. and Roberts, H. (1984) *Miscarriage*, Fontana, London.

BOOKLETS/LEAFLETS
The Loss of Your Baby, Stillbirth and Neonatal Death Society, Argyle House, 29–31 Euston Road, London, NW1 2SD.
Mothers Writing about the Death of a Baby, National Childbirth Trust, 9 Queensborough Terrace, London, W2 3TB.
Series of leaflets, Foundation for the Study of Infant Deaths, 5th Floor, 4 Grosvenor Place, London, SW1X 7HD.

PERIODICALS
Miscarriage Association Newsletter, Miscarriage Association, Mrs K.

Ladley, 18 Stoneybrook Close, West Bretton, Wakefield, West Yorkshire, WF4 4TP.

Thyroid

BOOKS
Bayliss, R.I.S. (1982) *Thyroid Disease: The Facts*. Oxford University Press.

Venereal disease

BOOKS
Barlow, D. (1981) *Sexually Transmitted Diseases: The Facts*, Oxford University Press.

BOOKLETS/LEAFLETS
Guide to a Healthy Sex Life; *Sexually Transmitted Infections*, Health Education Council, 78 New Oxford Street, London, WC1A 1AH.

Women's health

BOOKS
Coleman, V. (1984) *Women's Problems A–Z*, Sheldon Press, London.
Phillips, A. and Rakusen, J. (1979) *Our Bodies Ourselves*, Penguin, Harmondsworth.

BOOKLETS/LEAFLETS
Series of leaflets, Health Education Council, 78 New Oxford Street, London WC1A 1AH.
Series of fact sheets and broadsheets, Women's Health Information Centre, 52 Featherstone Street, London, EC1.

For Health Education Council publications contact local health education services first.

SOURCE GUIDES

A number of other bibliographies, source guides and core lists have been produced which may provide further suggestions for suitable material. The following is a selection.

Health and patient education

Ash, J. and Stevenson, M. (1976) *Health: A Multimedia Source Guide* Bowker, New York.

American Academy of Family Physicians (1975) *Compendium of Patient Education Materials*, AAFP, Chicago.

Communication: An Information Series to Assist Patient/Staff Communication Titles available: *Allergies, Epilepsy, Hip conditions in Childhood, The Loss of a Baby, Premenstrual Syndrome, Multiple Sclerosis, Schizophrenia, Stroke*. Wessex Regional Library and Information Service, Southampton General Hospital, Southampton, SO9 4XY.

Eisenstein, E. (1984) *Selected List of Health Information Titles for Public Libraries: A Recommended Core Bibliography*, Community Health Information Resource Project, Oak Park, Illinois.

Ferguson, T. (1980) *Medical Self Care: Access to Health Tools*, Summit Books, New York.

Consumer Health Information Service, Microfilming Corporation of America, 1620 Hawkins Avenue, PO Box 10, Sanford, North Carolina, 27330.

Health Education Index and Guide to Voluntary Organisations (1983) Edsall, London.

Martyn, D. (1978) *Source List for Patient Education Materials*, HESCA (Health Services Communications Association), Milledgeville, GA.

Philbrook, M. (1976) *Medical Books for the Lay Person*, Boston Public Library.

Rees, A.M. and Janes, J. (1984) *The Consumer Health Information Sourcebook* 2nd edn. Bowker, New York.

Sources of Health Information for Public Libraries (1976) University of Illinois Medical Center.

Ulene, A. and Feldman, S. (1980) *Help Yourself to Health: A Health Information and Services Directory*, Putnams, New York.

US Department of Health and Human Services, Public Health Service (1984) *Staying Healthy: A Bibliography of Health Promotion Materials*, US DHHS, Office of Disease Prevention and Health Promotion.

Children

Azarnoff, P. (1983) *Health, Illness and Disability: A Guide to Books for Children and Young Adults*, Bowker, New York.

Bernstein, J.E. (1983) *Books to Help Children Cope with Separation and Loss*, Bowker, New York.

Chabon, S.S. (1979) Annotated Bibliography of Health Care Books for Children, *American Journal of Diseases of Children* vol. 133 (2), pp. 184–6.

Friedberg, R.B., Mullins, J.B., and Sukiennik, A.W. (1985) *Accept Me as I am: Best Books of Juvenile Non-Fiction on Impairment and Disabilities*, Bowker, New York.

Knowles, J.W. (1978) Pamphlets for Parents [of handicapped children] *Child: Care, Health and Development* vol. 4, pp. 337–44.

Fiction and biography

Baskin, B.H. and Harris, K.H. (1977) *Notes from a Different Drummer: A Guide to Juvenile Fiction Portraying the Handicapped*, Bowker, New York.

Baskin, B.H. and Harris, K.H. (1984) *More Notes from a Different Drummer: A Guide to Juvenile Fiction Portraying the Disabled*, Bowker, New York.

Quicke, J. (1984) *Disabilities in Modern Children's Fiction*, Croom Helm, London.

Tabor, R.B. (1983) *Reflections: A Subject Guide to Works of Fiction, Biography and Autobiography on Medical and Related Topics*, Wessex Regional Library & Information Service, Southampton.

Trautmann, J. and Pollard, C. (1982) *Literature and Medicine: an Annotated Bibliography*, University of Pittsburgh Press.

Material from pharmaceutical companies

Allen, K.F. and Sweeney, S.J. (1985) 'The availability and design of patient information leaflets (including list of materials available from pharmaceutical companies)'. *Pharmaceutical Journal*, 10 August pp. 181–3.

Sloan, P.J.M. (1984) 'Survey of patient information booklets', *British Medical Journal* vol. 288, pp. 915–9.

Alternative medicine

Thompson, I. (1981) *Alternative Medicine: Readers Guide*, Library Association Public Libraries Group, London.
West, R. and Trevelyan, J.E. (1985) *Alternative Medicine: A Bibliography of Books in English*, Mansell, London.

Disability

Matthews, G. (1984) *Disability: Readers' Guide*, Library Association Public Libraries Group, London.
Self, P.C. (1984) *Physical Disability: An Annotated Literature Guide*. Marcel Dekker, New York.
Velleman, R. *Serving Physically Disabled People: An Information Handbook for all Librarians*, Bowker, New York.

Other useful guides

Directories and Resources for Volunteer Projects (1985), Select Bibliography Series No. 8, Volunteer Centre, Berkhamsted.
Graves, N. (1984), *A Directory of Free Leaflet Providers*, CINDEX, St Pancras Library, 100 Euston Road, London, NW1 2AJ.
Health education resources on women's health, Paddington and North Kensington Health Education Department, 304 Westbourne Grove, London, W11.
Morby, G. (1982), *Know How: To Find Out Your Rights*, 2nd edn. Pluto Press, London.
Rubin, R.J. (1978) *Bibliotherapy Sourcebook*, Oryx Press, Mansell, London.
Simpson, M.A. (1979), *Dying, Grief and Death: A Critically Annotated Bibliography*, Plenum, New York.

SUBJECT HEADINGS: ORGANISING THE COLLECTION

This list of subject headings was developed to index the Help for Health collection and to provide the keywords for the Help for Health database of voluntary organisations and self-help groups. It provides for indexing by parts of the body; diseases; and types of care. Most terms are compatible with the National Library of Medicine's *Medical Subject Headings* (MESH) and extra terms may be added from MESH if required. Non-MESH terms are identified with an asterisk (*). Wherever possible we have tried to use MESH terms but English spellings are used and, on occasions, an English term is preferred to a less familiar or American one (for example, STILLBIRTH not FETAL DEATH). Cross references are made from terms not used to preferred terms (aids *see* EQUIPMENT) and also to related terms (ALTERNATIVE MEDICINE *see also* ACUPUNCTURE). To aid more precise indexing and to reduce the number of cross references, *see also* references are made to narrower but not to broader terms.

Thesaurus of subject headings

abnormalities	*see*	CONGENITAL DISORDERS
ABORTION	*see also*	MISCARRIAGE
*ACCESS	*see also*	DESIGN; MOBILITY
ACCIDENTS		
*ACCOMMODATION	*see also*	DESIGN; RESIDENTIAL CARE
achondroplasia	*see*	GROWTH
ACNE		
acquired immune deficiency syndrome	*see*	AIDS
ACTIVITIES OF DAILY LIVING	*see also*	EQUIPMENT
ACUPUNCTURE		
adenoid	*see*	EAR, NOSE AND THROAT
ADOLESCENCE		
ADOPTION		
adventure playgrounds	*see*	PLAY
*ADVICE SERVICES		
AGED	*see also*	RETIREMENT
agoraphobia	*see*	PHOBIAS
aids and equipment	*see*	EQUIPMENT
AIDS		
ALCOHOLISM		
*ALLERGY	*see also*	HAY FEVER; FOOD ADDITIVES
allowances	*see*	SOCIAL SECURITY
alopecia	*see*	HAIR
*ALTERNATIVE MEDICINE	*see also*	ACUPUNCTURE; CHIROPRACTIC; HERBALISM; HOMOEOPATHY, OSTEOPATHY; HYPNOTHERAPY
amenorrhoea	*see*	MENSTRUATION
AMPUTATION		
ANATOMY		
anaemia	*see*	BLOOD

232

duodenal ulcer	*see*	ULCER
dwarfism	*see*	GROWTH
DYSLEXIA		
dysphasia	*see*	LANGUAGE

*EAR, NOSE & THROAT		
ECZEMA		
EDUCATION		
elderly	*see*	AGED
embryo	*see*	PREGNANCY
emergencies	*see*	ACCIDENTS
emphysema	*see*	LUNG
EMPLOYMENT	*see also*	SHELTERED WORKSHOPS; UNEMPLOYMENT
ENDOCRINE GLANDS	*see also*	DIABETES; THYROID
enuresis	*see*	INCONTINENCE
ENVIRONMENTAL HEALTH	*see also*	ACCIDENTS
EPILEPSY		
*EQUIPMENT	*see also*	DESIGN; WHEELCHAIRS
ETHNIC GROUPS		
EUTHANASIA		
exercise	*see*	PHYSICAL FITNESS
EYE		

faecal incontinence	*see*	INCONTINENCE
false teeth	*see*	TOOTH
FAMILY	*see also*	MARRIAGE; ONE PARENT FAMILY; PARENTS; SIBLINGS
FAMILY PLANNING		
fathers	*see*	PARENTS
FERTILITY		
*FICTION		
*FINANCIAL ASSISTANCE		
FINANCING, PERSONAL	*see also*	FINANCIAL ASSISTANCE; SOCIAL SECURITY
FIRST AID		
fitness	*see*	PHYSICAL FITNESS
fleas	*see*	PARASITES
foetus	*see*	PREGNANCY
food	*see*	DIET
FOOD ADDITIVES		
food allergy	*see*	ALLERGY
FOOT	*see also*	SHOES
forces	*see*	ARMED SERVICES
*FOSTER CARE		
FRACTURES		
FRIEDREICH'S ATAXIA		
friendly societies	*see*	BENEVOLENT SOCIETIES

*GAMBLING		
*GARDENING		
gastric ulcer	*see*	ULCER
gastrointestinal system	*see*	DIGESTIVE SYSTEM
general practice	*see*	PRIMARY CARE
GENETIC COUNSELLING		
geriatrics	*see*	AGED
german measles	*see*	RUBELLA
gigantism	*see*	GROWTH
*GLANDULAR FEVER		
glasses	*see*	VISION
glaucoma	*see*	EYE
glue sniffing	*see*	SOLVENT ABUSE
gonorrhoea	*see*	VENEREAL DISEASES
grief	*see*	BEREAVEMENT
GROWTH		
guide dogs	*see*	BLINDNESS
gynaecology	*see*	WOMEN
haemodialysis	*see*	KIDNEY
HAEMOPHILIA		
HAEMORRHOIDS		
HAIR		
HALF WAY HOUSES		
HAND		
handedness	*see*	LEFT HANDED
HANDICAPPED	*see also*	CHILD HANDICAPPED; MENTAL HANDICAP; PHYSICAL HANDICAP
HAY FEVER		
HEAD		
HEAD INJURIES		
head lice	*see*	PARASITES
HEADACHE	*see also*	MIGRAINE
HEALTH	*see also*	MENTAL HEALTH; PHYSICAL FITNESS
health authorities	*see*	HEALTH SERVICES
HEALTH EDUCATION		
HEALTH PROMOTION		
HEALTH SERVICES	*see also*	COMMUNITY HEALTH COUNCILS; HOSPITALS; MENTAL HEALTH SERVICES; PRIMARY CARE
health visitors	*see*	PRIMARY CARE
hearing aid	*see*	DEAFNESS
HEARING	*see also*	DEAFNESS
HEART		
HEMIPLEGIA		
hepatitis	*see*	LIVER
HERBALISM		
HEREDITARY DISEASES	*see also*	GENETIC COUNSELLING

234

HERNIA		
HIP		
hobbies	*see*	RECREATION
HODGKIN'S DISEASE		
HOLIDAYS	*see also*	PILGRIMAGES
*HOME CARE	*see also*	CARERS
home helps	*see*	HOME CARE
*HOMELESS		
HOMOEOPATHY		
homes	*see*	ACCOMMODATION
HOMOSEXUALITY		
hormones	*see*	ENDOCRINE GLANDS
horticulture	*see*	GARDENING
HOSPICES		
HOSPITALISATION	*see also*	CHILD, HOSPITALISED
HOSPITALS		
HOSPITALS, PSYCHIATRIC		
housebound	*see*	HANDICAPPED
housing	*see*	ACCOMMODATION; DESIGN
HUNTINGTON CHOREA		
HYDROCEPHALUS		
*HYPERACTIVITY		
hypersensitivity	*see*	ALLERGY
HYPERTENSION		
HYPNOTHERAPY		
HYPOTHERMIA		
HYSTERECTOMY		
ileostomy	*see*	STOMA CARE
immigrants	*see*	ETHNIC MINORITIES
IMMUNISATION		
*INCONTINENCE		
INFANT		
infant death	*see*	SUDDEN INFANT DEATH
infectious diseases	*see*	COMMUNICABLE DISEASES
infectious mononucleosis	*see*	GLANDULAR FEVER
infertility	*see*	FERTILITY
INFLUENZA		
INFORMATION SERVICES		
INSEMINATION, ARTIFICIAL		
insomnia	*see*	SLEEP
insurance	*see*	FINANCING, PERSONAL
INTESTINES		
isolation	*see*	LONELINESS
JEWS		
JOINTS		

KIDNEY
KNEE

labour	*see*	CHILDBIRTH
LANGUAGE	*see also*	LITERACY; READING; SPEECH, WRITING

LARYNGECTOMY

laryngitis	*see*	EAR, NOSE AND THROAT
laws	*see*	LEGISLATION
leagues of friends	*see*	HOSPITALS

*LEFT HANDED

LEG	*see also*	FOOT; HIP; KNEE

LEGISLATION

leisure	*see*	RECREATION

LEPROSY
LEUKAEMIA

libraries	*see*	INFORMATION SERVICES
lifting	*see*	NURSING CARE

*LITERACY
LIVER

LONELINESS	*see also*	CONTACT ORGANISATIONS

LUNG
*LUNG CANCER

maladjusted children	*see*	CHILD PSYCHIATRY

MALNUTRITION

MARRIAGE	*see also*	SEPARATION

MASTECTOMY

meals on wheels	*see*	HOME CARE

MEASLES

medicines	*see*	DRUGS

*MEN
MENINGITIS
MENOPAUSE
MENSTRUATION

*MENTAL HANDICAP	*see also*	CHILD, HANDICAPPED; DOWN'S SYNDROME

MENTAL HEALTH

MENTAL HEALTH SERVICES	*see also*	CHILD PSYCHIATRY; COUNSELLING; HALF WAY HOUSES; HOSPITALS, PSYCHIATRIC; PSYCHOTHERAPY; SHELTERED WORKSHOPS
MENTAL DISORDERS	*see also*	ANOREXIA NERVOSA; ANXIETY; CHILD PSYCHIATRY; DEPRESSION; NEUROSES; PHOBIAS; SCHIZOPHRENIA; STRESS

METABOLIC DISORDERS
MIDDLE AGE	*see also*	MENOPAUSE
midwifery	*see*	CHILDBIRTH

MIGRAINE
military	*see*	ARMED SERVICES

*MISCARRIAGE
*MOBILITY	*see also*	DRIVING; TRANSPORT; WHEELCHAIRS
mongolism	*see*	DOWN'S SYNDROME
mothers	*see*	PARENTS

*MOTOR NEURONE
   DISEASE
MOVEMENT
MOUTH
MULTIPLE SCLEROSIS
MUMPS
MUSCLES
MUSCULAR DYSTROPHY
MUSCULOSKELETAL
SYSTEM	*see also*	BONES; JOINTS; SPINE

MUSIC
mutism	*see*	DUMBNESS

MYASTHENIA GRAVIS

narcotics	*see*	DRUG ABUSE
national health service	*see*	HEALTH SERVICES
natural childbirth	*see*	CHILDBIRTH

NECK
neonates	*see*	INFANT
neoplasms	*see*	CANCER
NERVOUS SYSTEM	*see also*	BRAIN

NEUROMUSCULAR
DISEASES	*see also*	MUSCULAR DYSTROPHY; MYASTHENIA GRAVIS

NEUROSES
newborn	*see*	INFANT
nose	*see*	EAR, NOSE AND THROAT

NURSING CARE
nutrition	*see*	DIET

OBESITY	*see also*	SLIMMING
obstetrics	*see*	CHILDBIRTH

*OCCUPATIONAL HEALTH
OCCUPATIONAL
   THERAPY
*ONE PARENT FAMILY
operations	*see*	SURGERY
ophthalmology	*see*	EYE
organisations	*see*	VOLUNTARY ORGANISATIONS

otorhinolaryngologic diseases	*see*	EAR, NOSE AND THROAT
osteoarthritis	*see*	ARTHRITIS
osteogenesis imperfecta	*see*	BONES
OSTEOPATHY		
OVARY		
paediatrics	*see*	CHILD
*PAGET'S DISEASE		
PAIN		
PARAPLEGIA		
PARASITES		
PARENTS	*see also*	ONE PARENT FAMILY
PARKINSON DISEASE		
partial sight	*see*	BLINDNESS
PATIENT EDUCATION		
PATIENTS	*see also*	HOSPITALISATION; SELF-HELP GROUPS
PENIS	*see also*	CIRCUMCISION
pensions	*see*	SOCIAL SECURITY
peptic ulcer	*see*	ULCER
personality disorders	*see*	MENTAL ILLNESS
pets	*see*	ANIMALS
pharmacology	*see*	DRUGS
PHENYLKETONURIA		
PHOBIAS		
PHYSICAL FITNESS		
PHYSICAL HANDICAP	*see also*	CEREBRAL PALSY; CHILD, HANDICAPPED; MULTIPLE SCLEROSIS; MUSCULAR DYSTROPHY; PARAPLEGIA; SPINA BIFIDA; THALIDOMIDE (and other specific disorders)
PHYSIOLOGY		
*PHYSIOTHERAPY		
piles	*see*	HAEMORRHOIDS
*PILGRIMAGES		
pituitary gland	*see*	ENDOCRINE GLANDS
*PLASTER CASTS		
*PLAY		
PNEUMONIA		
POISONING		
POLIOMYELITIS		
pollution	*see*	ENVIRONMENTAL HEALTH
POSTNATAL CARE		
POSTURE		
POVERTY		
*PRECONCEPTUAL CARE	*see also*	GENETIC COUNSELLING
PREGNANCY	*see also*	MISCARRIAGE
premenstrual tension	*see*	MENSTRUATION

*SEPARATION		
services, armed	*see*	ARMED SERVICES
SEX	*see also*	HOMOSEXUALITY
SEX EDUCATION		
sexually transmitted diseases	*see*	VENEREAL DISEASES
SHELTERED WORKSHOPS		
SHOES		
SIBLINGS		
sight	*see*	VISION
single parent family	*see*	ONE PARENT FAMILY
SKIN	*see also*	ACNE; ECZEMA; PSARIASIS
skull	*see*	HEAD
SLEEP		
*SLIMMING		
SMOKING		
SOCIAL PROBLEMS	*see also*	CRIME; HOMELESS
SOCIAL SECURITY		
SOCIAL WELFARE	*see also*	SOCIAL SECURITY; SOCIAL SERVICES; VOLUNTARY ORGANISATIONS; VOLUNTARY WORKERS
SOCIAL SERVICES	*see also*	ADOPTION; DAY CARE; FOSTER CARE; HOLIDAYS; HOME CARE; RESIDENTIAL CARE; SHELTERED WORKSHOPS
social work	*see*	SOCIAL SERVICES
societies	*see*	VOLUNTARY ORGANISATIONS
*SOLVENT ABUSE		
spasticity	*see*	CEREBRAL PALSY
spectacles	*see*	VISION
SPEECH	*see also*	DUMBNESS
SPINA BIFIDA		
SPINE	*see also*	PARAPLEGIA
spiritual guidance	*see*	RELIGION
SPORTS		
SPRAINS AND STRAINS		
stammering	*see*	SPEECH
STATISTICS		
sterility	*see*	FERTILITY
*STILLBIRTH		
still's disease	*see*	ARTHRITIS
STOMA CARE		
STOMACH		
STRESS	*see also*	RELAXATION
*STROKE	*see also*	HEMIPLEGIA
students	*see*	EDUCATION
SUDDEN INFANT DEATH		
SUICIDE		
SURGERY		
syphilis	*see*	VENEREAL DISEASES

240

TAPE RECORDING		
teaching	*see*	EDUCATION
teenage	*see*	ADOLESCENCE
TERMINAL CARE	*see also*	EUTHANASIA; HOSPICES
tetraplegia	*see*	PARAPLEGIA
THALIDOMIDE		
therapeutic cults	*see*	ALTERNATIVE MEDICINE
thoracic diseases	*see*	RESPIRATORY SYSTEM
throat	*see*	EAR, NOSE AND THROAT
thrush, vaginal	*see*	VAGINA
THYROID		
TINNITUS		
tonsil	*see*	EAR, NOSE AND THROAT
TOOTH		
toys	*see*	PLAY
TRANSPLANTATION		
*TRANSPORT		
travel	*see*	' TRANSPORT
TUBERCULOSIS		
TWINS		
ULCER		
UNEMPLOYMENT		
urinary diversion	*see*	STOMA CARE
urinary incontinence	*see*	INCONTINENCE
URINARY TRACT		
INFECTIONS	*see also*	CYSTITIS
UTERUS	*see also*	HYSTERECTOMY
vaccination	*see*	IMMUNISATION
VAGINA		
VARICOSE VEINS		
VASECTOMY		
vegetarianism	*see*	DIET
veins	*see*	BLOOD VESSELS
VENEREAL DISEASES		
VIOLENCE	*see also*	CHILD ABUSE; RAPE; WIFE ABUSE
VISION	*see also*	BLINDNESS
VOICE		
*VOLUNTARY		
ORGANISATIONS	*see also*	SELF-HELP GROUPS
VOLUNTARY WORKERS		
welfare	*see*	SOCIAL WELFARE
WHEELCHAIRS		
widow	*see*	BEREAVEMENT
*WIFE ABUSE		
WOMEN		
work	*see*	EMPLOYMENT

| wounds | *see* | FIRST AID |
| WRITING | | |

| young person | *see* | ADOLESCENCE |

Other thesauri

The major thesauri of subject headings in the health field are:

Medical Subject Headings (annual), National Library of Medicine, 8600 Rockville Pike, Bethesda, Maryland, 20209, USA. US Department of Health and Human Services NIH Publication No. 85–265.

DHSS Data Thesaurus: The Thesaurus of the Department of Health and Social Security Library, London (1985), DHSS Leaflets Unit, PO Box 21, Stanmore, Middx. HA7 1AY.

Health Education Thesaurus (1986), Health Education Council, 78 New Oxford Street, London, WC1A 1AH.

These are very detailed lists which could be used to index a large collection or database.

Index

128, 130
computer assisted learning (CAL) 64, 65–8
computers *see* microcomputers
consortia, health promotion 132–3
consumer health information (in United States) 13, 130–2, 136–48
Consumer Health Information Program and Services (CHIPS) 140
Consumer Health Information Service (CHIS) 136
consumerism in health care 49–51, 112, 144–5, 157
Consumers' Association 58, 67, 80, 91, 98, 112
Contact A Family 108, 184
cost effectiveness of health information 34, 129–30
Council of Complementary and Alternative Medicine 182
councils for voluntary service 106–7, 190
Croatia 156
Crossroads (television programme) 53
Croydon Health Education Service 72
current awareness services 201–2
cystic fibrosis 210

databases
    cancer resources 111
    CHID: Combined Health Information Database 148
    community information 94–5, 134
    DIRLINE 148
    health education 72, 163
    MEDLINE 133, 143, 148
    self help groups and voluntary organisations 99, 102, 107, 113, 142,
deafness 70, 184, 210–1
death rates 1

dementia 211
Denmark 54, 164
dental health 54
Department of Health & Human Services, USA 145–7
Department of Health & Social Security 1, 26, 49, 70, 92, 103, 191
depression 211
developing countries 166–9
Devon 64–5, 94, 113
diabetes 28, 31, 59, 64, 67, 130, 161, 168, 211
DIAL: Disablement Information & Advice Lines, 52, 88–91, 189
diaries, patient 164
dictionaries 192
diet 67, 68
DIRLINE 148
Disability Alliance 185
Disabled Living Foundation 91, 185, 197
disabled people
    aids and equipment 91–2
    citizens' advice bureaux and 85
    DIAL groups 88–91
    information needs 136
    information sources 185–6, 195–6, 212, 228
Disabled Electronic Aids and Reference Service (DEARS) 92
Disablement Income Group 92, 185
display machines 60–2
Down's syndrome 212
drug abuse 187, 213
drugs *see* medication
Dutch Health Education Centre, Utrecht 163–4
dyslexia 214

eczema 214
Edinburgh 72, 74
Education Act 1981 48
education departments 191
elderly 22, 51, 102, 108, 186, 204
epilepsy 59, 214–5

incontinence 218–9
indexes 201–2
India 167
informed consent 35–9, 129
Institute for Complementary Medicine 182
Institute for the Study of Drug Dependence 187
International Information Centre on Self Help and Health, Leuven, Belgium 108, 155–6
International Year of Disabled People, 1981 53, 185
Iran 166, 168–9
Ireland 69, 72

journals and magazines 20–22, 51, 53, 54, 58–9, 97, 196–201

Kaiser Permanente Health Library, Oakland, California 137
Kentish Town Health Centre, London 76
kidney disease 29, 217
King's College Hospital, London 67
Kingston Hospital, London 59–60
Körner Committee on Health Services Information 103
Kropotkin, Peter A 11

Lapland 156
law centres 87–8, 89, 157
Leeds 66, 70, 73, 76, 85–6
legal aspects of health information 37–8, 48, 128–9
leukaemia 217
libraries, health care
in Netherlands 163–4
in United Kingdom 95–103, 189
in United States 133–40
libraries, patient, in general practice 76–7
libraries, public
community information 92–5
in Canada 151
in Netherlands 163

in United Kingdom 69, 92–5, 97, 189
in United States 132–4
Prestel and 69
libraries, university 96
Library Association 94
Medical Health & Welfare Libraries Group 95
life assurance companies 130
lifestyles 3
Lisson Grove Health Centre, London 77
literacy 33, 168
Liverpool 73, 89
London School of Economics 67

McMaster University Medical Centre, Ontario 152
'Maggie's Place' community information service, Colorado 134
Manchester 9, 110
Manpower Services Commission 73, 86, 89, 90
maternity services 26–7, 51, 66
media 51, 52–7, 73
Medical Information Research Unit, Leeds 70
Medical Library Association, USA 133–4
medical records 40, 77, 164
medication 5, 29, 30–34, 56, 128, 157, 213–4
Meditel 70
MEDLINE 133, 143, 148
MENCAP: Royal Society for Mentally Handicapped Children and Adults 8, 58, 187, 197, 200
menopause 217
mental handicap 65, 187, 212, 217–8
mental health 21, 86, 136, 187, 218
microcomputers
computer assisted learning 64–8
databases of organisations 99, 107, 142
in information and advice services

81, 90, 94–5, 190
Prestel and 70
welfare rights assessment 77
Micronet 800 70
Midwives Information & Resource
Service 188, 199
migraine 218
MIND: National Association for
Mental Health 50, 58, 59, 63,
87, 108, 187–8, 200
Ministry of Agriculture, Fisheries
and Food 70
miscarriage 224–5
mobile information services 84,
86–7
motor neurone disease 218
multiple sclerosis 199, 219
muscular dystrophy 219

National Association for the Wel-
fare of Children in Hospital 50,
184
National Association of Citizens'
Advice Bureaux 81, 84, 188
National Association of Patient
Participation Groups 76
National Cancer Institute, USA 111
National Childbirth Trust 50, 58,
199–200
National Children's Bureau 108, 184
National Library for the Handi-
capped Child 184
National Consumer Council 48, 81
National Council for Voluntary
Organisations 81, 105–6, 107,
182, 202
National Health Information Clearing-
house, USA 145, 148
National Health Promotion and
Disease Prevention Act 1976,
USA 128
National Health Service 8, 24, 49–
51, 71, 81, 191, 193, 219
National Information Forum 185
National Self Help Clearinghouse,
USA 147

National Self Help Support Centre
107
National Tuberculosis Association,
USA 128
neighbours 51, 60
Netherlands 160–4
New Zealand 153
Newcastle 83, 89, 92
newspapers 51, 52, 53–4, 70
Northampton General Hospital 63–
4
Northwick Park Hospital, Harrow,
London 87
Nottingham 76, 107
nurses
as health and patient educators
28, 35, 71–2, 134–5, 151
and cancer information 109–10,
111–2
nursing process 28
see also health visitors

occupational health 76
Open University 55, 104
oral tradition 168–9
Osler, William 52

Paddington and North Kensington
Health Authority, London 78,
85
Pakistan 166
Papua New Guinea 169
Parkinson's disease 219
Patient Counselling and Patient
Organisation (PACO) project,
Maastricht, Netherlands 163
patient education
bibliographies 226
cost benefits 130
definition 12
development 128
in cancer 109–10
Netherlands 160–2
nursing and 28, 35, 71–2, 134–5,
151
Patient Education Newsletter

248

150, 159
databases of 99, 102, 113, 142
definition 7–9, 12, 155
directories of 193–4
history and development 7–9
in France 157–8
in Germany 159
in Netherlands 162–8
information sources 181–2, 193–4
see also voluntary organisations
Self Help Team, Nottingham 107, 156
sex 21, 222
SHARE Community 201
Sheffield 76, 82, 87
Sidaway v the Board of Governors of Bethlem Hospital 37
Smiles, Samuel 10
smoking 222
Snowdon Report *Integrating the Disabled* 77–8
social aspects of ill health 20, 77, 104–5
social class 23, 104–5
social services departments 192, 193
South Western Regional Health Authority 64
Southampton 32–3, 98–103
Soviet Union 156
Spastics Society 8, 58, 92, 198
spina bifida 222
spinal injuries 73, 223
Springfield Hospital, Wandsworth, London 88
Stevenage 96–8
Stockport 83
Stockton on Tees 76
stillbirth 224
stoma care 29, 223
stress 29–30, 223
stroke 34–5, 224
Sudan 166
sudden infant death 224
surgery, preparation for 29–30, 59–60, 195
surveys 50, 73, 131–2, 153

Sweden 164–6
syndromes, rare 59, 108

Tanzania 166
Teaching Aids at Low Cost (TALC) 167
Tel Med 59, 113, 138, 140–1, 142
telephone information services 59, 111–2, 113–4, 140–1, 142, 160, 165
television 51, 52–3, 54–7, 62–5, 70
closed circuit 62–3
cable 65
video 62–5, 160
terminology, medical 18, 26
tests, medical 30, 194
theatre projects 169
thesauri of subject headings 99, 164, 228–42
third world *see* developing countries
thyroid 225
Tooting Bec Hospital, London 87–8
training of information and advice workers 73, 83, 89, 110, 111, 133–4, 136, 139, 140
trolleys, information 86, 135, 140
tuberculosis 128

unemployment 73, 104
United States of America 10, 37, 38–9, 59, 62, 127–49
California 130, 134, 135, 137–8, 140
Colorado 134
Florida 138
Illinois 133, 135
Maryland 135
Massachusetts 62, 139–40
Minnesota 66, 129, 138–9
New Jersey 131, 134, 135, 142–3
New York 132–4, 135, 141–2
North Carolina 134
Ohio 62, 136
Oklahoma 133
Pennsylvania 65, 135
South Carolina 134